TEXAS

From the Frontier to Spindletop

Also by James L. Haley

APACHES:
A History and Culture Portrait

THE BUFFALO WAR:
The History of the Red River Indian Uprising of 1874

TEXAS

From the Frontier to Spindletop

JAMES L. HALEY

St. Martin's Press
New York

LIBRARY OF CONGRESS CATALOGING-IN-PUBLICATION DATA

Haley, James L.
    Texas : from the frontier to spindletop / James L. Haley.
      p.   cm.
    ISBN 0-312-06479-9 (pbk.)
    1. Texas—History. I. Title.
    F386.H236 1991
    976.4—dc20   91-20614
                                       CIP

First published in the United States by Doubleday & Company, Inc., under the title *Texas: An Album of History*.

10 9 8 7 6 5 4 3 2 1

To Kim and Laurie Lou
with love . . .

. . . and with a thought for JOHN MARSHALL,
who went to Law School to be a better writer.

Contents

Acknowledgments

IN preparing a book of this kind the writer is necessarily dependent upon the goodwill of archivists and librarians who care for the material. Access is not always automatic, and I recall once bribing my way into a photo collection with flattering comments on a snapshot of the attendant's grandchildren. Such maneuvers have been unnecessary for the present volume, for aid in finding and assessing materials has been uniformly warm and generous. The following people deserve particular thanks:

At the Texas State Library in Austin, Mike Dabrishus, Carol Finney, and Mike Green, and Jean Carefoot;

At the University of Texas at Arlington Library, Special Collections, Mary Van Zandt and Carol Thurman;

At the Institute of Texan Cultures in San Antonio, Tom Shelton;

At the San Jacinto Museum of History, James C. Martin;

At the Panhandle-Plains Historical Museum in Canyon, Claire Kuehn;

At the Museum of the Daughters of the Republic of Texas in Austin, Jane Baker;

At the Museum of the United Daughters of the Confederacy in Austin, Mrs. Ethel McCutcheon, and Mrs. Retta Riefkohl;

At the El Paso Public Library, Itoko McNully;

At the Rosenberg Library in Galveston, Uli Haller;

At the Fort Bend County Museum, Priscilla Hauger;

Of the Daughters of the Republic of Texas, at the Alamo, Fleta Johnson and Martha Utterback.

Also, for their unfailingly courteous attention, thanks to the staffs of the Austin Public Library, Austin History Center; the National Archives; the Library of Congress; the Defense Audiovisual Agency; the Museum of the Confederacy; the Confederate Research Center; Fort Richardson State Historic Park; the Fort Concho Museum; the Old Stone Fort Museum; and the Star of the Republic Museum.

For sharing his expertise on the Gonzales cannon, thanks to Dr. Pat Wagner of Shiner, Texas. For similar help, thanks to Charles G. Anderson of Snyder, Texas, Chuck Parsons of Silver Lake, Minnesota, Frank M. Temple of Lubbock, Texas, and Maurice Stack of Center, Texas. For important practical and financial assistance in getting through this book, thanks as usual to my mother, to Michael C. Alexander of Austin, and to Craig and Alyne Eiland of Tulsa, Oklahoma.

Preface

As grist for historians, "Texana" wears well. The more we try to strip away its romance and get at facts, the more romantic it becomes to spite us. The more we rub at it, the more it shines. It is one of those topics of American history in which the romance lies in the experience itself, rather than in some later conjuring of it. That is, I think, part of the magic that has enchanted an international readership throughout the twentieth century. If that is true, then it might follow that the most transporting dose a modern reader can have of the Texas experience is to see it through the eyes of those who saw it, and heard it, and breathed it, and—fortunately for us—photographed it. This is therefore a fairly straightforward narrative, with a great many pictures and large blocks of original accounts.

It is a simple format, but it has come near to killing me, because many historians, myself included, sometimes feel we shall burst if we cannot spend as much space writing *about* the history as we do writing the history itself. However, a reader can probably best enjoy the Texas experience if as much as possible of the intervening acculturation and technologifying is removed from interference. Part of that interference, one must admit, is the historian's tendency to want to explain and hypothesize. At least in the trade literature, that method inevitably is like lecturing a class on a filmstrip while standing in front of the screen. The task of the writer who wants to get his interpretation across, yet remove himself from the picture, lies in the nuance of his selection and arrangement of the material. He wishes to let the reader feel he is in the past, without letting on that there has been an art to the selection. In a way, it is a dangerous method to prepare a history, because modern minds can interpret the same original material many different ways, depending upon how much—or little—a reader already knows about the contexts involved. By and large, one should understand that the original materials contained herein, from posturing jingoism to breathtaking racial slurs, are stopped frames from the motion of the past, and not my own sentiments. For instance, when Frederick Law Olmsted used the term "pickininnies," it wasn't because he was a racist. In fact, he was a crusading abolitionist. "Pickininnies" was at the time an unloaded word, but would not be read so today. Thus, its use is as much part of the history as the events described.

A second point of explanation is necessary. To prepare this short a montage of early visual and literary Texana, and still have it be cohesive to a largely non-Texan audience, I have had to shortcut some chronological and spatial details of the history. I regret the necessity of this, and have done it only where strongly indicated. For instance, Noah Smithwick's story of Mrs. Varner's biscuits was, in his book of 1900, followed by a very brief aside telling of his visit to the family of Thomas B. Bell. Here I have omitted mention of Bell and finished the paragraph as though Smithwick were still referring to the Varners. If this concession were not allowed me, then anyone who

has ever been cornered by a tennis-shoed genealogist knows what endless particulariz-
ing ramifications can follow. This departure from factual precision is probably not great
enough for anyone to quarrel with—except, of course, descendants of Bell who could,
with some justification, feel shortchanged.

That is in itself an important point. No group of Americans is more proudly assert-
ive of the rights of their ancestors, as against those of the historian, than are we Texans,
and I wish at once to make my peace with deep-rooted natives who will not find their
forebears within. They must keep in mind that in an album history designed to show-
case fine old photographs, extensive—and painful—editing has been necessary to result
in an affordable volume.

Similarly, I should probably also expect some modicum of critical snorting over
what has been left out. It is not hard to envision the reviewer leafing through these
pages looking for that topic on which he is particularly expert, only to discover to his
pious horror that I have given it short shrift or omitted it entirely. Indeed, there are
omissions to flog me for. Sterling Robertson's colony was in some respects as successful
as Austin's; had I the space I would have covered it, as well as the Philosophical
Society, the influence of the Masonic orders in early Texas, and the careers of such
fascinating stalwarts as Gail Borden and Ashbel Smith. They, and topics varying from
the German breweries to the invention of the hamburger, were excised.

Again, affordability of the volume was of paramount concern. There is little sense
to writing a book if when it is produced nobody can buy it. What is presented here is
broad and a bit impressionistic—rather like a time line sketched by a literary cubist.
The object was not to produce a definitive history, but to produce, textually, an engaging first read for someone new to the subject; interpretively, new lighting on some
topics that have become hidebound either by tradition or in revision; and visually, a
window into what it was like to live in that magical period.

Austin, Texas
October 1984

A stagecoach disembarks in Austin,
circa 1870.

A man on the stage who sat near said—
"Reckon you've read a good deal, hain't you?"
"Oh, yes; why?"
"Reckoned you had."
"Why?"
"You look as though you like to read. Well, it's a good thing. S'pose you take a
pleasure in reading, don't you?"
"That depends, of course, on what I have to read. I suppose everybody likes to
read when they find anything interesting to them, don't they?"
"No; it's damn tiresome to some folks, I reckon any how, 'less you've got the
habit of it. Well, it's a good thing; you can pass away your time so."

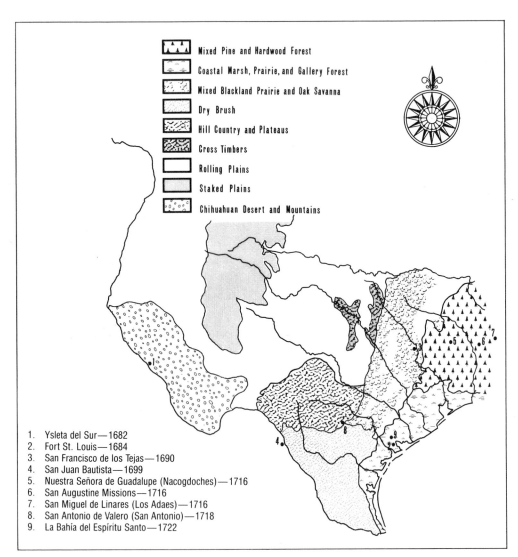

Legend:

- Mixed Pine and Hardwood Forest
- Coastal Marsh, Prairie, and Gallery Forest
- Mixed Blackland Prairie and Oak Savanna
- Dry Brush
- Hill Country and Plateaus
- Cross Timbers
- Rolling Plains
- Staked Plains
- Chihuahuan Desert and Mountains

1. Ysleta del Sur—1682
2. Fort St. Louis—1684
3. San Francisco de los Tejas—1690
4. San Juan Bautista—1699
5. Nuestra Señora de Guadalupe (Nacogdoches)—1716
6. San Augustine Missions—1716
7. San Miguel de Linares (Los Adaes)—1716
8. San Antonio de Valero (San Antonio)—1718
9. La Bahía del Espíritu Santo—1722

SPANISH TEXAS

At the time France acquired Louisiana from Spain, no boundary had been marked between that province and Texas, a condition still extant when the United States bought the tract in 1803. President Jefferson therefore claimed Texas as part of the deal, an assertion disputed by the King of Spain. Both countries rushed armies to the region to uphold their respective national dignities.

Commanding the American force was General James Wilkinson, who took a bold initiative. Without authority, he wrote the Spanish governor of Texas, Antonio Cordero, explaining that "operations are at issue a thousand miles from the source of authority . . . and [except for] the point of Honor, the subject of our test is scarcely

Introduction

FROM the time the northwestern coast of the Gulf of Mexico was first mapped, by the Spaniard Alonso Álvarez de Piñeda in 1519, no European ventured there until another Spaniard, a naked, shipwrecked Alvar Núñez Cabeza de Vaca, washed ashore like a piece of hairy flotsam.

It was November 6, 1528. Henry VIII was King of England, still married to his first wife. Titian was the greatest artist in Europe, and Martin Luther was reforming the church. Charles V, the Holy Roman Emperor, had just sacked Rome and captured the Pope. Suleiman the Magnificent ruled the Ottoman Empire and was preparing to lay siege to Vienna. In the New World the struggle for survival was simpler, as Cabeza de Vaca and his three companions eluded the coastal cannibals and made their way inland. They took little notice of the geography of the new wilderness; its sheer vastness was an enemy. Sometimes alone and sometimes in the servitude of Indians who spared their lives, they wandered through brackish marshes and dark, moss-hung gallery forests along the rivers. Heading west and northwest, they encountered lush, mild prairies, followed by a higher region of swift, shallow rivers and rocky, broken hills. The vegetation thinned and dried as they continued, into brushy scrub and finally the cactus deserts of their own New Spain.

Having regained civilization, Cabeza de Vaca uttered the magic word—Cíbola—and in 1540 an expedition led by Francisco Vásquez de Coronado set out to find the Seven Cities of Gold. Traveling north and then east, they found instead mud-walled pueblos before encountering a high, dry, buffalo-crowded grassland so bare of trees that at night they had to tether their horses to spikes driven into the ground. The region became known as the Staked Plains.

Other Spaniards saw different faces of the new land. When Hernando de Soto died in 1542 without finding the riches he had envisioned upon landing in Florida, some of his men continued west. Led by Luís Moscoso de Alvarado, they crossed the mighty river that split the continent and entered a region of sticky red soil that supported rolling, fragrant pine forests. As they pressed onward, the soil changed and with it the trees, first a belt of cedar breaks and then one of tall, spreading post oaks, and finally a

---

worth the blood of one brave man." Wilkinson offered to pull his troops back to the line claimed by Spain, the Arroyo Hondo, if his counterpart, General Symon de Herrera, pulled his troops back to the line claimed by the United States, the Sabine River, until the two countries could agree on a boundary.

Herrera answered that "Your Ex'cy manifesting by these operations, the peaceful ideas that possesses [sic] you . . . these proceedings oblige me" to agree. The Neutral Ground Agreement, November 6, 1806, muddied the boundary question for a generation, but averted a war and reflect credit on the officers who dared it.

low, lush prairie studded with patches of forest. By the time they reached the river that became known as the Brazos de Dios—the Arms of God—they had acquired some appreciation for the scale of the new geography, and turned back. In 1582 Antonio de Espejo took a closer look at the hostile desert country that lay just beyond the river which led up to Coronado's pueblos. The Indians there called the stream Po-so-ge, Mighty Water. Espejo when he crossed named it the Rio del Norte. In 1598 Juan de Oñate arrived at the same stream and called it the Rio Grande. Exercising his royal commission, Oñate thrust his sword into the ground and claimed the entirety of the new empire for the King of Spain.

None of the early explorations yielded any trace of gold or silver, however. All they found were Indians: the natives of the pueblos were easy enough to subdue at first, but all around them roamed the fierce raiders that Oñate named Apaches. In the coastal marshes and forests lurked Karankawas, six-foot cannibals smeared with alligator grease against mosquitoes. More to the northeast, on the prairies, were a host of smaller tribes whose demeanor swayed from indifferent to ferocious. With no precious metals to exploit and no willing colonists to hazard a settlement, Spain seemed content to let the place alone. The only permanent towns, Ysleta del Sur and Socorro del Sur on the upper Rio Grande, were started in 1682 by survivors fleeing a sudden pueblo uprising farther north.

Still, a claim had been staked, and the other colonial powers in Europe took notice. Robert Cavelier, Sieur de la Salle, a French explorer, spent the years 1679 to 1682 probing up and down the Mississippi River. When he returned home, Louis XIV commissioned him to start a settlement at the great river's mouth, close enough to post a challenge to Spanish claims. La Salle, either by accident or secret design, sailed past that point and landed at La Bahía del Espíritu Santo, now Lavaca Bay. Several expeditions sortied from his Fort St. Louis, some west to learn what the Spanish were up to, then some east to locate the Mississippi. The Spanish were suitably jarred to learn of the French incursion, but by the time a column could be sent to attack it, in 1689 under the governor of Coahuila, Captain Alonso de Léon, La Salle was dead—murdered by one of his own—and Fort St. Louis was a deserted shambles, the victim of disease, mutiny and Karankawas. De Léon could not know that, and as his expedition neared the bay marked Espíritu Santo, tensions mounted. "In the villages through which we passed," he reported, "we found some books that the Indians had in the French language, and in very good condition, with other trinkets of little value." Making inquiries through a captive interpreter, de Léon learned that, not counting those French who had marched off overland and never returned, "the rest had been settled on the little Sea (that is, the Bay), and that all had died at the hands of the Indians of the coast; . . . and that it had been three months since it had happened; and that previously, an epidemic of small pox had killed the rest." Governor de Léon asked to be guided to the place. "We went through some great plains in which there were not many trees in great distances. We went eight leagues until we reached a creek of good water [probably the Lavaca]. . . . The land all seemed pleasant, and we saw many buffalo." On a rainy Thursday, April 22, 1689, "we found it, and having stopped the force [the distance of] an arquebus shot from it, we went to look, and found all the houses sacked, the boxes all broken, and the bottle cases, also the other furnishings that the settlers had had; more than 200 books (it seemed) in the French language, broken, and the pages thrown in the patios were rotten.

"We found three dead bodies strewn in the field, one of which seemed to be a woman by the clothes that still clung to the bones, which we gathered and gave burial to with a Mass sung with the bodies present. . . .

"We looked for more dead bodies, and could not find them, which caused us to conclude that they had been cast into the arroyo and that the alligators, many in number, had eaten them. The settlement was located in a good place, on a plain good enough for defense from whatever might happen.

"The principal house of this settlement is of ships' timber made in the manner of a boarded fort. . . . On the doorcase of the principal door was located the year of the settlement, which was 1684."

Governor de Léon was relieved that the French threat had disappeared, but one other discovery aroused his consternation: "We found more than a hundred stocks of

MISSION SAN LUÍS DE LAS AMARILLAS. Of all the Spanish missions in Texas, the history of none was more bizarre than of this one, near the San Saba River some hundred miles northwest of San Antonio de Béxar.

From their earliest *entradas* the Spanish had considered the Apaches the most dangerous of the Indians in Texas, and enlisted the aid of as many other tribes as they could to fight them, including Comanches—fierce, mounted nomads who were showing up in Texas in increasing numbers as their Sioux rivals pushed them off the North Plains. By the mid-1700s the Comanches had driven the Apaches out of most of their Texas haunts, including the limestone hills northwest of Béxar.

In 1749 a group of Lipan Apaches rode into that settlement, won a truce, and requested that a mission be built for them in their country on the San Saba. What they did not tell the gullible Franciscan friars was that they had lost the San Saba country to the Comanches years before. The Spanish bureaucracy considered the proposal for eight years, during which the Apaches not only obtained a fortune in food and trade gifts in Béxar, but raided Comanche villages, leaving some of the Spanish hardware behind. The San Saba mission was finally built in 1757, and the following spring its small Apache constituency vanished shortly before the garrison and clergy were butchered by two thousand howling, buffalo-horned Comanches.

Not until 1790 could the Spanish exact a full measure of revenge, when the governor of Coahuila, Don Juan de Ugalde, with Comanche help trapped and massacred most of the Texas Lipans in a canyon west of Béxar.

flintlock arquebuses. . . . There were near and in the fort and the houses eight pieces of Artillery of Iron, of medium weight of four and six pound shot, and three very old swivel guns. . . . [T]here were some ship's guns from off the ships; and as all were in the street it was no accident."

The empty wedge of continent now held importance as a buffer against French ambitions, and the Spanish decided to colonize, relying on their tried, if not always true, mission system. The dual objectives of the missions were, first, to show the flag of empire in new territories, while second, Christianizing the native inhabitants. When

THE OLD STONE FORT. The Spanish decision to abandon East Texas in 1773 was the result of a report by the Marqués de Rubí, whom the king had sent to investigate the condition of internal defenses. Rubí recommended that Spain should contract her frontiers and consolidate her holdings for them to be defended adequately.

Some settlers in the region lost a great deal of property with the forced evacuation. One of them, Antonio Gil Ybarbo, born at Los Adaes in 1729 to Andalusian immigrants, petitioned the government to go back, "begging your lordship (Commandant General of the Interior Provinces Teodoro de Croix) to be pleased to take pity on us."

As "your most attentive and grateful subject kisses your lordship's hand," he was allowed to return as far east as Nacogdoches in 1779. La Casa Prieta was erected under Ybarbo's direction during the reoccupation. Although called a fort, it was more frequently used as a warehouse and jail; members of the Nolan expedition were locked up here in 1801. The Gutiérrez-Magee Republic took the building for their "Green Flag" in 1813, and it served as the capitol of the abortive republics of Dr. James Long in 1819 and Haden Edwards in 1826.

Volunteers were sworn into the Republic of Texas army here, and Texas' first district court convened here in March 1837. Efforts to save the building shown here failed, and it was torn down in 1902. It was reconstructed in 1936 on a different site, from the identical plan and using the same stones.

the first one in this quarter was established it was in the tall, damp pine forests that bordered right on French Louisiana. The Indians there were passive and easygoing; The Spanish called them by one of the natives' own words: *tejas,* or as de Léon spelled it, *texas,* meaning "friend" or "ally." Their mission, San Francisco de los Tejas, was built on the Neches River in May of 1690, and a second soon followed.

The entire region, ill-defined but bounded approximately by the flow of the Red River, was proclaimed Spanish and a governor, Domingo Terán de los Ríos, was appointed. He inspected his wilderness in 1691, but as the French excitement diminished,

José Antonio Navarro, an early view of the rancher, merchant, lawyer and politician who was preeminent in early Texas affairs. A San Antonio de Béxar native of Corsican extraction, born in 1795, Navarro was active in the Gutiérrez-Magee Rebellion, and after its collapse he lived in exile in Louisiana until 1816. During Stephen Austin's first visit to San Antonio in 1821 the two became friends. Navarro represented Texas in the legislature of Coahuila y Texas when the dual state was created in 1824, and he assisted Ben Milam and others in obtaining empresario grants before receiving land of his own.

He was elected to the National Congress in 1833, but upon elevation to senator in 1835 he faked an illness to avoid Mexico City during the Santanista upheaval. Navarro signed the Declaration of Independence in 1836, helped draft the Constitution, and was elected to the Third and Fourth Congresses of the Republic of Texas.

President Lamar persuaded him to accompany the Santa Fe Expedition in 1841. When the group was captured, Navarro was surrendered on a guarantee of protection, but he was condemned to death by Mexican President Santa Anna. Eventually, he was paroled from San Juan de Ullóa dungeon, escaped the country on a British vessel, and reached home in February of 1845. Navarro favored annexation to the United States, and was the only Mexican native in the Convention of 1845. While he distinguished himself in the state legislature, he also espoused secession in 1861. He died in 1871.

the missions were withdrawn. The Spanish retired as far southwest as San Juan Bautista, an outpost on the Rio Grande near present Eagle Pass, and the Texas matter rested for more than twenty years. In 1714, though, a traveler arrived there: Louis Juchereau de St. Denis, a French adventurer who had crossed the breadth of Texas undetected. His arrival hit the Spanish like a bucket of water.

St. Denis argued that he was only in search of trade, but was hustled off in arrest to Mexico City to tell his story there. Soon Captain Domingo Ramón and Father Francisco Hidalgo headed east from San Juan Bautista to penetrate deep into eastern Texas and post a whole picket line of missions. Near the original San Francisco de los Tejas

JANE HERBERT WILKINSON LONG, niece of the American officer who devised the Neutral Ground Agreement in 1806, was the wife of Mississippi filibuster Dr. James Long. General James Wilkinson was one of Long's backers, and Jane too was active in his schemes. She had been in Nacogdoches when the Spanish retook it; she fled, joining her husband at Jean Lafitte's pirate base on Galveston Island. She begged her husband to let her join his Goliad march, but he refused. Lafitte's camp was shut down by the United States Navy after an attack on an American ship, and Jane spent the frigid winter on the island, alone except for her five-year-old daughter and her slave, Kiamatia. Four days before Christmas 1821, Jane was delivered of a baby girl, Mary James, the first known Anglo born in Texas. For this feat Jane Long is sometimes awarded the sobriquet "Mother of Texas."

She was rescued the following summer but returned to Texas as one of Austin's colonists. A resident of Brazoria before opening a hotel in Richmond, Jane Long hobnobbed with all the best. She was romantically linked with Ben Milam, and President Lamar dedicated poetry to her. She died in 1880 at the age of eighty-two.

they placed a new one in 1716, followed farther east by Nuestra Señora de Guadalupe, with its settlement that became Nacogdoches. Eastward still, three missions marked the beginnings of the town of San Augustine. A fifth mission, San Miguel de Linares, was established about halfway between the Sabine and Red rivers. Once these were in place, other missions were placed closer in, linking them to the Spanish mother world. Of these the most important were San Antonio de Valero, with its protective presidio, San Antonio de Béxar, built in 1718 at a halfway point, and four years later near La Salle's ruined fort, Mission La Bahía del Espíritu Santo. The capital of the new province was established at its distant outpost, Mission San Miguel, and called Los Adaes, near present Robeline, Louisiana. The linking route, from San Juan Bautista through San Antonio de Béxar to Los Adaes, became El Camino Real, the King's Highway.

From 1720 four new missions were added to San Antonio, and in 1731 fifteen families of Canary Islanders were imported to strengthen the colony. San Antonio survived, but the eastern theater of missions eventually fizzled. They were simply too remote to be supplied or protected adequately. In 1772 the capital was moved from Los Adaes to San Antonio de Béxar, and in 1773 all the eastern outposts were evacuated. Some settlers lost considerable property with the abandonment and petitioned the government until they were allowed to return as far east as Nacogdoches in 1779. This time the town stuck.

Spanish suspicion of activities in French Louisiana became more complicated after Great Britain's American colonies gained their independence in 1783. France had aided their revolution, and the increasing numbers of rowdy American rustics—they became known collectively as filibusters—along the eastern border concerned the Spanish. Their fears seemed confirmed in 1801 when one American named Philip Nolan was discovered with a force of armed men deep in the central Texas prairies. Apparently, they were catching wild horses and had some dealings with Indians; when the Spanish attacked, Nolan was killed and nine of his men taken prisoner to Mexico. Only one was ever seen again.

There was much about the Nolan affair that foreshadowed the next fifty years' friction between Americans and Spanish. The latter attacked with overwhelming odds, more than ten to one, and opened fire without any attempt to learn the Americans' intentions. Then, according to the lone Nolan survivor, Peter Ellis Bean, "about three o'clock in the afternoon they hoisted a white flag, and (through an American that was with them) told us that the commander wanted us to return to our own country, and not remain there with the Indians. We quickly agreed to go as companions with them, but not give up our guns. . . .

"In some days after we arrived at Nacogdoches, the commandant told us he was waiting for orders from Chihuahua to set us at liberty and send us home. We waited in this hope for about a month, when, instead of our liberty, we were seized and put in irons, and sent off under a strong guard to San Antonio. Here we lay in prison three months. Then we were started to Mexico, but were stopped at San Luis Potosí, where we were confined in prison one year and four months. . . .

"[After] we had passed five years, in all, in Mexico . . . a colonel read to us the king's order—which was, that every fifth man was to be hung, for firing on the king's troops. This was to be decided by throwing dice on the head of a drum. Whoever threw lowest, was to be executed."

The Spanish practices of surprise attack, capture by treachery, imprisonment without charge or trial, and execution by lottery, were all aspects of the Hispanic way of doing things that disgusted and outraged border ruffians like Bean and Nolan. "These are a people," wrote Bean, "in whom you should put no trust or confidence whatever."

Soon after the United States purchased Louisiana in 1803 a more sinister plot was uncovered. Aaron Burr, once American Vice President and now on the lam for killing the Secretary of the Treasury, concocted a scheme to wrest an empire in Texas from the Spanish. The "Burr Conspiracy" was timely thwarted, but it left Spain more suspicious than ever.

The filibusters were not alone in perceiving evil in the Spanish regime, and Mexico's internal difficulties also led to trouble in Texas. The rebellion of Father Miguel Hidalgo y Costilla to free Mexico in 1810–11 failed, but one of his followers, Bernardo Gutiérrez de Lara, kept the cause alive. He won the support of an American army officer in Louisiana, Augustus Magee, who resigned his commission and helped Gutiérrez raise an expeditionary force. They called themselves the Republican Army of the North, and marching under their Green Flag captured Nacogdoches, Goliad, and San Antonio de Béxar—the only towns in the province. Independence was declared and a constitution drafted; spring of 1813 saw Texas standing as an independent state. On August 18, however, Gutiérrez' army of a thousand was crushed by royalist forces in a battle southwest of San Antonio, on the Medina River. Most were massacred.

Then came more ambitious Americans. In 1819 Dr. James Long of Mississippi invaded, and again Nacogdoches fell. The Spanish retook it while Long was absent, trying to enlist help from a French pirate, Jean Lafitte, who ruled over a robbers' roost on Galveston Island, near the Louisiana border. Long struck again in 1821, from near Lafitte's camp, and managed to take Goliad, but he was captured and sent, like his predecessors, to a mysterious death in Mexico.

Moses and the Promised Land

MOSES AUSTIN.

THE chronically unstable and unproductive state of affairs in Texas might have continued indefinitely but for the appearance of an enterprising Connecticut Yankee named Moses Austin. From New England he had moved to Virginia and then west, a successful financial venturer who came to own interests in a bank and a lead mine. He also had an eye for real estate, and in 1797 he moved into that part of Spanish Louisiana which eventually became Missouri, to take advantage of the more pliable land laws. He did so well there that he renounced his American citizenship, became a subject of the Spanish king, and enjoyed a good relationship with local officials. In 1800, however, the huge tract of Louisiana was ceded to France and then sold, in 1803, to the United States, and Austin found himself an American again. He was not pleased, but he was adaptable and continued to prosper. He had a spacious home in the town of Potosi, Missouri, and his elder son, Stephen, studied two and a half sessions at Transylvania University in Kentucky before assuming responsibilities in the family businesses.

Moses Austin carried in the back of his mind a scheme for a trade mission to the Southwest, in Spanish Texas, perhaps as early as 1813, but it was vague, unformed, and unimportant. In 1819, however, there was a financial panic, and Austin was suddenly a ruined man. With nothing to do but begin anew, and knowing that he had done very well under Spain before, the Texas scheme reasserted itself. "I found nothing I could do would bring back my property again," he wrote, "and to remain in a Country where I had enjoyed wealth in a state of poverty I could not submit to." Details were probably lacking even in his own mind, but in January of 1820 he wrote to Washington to obtain a copy of his Spanish passport in case it should prove handy. Spain was known to have been encouraging its Mexican subjects to move into the uninhabited portions of Texas to secure the wilderness from the Indians and begin to make the region productive. Moreover, Spain knew as well as any colonial power that possession was the greater part of establishing ownership, and to settle the region would lessen any claims that foreign governments could lay on it. During the summer Austin's plans became firmer: to establish an Anglo-American colony in Texas, loyal to Spain, with himself as empresario. Between the land grant he would receive from the government and the settling fees charged to immigrants, his fortune could be remade. He broached the idea to Stephen, who, with tact and respect, discouraged the scheme as too improbable to succeed. The greatest threat to Spain's territorial entity was now the United States, which had strong-armed the cession of Florida only the year before. Spain could not be expected to trust expatriate Americans to hold the frontier against the near religion of expansion from their homeland.

Stephen F. Austin's financial plight was nearly as precarious as his father's, although for a man of twenty-seven he had remarkable experience. Besides working in his father's enterprises, he had served six years in the territorial legislature of Missouri, done a stint as adjutant of militia, and been chief officer of the Bank of St. Louis until it was wrecked by the panic of 1819. He then moved to Arkansas and accepted an ap-

DURHAM HALL, the Austin family seat in Potosi, Missouri.

MOSES AUSTIN'S PETITION to establish an American colony,
in "Baron" Felipe de Bastrop's handwriting.

pointment as district judge, and it was in Little Rock that Moses Austin visited his son
in October 1820 and pressed his Texas scheme. Stephen's circumstances were now
better than his father's, although just barely; unable to turn him away, he relented and
backed Moses' trip to Texas' provincial capital of San Antonio de Béxar. Stephen provided him a horse, a pack mule, a slave, and fifty dollars, for all of which he was duly
receipted, and Moses set off for Natchitoches, Louisiana. That town was the eastern
terminus of El Camino Real, the royal road, a dirt trace down which, four hundred
miles to the west, lay Béxar and the governor. Stephen himself left Arkansas for New
Orleans to try to find a better job, but times were bad. Nearly two months after his
father had ridden into Texas, Stephen wrote his mother, "I offered to hire myself out as
a clerk, as an overseer, or anything else, but business here is too dull. . . . There are
hundreds of young men who are glad to work for their board."

When Moses Austin struck into Texas late in November, the lushness of the country surpassed even his expectations. In heading west he passed through a succession of
broad belts of timber, first tall pine, then cedar breaks, and finally open forests of post
oak, before emerging onto rippling grass prairies. The rivers were clear and strong,
game abundant. He entered Béxar two days before Christmas 1820.

Antonio de Martínez had been royal governor of Texas since 1817, which was, for
that position, a long tenure (he had been the fourth man to assume the title in that year
alone). He was apparently a deft politician, sensitive to prevailing winds of sentiment,

but nevertheless a part of the Spanish hierarchy that placed as much emphasis on manners, minutiae, and genuflection as it did on policy or results. His view of Americans seems to have been just what Stephen expected it would be.

Moses Austin was a man of energy, persuasion, and optimism, but the good relationship he'd had with the royal bureaucracy twenty years before had been a fortunate accident. The level of diplomacy required for moving in higher Spanish political circles was beyond him. Instead of making his presence in Béxar known and awaiting an invitation from the governor, Austin presented himself and his deal to Martínez directly. When the governor learned that the boor before him was an American, he had heard enough. He didn't even look at Austin's papers before ordering him out of the city at once, and to return whence he came "with all possible speed." Crestfallen, Austin headed toward his lodging, but then had a remarkable stroke of luck: in the plaza he met an old friend from his Louisiana days, the Baron Felipe de Bastrop. Actually, he was not a baron at all but a shady Dutch tax collector whose successful embezzling had financed his start in the New World. He had conferred the title on himself— although he had owned considerable property in Louisiana when Austin knew him— and he wore it convincingly. His debonair manners and facile tongue had gained him entry into all the best houses, and he counted Martínez among his friends. Austin did not know he wasn't a baron.

Austin confided his hopes and his frustration to his old friend, and Bastrop, sensing the merits of the enterprise and also a chance to advance his own fortunes, agreed to exert his influence. He redrafted Austin's proposal into a petition of the obsequious formality required by the Spanish Government, calling attention to Austin's Catholicism, his past Spanish citizenship and faithful service to the king. In talking to the governor, Bastrop doubtless focused Martínez' attention on the crux that somebody must populate the frontier to hold it against the Indians, and that other Mexicans had refused to leave the more established areas; in fact, the population of Texas had been declining. As long as the colonists were Catholics and swore allegiance to the Spanish crown, the future tax revenues to be gained would more than offset the onus that they came from North Americans. It was virtually the only prospect to change Texas' dismal complexion, and Martínez probably needed no reminding how much more he stood to gain by governing a rich province than a paupered one. Moreover, King Ferdinand VII had reestablished the liberal Constitution, and it could not hurt to make a good impression by implementing the king's policy that former subjects displaced by the Napoleonic upheavals—of which the loss of Louisiana was one—be allowed to resettle.

Bastrop's persuasive powers carried the day, and Austin was granted a second audience. The town council—the *ayuntamiento*—was called into session to discuss the proposal, and three days later Martínez agreed to forward Austin's plan with a favorable endorsement to his superior. The man with authority in the matter was Joaquín de Arredondo, Commandant General of the Eastern Interior Provinces. If Arredondo approved, Austin would be granted two hundred thousand acres of his choice. On this tract he would settle three hundred families, loyal to Spain, and for whose good character Austin would be responsible.

Buoyantly, Austin set off on the road to Louisiana, but the return trip was one of terrible difficulty. One of his traveling companions, a man named Kirkham, proved to be a scoundrel who had used his time in Béxar to make black market connections.

Austin, stricken with the fear that his own venture could suffer for the unfortunate association, quickly sent a full disclosure of the mischief to Bastrop. What was worse, Austin's gunpowder became ruined, and for the last week or more of the journey the fifty-three-year-old man and his servant had to subsist entirely on roots and acorns. The slave was so broken down that he had to be left with an acquaintance at the international boundary, and on January 15, 1821, Austin reached McGuffin's Inn near Natchitoches, "after undergoing," as he wrote, "everything but death." His physical constitution was broken, and he was bedridden for three weeks before he could resume his trip to Missouri.

STEPHEN FULLER AUSTIN, a portrait
attributed to George Catlin.

His recuperation was slow, but his spirits soared during the spring when he received word that Commandant General Arredondo had approved the colony. Austin had received applications or inquiries from enough families to fill his contract already, and he calculated his empresario fees—when paid—at eighteen thousand dollars. "I can now go forward with confidence," he wrote Stephen on May 22, "and I hope and pray that you will Discharge your Doubts as to the Enterprise . . . Raise your Spirits[.] Times are changing[,] a new chance presents itself." Three weeks later he was dead of pneumonia.

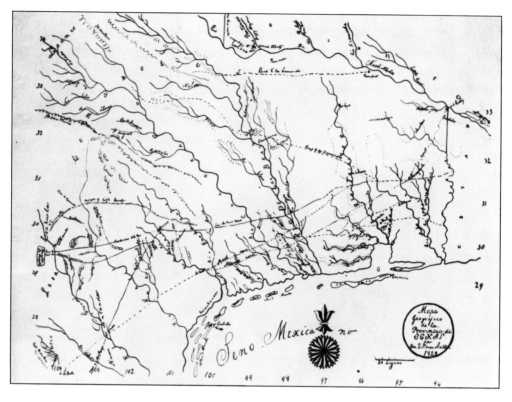

AUSTIN'S SKETCH MAP of the Texas lands he
explored in the fall of 1821.

During his father's absence Stephen remained dubious; he was not anxious to leave New Orleans just when things were looking up. He had a job helping to edit the *Advertiser,* and still better, he had become friends with a lawyer, Joseph Hawkins. The younger Austin had known Hawkins' brother at school in Kentucky, and after a brief acquaintance Joseph offered to keep Austin up while he studied the French language and law to enter practice. "An offer so generous," he wrote his family, "and from a man who two months ago was a stranger to me, has almost made me change my opinion of the human race." He was still worried that his Missouri creditors might prosecute him, and he estimated it would take a year and a half to study. During that time, he was sorry to say, he could send them no money. But once he learned the law, "I then shall have the means of fortune within my reach. I am determined to accept of Hawkins' offer." Just when things seemed to have some pattern and progression, he received the news from his father, along with the suggestion that Hawkins, a man of means, be brought into the venture. Stephen was to outfit a vessel with supplies and send it to the mouth of the Colorado River to begin the port of Austina, and then meet Moses in Natchitoches at the beginning of summer with a crew of explorers and laborers. Before many inquiries had been made, however, Stephen received two letters, one from his mother and one from his brother-in-law, James Bryan, telling him that his father, never fully recovered from the ordeal of returning from Béxar, was desperately ill. But events had now been set in motion; Governor Martínez had sent a delegation to meet the

Austins in Natchitoches, and Stephen, after arranging with Hawkins to open his mail for news of his father, went up to meet them.

Whatever personal doubts Martínez had about the venture, he now seemed willing to cooperate, and the escort he dispatched for the Austins was impressive. Aside from several traders, it included Béxar's *alcalde* (the Mexican equivalent of mayor), Josef Erasmo Seguín, and a scion of the town's most prestigious family, Juan Martín de Veramendi. Stephen arrived on board a Red River steamer on June 26, and soon after a messenger from Hawkins informed him of his father's decease. The letter forwarded from his mother urged on him Moses Austin's dying wish: "He called me to his bedside and with much distress and difficulty of speech beged *[sic]* me to tell you to take his place and if god *[sic]* in his wisdom thought it best to disappoint him in the accomplishment of his wishes and plans formed, he prayed him to extend his goodness to you and enable you to go on with the business in the same way he would have done."

Doubtfully but dutifully, Austin assumed his father's place in the venture. Accompanied by Seguín and Veramendi and the others, as well as his own party of men to explore possible sites for the colony, he departed for San Antonio de Béxar on July 3. Martínez received him warmly, and Austin made a profound impression on the governor, who characterized the young empresario as "a man of high honor, of scrupulous regard for formality, and of desiring to learn how to discharge faithfully the duties proposed by his late father." And he was befriended as well by the Baron de Bastrop.

During ten days in Béxar, Austin worked out the details of his settlement plan. Each immigrating man would receive 640 acres, with additional allotments for his

THE OLD HAND-PULLED FERRY, SAN FELIPE. The Colorado River was not a barrier to settlement for long. This hand-pulled ferry went into service in 1823 and stayed in business for over a century, as shown by its cargo in this photograph.

women and children. After Martínez gave his permission to explore the valley of the Colorado River down to its mouth, Austin pushed southeast to La Bahía, the only other settlement in the interior. He presented his credentials to the alcalde there, obtained a guide (who got lost), and set off, still unpersuaded of his scheme's feasibility, into the wilderness.

Exceeding his commission, Austin explored through the late summer and fall, mapping the Guadalupe River to its mouth, northeast to the Colorado and down to its mouth, then northeast again to the Brazos River and down to its mouth. During this time his attitude toward the venture changed profoundly. As he recalled to his cousin Mary Austin Holley some years later: "When I explored this country in 1821, it was a wild, howling interminable solitude from Sabine to Bexar. . . . [But] I found the country so much more valuable than I expected that the idea of contributing to fill it with a civilized and industrious population filled my soul with enthusiasm." At last, Austin's abundant but undirected talent had, not just a job to do, but something to live for, a life's work that became "the idol of my existence—it . . . assumed the character of a *religion* for the guidance of my thoughts and actions." From La Bahía he had sent a flier of sorts back to Louisiana for publication, inviting inquiries from the general public. But his motives, he insisted, were pure. "I can with truth and a clear conscience say that none of the sordid and selfish motives which influence the mass of adventurers had any weight in determining me to attack the wilderness. I commenced on the solid basis of sound and philanthropic intentions and of undeviating integrity."

Fall of 1821 found Austin back in Natchitoches, writing replies to the hundred or so letters he had received in response to his announcement. When he wrote a report for Martínez, he requested not the two hundred thousand acres granted his father but a huge tract over fifty times that size. Austin needed time to arrange details in New Orleans, and so let some of the colonists precede him to Texas, to be managed in his absence by an Arkansas acquaintance, Josiah Bell. Needing capital, Austin sold half his interest to Hawkins for four thousand dollars, which allowed him to buy a small ship, the *Lively*. He outfitted her with goods for his colonists, and instructed the crew to anchor at the mouth of the Colorado and wait for him. Austin then traveled to San Antonio de Béxar to clarify the land policy with Governor Martínez but received a shock: the revolutionary government in Mexico that had just ousted the Spanish had repudiated his land grant. Martínez' only advice was for Austin to go to Mexico City himself and try to rescue the scheme.

Nor was that the extent of Austin's trouble. The *Lively* had anchored at the mouth of the Brazos instead of the Colorado, waited, returned to New Orleans, and set out again. She got as far as Galveston Island before running aground, losing the entire cargo. Austin was ignorant of her fate as he waited for her in early March on the Colorado. He was in a worried frame of mind when he left Bell and the early arrivals on their own and struck out for Mexico City.

Fearing to be looted by highwaymen, Austin and his small party dressed as beggars. The bandits did not molest them, but they were briefly waylaid by Comanche Indians, who mistook them for Mexicans. When the warriors discovered their error, they apologized and returned all the goods they had taken, except for a Spanish-English dictionary. It was in April when Austin finished the twelve-hundred-mile trip, entering Mexico City, as he lamented in a letter, "without acquaintances, without

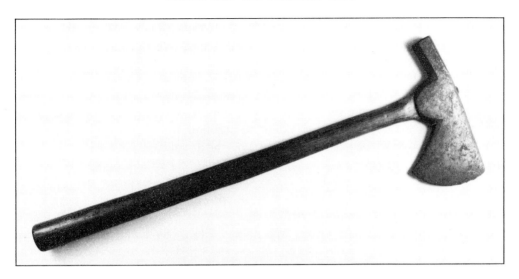

STEPHEN AUSTIN'S HATCHET, by which he literally as well as figuratively
brought civilization to Texas' unsettled wilderness.

friends, Ignorant of the Language, of the Laws, the forms, the disposition and feelings
of the Government, with barely the means of paying my expenses for a few months."

With Spanish authority overthrown, two major political parties emerged and grap-
pled for control: Centralists, who insisted on the strict maintenance of power in Mexico
City, and Federalists, who contended for a looser confederation of more autonomous
states. Each party contained subfactions whose loyalties varied with the passage of
time, bribes, and circumstances. Austin summarized that he "found the City in an
unsettled state, the whole people and country still agitated by the revolutionary con-
vulsion, public opinion vacillating—Party spirit raging."

Typically, though, he set to work, playing it safe, offending none, seeking to persuade all factions of the merits of his colony, generally getting a more sympathetic
hearing from Federalists anxious to develop that underpopulated sector of the frontier.
In May of 1822 the opposing Centralists declared General Agustín Iturbide emperor,
and Austin's petitions got nowhere in the Congress. Still, he worked on patiently. He
learned Spanish; he honed his skills in Mexican politics, learning in his advocacy to
strike the crucial balance between deference and machismo, between reason and his
hearer's self-interest.

Iturbide dissolved Congress in October, but in January 1823 Austin managed to
change the emperor's mind, and a colonization law was promulgated. And then no
sooner did Austin taste victory than the kaleidoscope of power shifted again. The
emperor was deposed and later shot, a new Congress called; the agreement was repudiated. Austin was widely respected by now, however, and in April he succeeded beyond
all his expectations.

Under the new law, each colonist would receive not the 640-acre section originally
conceived, but a maximum of a *league* (4,428 acres, for ranching) and a *labor* (177 acres,
for farming), with a clear title to be issued by Baron de Bastrop, who had become
Austin's land commissioner. Because the central government lacked funds to either

develop the new territory or provide even the most rudimentary services, Austin was proclaimed civil commandant, and 100,000 acres were appropriated as his own. Further, Austin was permitted to charge his settlers 12½¢ per acre to survey and defend the colony, and no taxes would be levied for six years. The central government required only that each colonist become a Mexican citizen and be baptized a Roman Catholic, but even here Austin won a concession for private religious toleration. His spectacular victory had taken a year of the most delicate negotiations and exhausting work, but when he returned to his people in August of 1823, he discovered that his labor had only begun.

The first corn crop, planted in the spring of 1822, withered in a drought. Karankawa Indians were intermittently hostile, and some immigrants had been killed. Others grew disgusted during Austin's year-and-a-half absence and went home. (When they heard the terms of the land policy, they came back.) Austin's contract called for him to settle three hundred families, and the document he submitted three

Austin House. After Stephen F. Austin established the Anglo-American settlement of Texas, many of his family followed either to visit or to reside permanently. Austin's own house was burned during the Runaway Scrape, after which he sometimes stayed with relatives at this family compound at Peach Point.

years later in fulfillment of the contract showed titles issued to 297. Soon known as the Old Three Hundred, they formed a root stock of Texas aristocracy.

In 1824 the Mexican Congress incorporated Texas into a new state, Coahuila y Texas, with the capital at Saltillo. When a companion law conferred on the states the power to set immigration laws, the Federalists in the state legislature of Coahuila y Texas granted not less than two dozen empresario contracts similar to Austin's, and the organized settlement of American-Texans turned into a chaotic land rush. For a time, however, the increase in numbers alone did not make life any easier.

One of the more important of the other empresarios, Green DeWitt, established the capital of his colony at Gonzales in 1825, at the confluence of the San Marcos and Guadalupe rivers. His settlers were so tormented by Indians that he removed them to the lower Lavaca River; it was at this latter location that he was visited by a young Kentucky blacksmith, Noah Smithwick. In his memoirs Smithwick recalled that as he disembarked and "set out on foot for DeWitt's colony . . . the beautiful rose color that tinged my visions of Texas paled with each succeeding step.

"The colonists, consisting of a dozen families, were living—if such existence could be called living—huddled together for security against the Karankawas, who, though not openly hostile, were not friendly. The rude log cabins, windowless and floorless . . . save as a partial protection against rain and sun were absolutely devoid of comfort.

"It was July, and the heat was intense. The only water obtainable was that of the sluggish river, which crept along between low banks thickly set with tall trees, from the branches of which depended long streamers of Spanish moss swarming with mosquitoes and pregnant of malaria. Alligators, gaunt and grim—certainly the most hideous creatures God ever made—lay in wait among the moss and drift for any unwary creature that might come down to drink. Dogs, of which every well regulated family had several, were their special weakness, and many a thirsty canine drank and never thirsted more. This was not perhaps from any partiality for dog meat; on the contrary, when the alligator went foraging under cover of night he evinced a decided preference for human flesh, particularly negroes. . . .

"The station being [temporary], they made no pretense of improving it, not even to the extent of planting corn, one of the first things usually attended to . . . so when the colonists used up the breadstuff they brought with them they had to do without until they raised it. [But] game was plenty the year round, so there was no need of starving.

"Men talked hopefully of the future; children reveled in the novelty of the present; but the women—ah, there was where the situation bore the heaviest. As one old lady remarked, Texas was 'a heaven for men and dogs, but a hell for women and oxen.' They —the women—talked sadly of the old homes and friends left behind . . . of the hardships and bitter privations they were undergoing and the dangers that surrounded them. They had not even the solace of constant employment. The spinning wheel and loom had been left behind. There was, as yet, no use for them—there was nothing to spin. There was no house to keep in order; the meager fare was so simple as to require little time for its preparation. There was no poultry, no dairy, no garden, no books . . . no schools, no churches—nothing to break the dull monotony of their lives, save an occasional wrangle among the children and dogs. The men at least had the excitement of killing game and cutting bee trees."

From DeWitt's coastal camp, Smithwick continued inland to Austin's capital at San Felipe, now a thriving town of perhaps two hundred which he found altogether more satisfactory. The second year's crops had been good, the colonists had become better acquainted, and life was easier. As Smithwick remembered, "they were a social people these old Three Hundred. . . . There were a number of weddings and other social gatherings during my sojourn in that section, the most notable one perhaps being the marriage of Nicholas McNutt to Miss Cartwright. . . . The bridegroom was a son of the widow McNutt, also among the early arrivals. The family, consisting of mother, two sons and three young daughters, came from Louisiana, where they had been very wealthy, but having suffered reverses they came to Texas to recoup their fortunes. Bred up in luxury, as they evidently had been, it was a rough road to fortune they chose, but they adapted themselves to the situation and made the most of it. Dr. Wells later married a Miss McNutt."

The men of Austin's colony still spent most of their time hunting, and trying to defend their encroachments against Comanche and Karankawa Indians. Smithwick earned a respectable living as their blacksmith, and he stayed around long enough to get a feel for the economic conditions: "Flour was $10 a barrel. Trading vessels came in sometimes, but few people had money to buy anything more than coffee and tobacco,

TWO OF THE OLD THREE HUNDRED. The Dr. Wells known to Smithwick was FRANCIS FLOURNOY WELLS of Virginia, born sometime around 1800. One of Austin's Louisiana recruits, he was granted a league and a labor of land on July 21, 1824, in Brazoria and Jackson counties. He had married MARTHA McNUTT by the time of the 1826 census, where she is cataloged as his wife "aged between sixteen and twenty-five." Wells' license to practice medicine in San Felipe was dated November 14, 1829, and he was appointed to the ayuntamiento's Board of Medical Examiners when it was created the following July. With his sister-in-law, Pamelia McNutt Porter, he founded the town of Texana, and was known to be still living in 1850.

VARNER PLANTATION, WEST COLUMBIA. This view of the old house built on the Varner grant was photographed before Governor James Hogg bought and massively renovated the place for his family seat in 1901.

which were considered absolutely indispensible. Money was as scarce as bread. There was no controversy about 'sound' money then. Pelts of any kind passed current and constituted the principal medium of exchange.

"Children forgot, many of them had never known, what wheaten bread was like. Old Martin Varner used to tell a good story of his little son's first experience with a biscuit. The old man had managed to get together money or pelts enough to buy a barrel of flour. Mrs. Varner made a batch of biscuits, which, considering the resources of the country, were doubtless heavy as lead. . . . When they were done Mrs. Varner set them on the table. The boy looked at them curiously, helped himself to one and made for the door with it. In a few minutes he came back for another. Doubting the child's ability to eat it so quickly, the old man followed him to see what disposition he made of the second. The ingenious youngster had conceived a novel and not altogether illogical idea of their utility. He had punched holes through the center, inserted an axle and triumphantly displayed a miniature Mexican cart. And I assure you, from my recollection of those pioneer biscuits, they were capable of sustaining a pretty heavy load.

"The repast was of the simplest, but served with as much grace as if it had been a feast, which, indeed, it became, seasoned with the kindly manners and pleasant conversation. . . . Not a word of apology was uttered during my stay of a day and night, and when I left them I did so with a hearty invitation to repeat my visit. It so happened that I never was at their place again, but was told that in the course of time the pole cabin gave place to a handsome brick house and that the rude furnishings were replaced by the best the country boasted, but I'll venture to say that the host and hostess still retained their old hospitality unchanged by change of fortune."

Austin's Dream Turns Sour

AUSTIN went to great lengths to ensure the character, industry, and literacy of his settlers, and almost to the last one they were ideal candidates for the enterprise.

However, after the last of his contracted colonists arrived, and after the state government of Coahuila y Texas threw wide the doors of immigration to other entrepreneurs, he lost control over what stripe of adventurer crossed the border. The "leatherstockings," as he called them, were moving in, and the deadly mix in the Deep South of a hot-blooded, chivalrous upper class and poor "white trash" kept a steady flow of fugitives splashing across the Sabine. Throughout the South, according to one observer, "G. T. T. (Gone to Texas) was the slang appendage . . . to every man's name who had escaped before the discovery of some rascality."

Most of the immigrants, of course, were just common folks looking to make a better life for themselves. Many came by their own hook, illegally, unaffiliated with any settlement contract. One unencumbered horseback traveler headed west overtook a number of the slower wagon trains. "Several families were frequently moving together, coming from the same district, or chance met and joined, for company, on the long road from Alabama, Georgia or the Carolinas. Before you come upon them you hear, ringing through the woods, the fierce cries and blows with which they urge on their jaded cattle. Then the stragglers appear, lean dogs or fainting negroes, ragged and spiritless. An old granny, hauling on, by the hand, a weak boy—too old to ride and too young to keep up. An old man, heavily loaded, with a rifle. Then the white covers of the wagons, jerking up and down as they mount over a root or plunge into a rut, disappearing, one after another, where the road descends. Then the active and cheery prime negroes, not yet exhausted, with a joke and a suggestion about tobacco. Then the black pickininnies, staring, in a confused heap, out at the back of the wagon, more and more of their eyes to be made out among the table legs and bedding as you get near; behind them, further in, the old people and young mothers, whose turn it is to ride. As you get by, the white mother and babies, and the tall, frequently ill-humored master, on horseback, or walking with his gun, urging up the black driver and his oxen. As a scout ahead is a brother, or an intelligent slave, with the best gun, on the lookout for a deer or a turkey. . . . They travel ten or fifteen miles a day, stopping wherever night overtakes them. The masters are plainly dressed, often in homespun, keeping their eyes about them, noticing the soil . . . generally dogged, surly, and silent. The women are silent, too, frequently walking, to relieve the teams, and weary, haggard, mud be-draggled, forlorn, and disconsolate, yet hopeful and careful."

Only one year after the state legislature at Saltillo passed their liberal immigration law, an incident occurred in Texas that appalled the central government and cost Coahuila much of the colonizing enthusiasm it had shown. They had granted some three hundred thousand acres near Nacogdoches to an American empresario named Haden

Edwards. Accompanied by his brother Benjamin, he arrived in the fall of 1825 and immediately began to bully the settlers already on the tract to pay him for permission to stay. Some of the titles he tried to expropriate derived from royal grants, and some of the families were the same who had resettled Nacogdoches with Gil Ybarbo in 1779. They protested. In June of 1826 the government revoked the Edwards' contract and ordered them to leave, but the two brothers, backed by a small band of followers beholden to them for their headrights, revolted. They declared the "Republic of Fredonia" and captured the stone fort erected by Ybarbo. Within six weeks they had fled to the United States, in the face of 250 Mexican soldiers and 100 militia drawn from Austin's colony.

Austin's loyalty was acknowledged, but the incident spotlighted wavering empresario authority, and Mexico began to understand that something was amiss with their plans for Texas.

To investigate the whole colonial matter the government sent one of its most intelligent and capable men, Don Manuel de Mier y Terán. A military figure of the Revolution, he had solidified his reputation in the defeat of the Tampico invasion. He had held a seat in the First Constituent Congress and served as Minister of War and

A DOGTROT CABIN. This was the favorite style of dwelling among Austin's colonists, so named for the open breezeway separating dual log pens. With time and prosperity, the passageway was often enclosed to form a central room, with sleeping lofts perhaps added under the eaves.

Admission to Austin's colony was stringently restricted. Each family head was required to submit affidavits of his good character, industry, and sobriety. Idlers, drunks, and interlopers were driven out of the settlements by force until they became too numerous to deal with. The terms of admission would probably be struck down in a court of law today, but for a few years, Austin's colony was peaceful and literate. Doors were left unlatched, and one observer was startled to hear a farmer reciting Tacitus while slopping his hogs.

The only vice tolerated was horse racing, which Austin allowed as an encouragement for stock improvement.

Navy. Best of all, he had several years' experience in colonial legislation and policy. Inspecting his way through Texas in the spring of 1828, Mier y Terán stopped in Nacogdoches and composed a report on June 28 to President Guadalupe Victoria. It was a document remarkable for its perception, forbearance, and common sense. Many of the Anglo complaints, he stated, were legitimate. The Mexican population, at least in the Nacogdoches region, was outnumbered ten to one, but retained political control and browbeat the colonists, who could not find legal redress nearer than Saltillo. The Mexicans "set themselves against the foreigners, deliberately setting nets to deprive them of the right of franchise and to exclude them from the ayuntamiento. The colonists find it unendurable that they must go three hundred leagues to lodge a complaint against the petty pickpocketing that they suffer from a venal and ignorant alcalde.

"The Mexicans of this town compris[e] what is in all countries called the lowest class—the very poor and very ignorant. [They] not only do not have sufficient means to establish schools, but they are not of the type that take any thought for the improvement of its public institutions or the betterment of its degraded condition. . . .

"It would cause you the same chagrin that it has caused me to see the opinion that is held of our nation by these foreign colonists, since, with the exception of some few who have been to our capital, they know no other Mexicans than the inhabitants about here.

"Thus . . . [there exists] an antagonism between Mexicans and foreigners, which is not the least of the smoldering fires which I have discovered. Therefore, I am warning you to take timely measures. Texas could throw the whole nation into revolution."

Another of the smoldering fires was slavery. Most of the Anglo families, even those of Austin's colony, who "are for the most part industrious and honest, and appreciate this country," owned at least one or two Negroes. This was not only odious, but increasingly dangerous, as the slaves learned that the state government was taking a position tolerant of their owners. Another was the increasing presence of criminals in the former No-man's Land on the American border. Most worrisome of all was the unanimity of opinion favoring Mexican statehood for Texas, separate from Coahuila.

"In spite of the enmity that usually exists between the Mexicans and the foreigners, there is a most evident uniformity of opinion on one point, namely the separation of Texas from Coahuila and its organization into a territory of the federal government. This idea, which was conceived by some of the colonists who are above the average, has become general among the people and does not fail to cause considerable discussion.

"They claim that Texas in its present condition of a colony is an expense, since it is not a sufficiently prosperous section to contribute to the revenues of the state administration; and since it is such . . . it ought not to be imposed upon a state as poor as Coahuila. . . ."

The economic argument was persuasive, and Texas had been promised full statehood, at an appropriate future time, by the law that created the dual state in 1824. The Americans had not become assimilated into Mexican culture. They were, he said, "more progressive and better informed than the Mexican inhabitants," and accustomed to having greater freedom. They viewed an enlightened political system as their birthright: "honorable and dishonorable alike travel with their political constitutions in their pockets, demanding the privileges . . . which such a constitution guarantees." Against these facts Mier y Terán had to consider that the Centralists were on the ascent again in Mexico City, and that statehood for Texas would probably not be granted in any case.

Thus, his recommendations were conciliatory to the Texan Anglos, but still Centralist. For political and judicial reform, a *jefe político* and court of appeals should be placed in Nacogdoches; and if Texas was poor, then the exemption from taxes which they had always enjoyed should be ended and customs houses placed at the ports. Mier y Terán did not advise expulsion of the American colonists. Rather, he preferred to make Texas more Mexican—to encourage emigration from the Mexican interior, even to the establishment in Texas of penal colonies, with land to be made available to convicts on their release.

HADEN EDWARDS, after bullying resident Mexicans until they got his contract revoked, was not personally present when his brother Benjamin launched the Fredonian Rebellion. In May of 1826 he had returned to the United States to drum up more capital for his troubled colony. After Mexican regulars and Austin's militia quelled the trouble, Edwards tried to revive the effort in Louisiana but failed, and went home to Kentucky. He returned to Nacogdoches when it was safe, and died there in 1849.

One of his thirteen children, Haden Hale Edwards, served with distinction in the Texas Revolution, and after annexation served two terms in the state legislature. Benjamin Edwards never hit a stride. One cause of the Fredonian failure was that the alliance he engineered with Texas Cherokee Indians never came through. He and the last of his insurgents escaped to Louisiana on January 31, 1827. When the Texas Revolution started he raised money and a regiment of volunteers in Mississippi, but the Battle of San Jacinto was fought before he could get them on the road. Frustrated again, he consoled himself by announcing for governor of Mississippi, but died before the election.

Mier y Terán was elevated to Commandant General of the eastern Interior States in 1829, but by the time legislative effect was given his Texas recommendations, the kaleidoscope of Mexican politics had rolled again. Guadalupe Victoria had left the presidency, the only one of this era to step down unaided. His successor was soon deposed and exiled by the Vice President, Anastasio Bustamante, a ruthless Centralist.

It was Bustamante's signature on the Law of April 6, 1830, which implemented Mier y Terán's Texas plans. Indeed, the Law of April 6 went the general one better. Article Eleven, the only one that Mier y Terán had not written, suspended unfilled empresario contracts and forbade any further immigration from the United States. The border was sealed, with entry by passport only.

One of the customs houses, with its garrison, was established at Anahuac, Texas' southeastern port of entry, on Trinity Bay. To enforce the Law of April 6, Mier y Terán sent out as garrison commander John (Juan) Davis Bradburn, a pompous, posturing ex-American soldier of fortune then in Mexican service. The first issue that aroused the settlers was his harassment and then arrest of the commissioner and surveyor sent by

GEORGE (JORGE) FISHER, born in Hungary in 1795, showed up in Mississippi sometime around 1817, having escaped merchants to whom he owed money under his redemption contract. He considered filibustering with James Long, but instead went to Mexico on his own to seek an empresario contract. He failed, but became a Mexican citizen in 1829 and picked up the lands forfeited by Haden Edwards for his Fredonian Rebellion.

After the Anahuac troubles, Fisher repaired to Matamoros, Mexico. Too conserva-tive for the Texans and too liberal for the Mexican Government, he was deported for publishing a newspaper critical of the regime. He was in New Orleans when the Revolution erupted. He returned to the town of Houston in 1837 and served in a variety of public posts after his admittance to the bar. Later adventures carried him to Panama and California, where he died in 1873.

This painting, possibly over a daguerreotype, was made shortly before he left Texas in 1850.

the state government to confirm land titles in the Anahuac area, which by this time had about a thousand American inhabitants. Before a year had passed, Bradburn had also impressed local slaves into his service without compensating the owners, annulled the ayuntamiento of the town of Liberty, and declared martial law along the coast.

Another American grabber in the Bustamante bureaucracy, George (Jorge) Fisher, became Bradburn's customs collector. He issued regulations for all Texas-bound cargo vessels to call at Anahuac for inspection, regardless of their destination or present location. One of the more forthright of the colonists, Edwin Waller of Virginia, owned the ship *Sabine,* then in port at Velasco, at the mouth of the Brazos some eighty miles from Anahuac. He joined other shipowners in refusing Fisher's order. When he was ready to sail, Waller offered the customs officer at Velasco an export duty of fifty dollars. The officer refused, but hinted that for a duty of one hundred dollars he could reconsider. The *Sabine*'s captain then sailed past the small harbor fort, musket balls peppering the vessel as she slipped by, and Waller was arrested.

Turmoil increased. Austin had several meetings with Bradburn to try to defuse the situation, but he was ready to throw up his hands: "I had an ignorant, whimsical, selfish and suspicious set of rulers over me to keep good natured, a perplexed, confused colonization law to execute, and an unruly set of North American frontier republicans to controul [sic] who felt that they were sovereigns, for they knew that they were beyond the arm of the Govt. or of law, unless it pleased them to be controuled."

In May of 1832 Bradburn arrested a twenty-two-year-old Alabama lawyer named Bill Travis on suspicion of intriguing against him, and then arrested a prominent local, Patrick Jack, who demanded Travis' release. More than 150 outraged settlers converged on the Anahuac garrison and captured a cavalry squadron that Bradburn sent out to intercept them. The colonists offered to exchange prisoners. Bradburn accepted, but after the soldiers were freed, the Texans learned that Travis and Jack were still held, and that Bradburn had used the time to fortify the garrison and train his cannon on the town. Led by John Austin, cousin of the empresario, some of the settlers departed to seize artillery warehoused at the port of Velasco.

The remainder retreated a few miles up Turtle Bayou to consider the situation. They knew they could be executed for what they were doing, yet they knew they were acting in justice. They also knew that the Bustamante regime was widely despised, and a strong rebellion had arisen in challenge. Its guiding force was Antonio López de Santa Anna, a prominent general who had, like Mier y Terán, played an important role in defeating the Spanish invasion at Tampico. What gave the Texans hope was that he had risen to influence as a Federalist. Rather than appear to all Mexico as traitorous freebooters, the colonists drafted and then published what became known as the Turtle Bayou Resolutions:

> *Resolved* That we view with feelings of the deepest regret, the manner in which the Gover't of the Republic of Mexico is administered by the present dynasty —The repeated violations of the constitution—the total disregard of the law— the entire prostration of the civil authority; and the substitution . . . of a military despotism, are grievances of such a character, as to arouse the feelings of every freeman, and impel him to resistance—
> *Resolved* That we view with feelings of the deepest interest and solicitude, the firm and manly resistance, which is made by the highly talented and distin-

guished Chieftain—General Santa Anna. . . . We pledge our lives and fortunes in support of the distinguished leader, who is now so gallantly fighting
in defence of Civil liberty.

The resolutions were voted on June 13. Similar ones were passed in the town of
Brazoria a week later as John Austin and his men passed through. As the force neared
Velasco, Austin took time to commandeer a small schooner, which was padded with
cotton bales and mounted with three small cannon. As expected, the garrison commander, Domingo de Ugartechea, refused them passage over the bar. Austin's men
attacked the fort on the night of June 26; ten Texans and five of the garrison were killed
before Ugartechea surrendered and was given safe passage to Matamoros.

Before any more violence could follow the "Lexington of Texas," Colonel José de
las Piedras arrived at Anahuac from Nacogdoches to set things straight. He freed the
jailed Texans and persuaded Bradburn to resign his post and leave, along with the
garrison. Much interpretation of this period of Texas history has centered on Bradburn
himself—whether he was an abusive incompetent, which he was, or whether he was
acting within the legal bounds of his military discretion, which he was. More to the
point, the situation reduced itself to Texas being sucked unwillingly into the fratricidal
abattoir of Mexican politics. The land commissioner and surveyor, sent by the state
legislature to confirm land titles, had been thwarted and finally arrested by a Centralist
officer. The Santanista rebellion had spread, and Piedras himself faced a mutiny when
he returned to Nacogdoches.

And, through it all, there was still the Law of April 6 to contend with. Stephen F.
Austin was quick to recognize the incendiary dangers of sealing the American border.
Writing Mier y Terán that "my hopes are fixed on you to save Texas," Austin per-
suaded him to interpret Article Eleven in such a way as would give it no effect.

"The affairs of Texas are understood by none but you and me," he answered
Austin, "and we alone are the only ones who can regulate them." Mier y Terán, himself
a Centralist, suffered a defeat in the field by Santa Anna. Sensing the end of his career
and the inevitable loss of Texas, he ended his life a few days after his last letter to
Austin.

It was increasingly apparent that Santa Anna would drive Bustamante from office.
When word of the troubles at Anahuac and Velasco reached Mexico, a column of four
hundred regulars under Colonel José Antonio Mexía headed north from Matamoros.
Mexía, a Santanista, was given a liberator's welcome. He was presented the Turtle
Bayou Resolutions, and returned satisfied that all was well. A political convention was
held in October at San Felipe which memorialized Santa Anna for reforms, including
statehood. Austin advised against taking action, however. Santa Anna hadn't won yet,
and besides, San Antonio de Béxar had spurned the convention, making it appear like a
rump gathering of Anglo troublemakers.

By January 1833, however, Santa Anna had won, and in April a second convention
met and renewed their petitions—resumption of American immigration, continuation
of tariff exemption, and Mexican statehood for Texas. Confident that statehood would
be granted, one committee drew up a proposed constitution, a dangerously American
document that no Mexican Government would have countenanced. Stephen Austin's
conservatism had so eroded his influence among the "leatherstockings" that when he
ran for president of the convention he was defeated. But he was the only man with the

experience and reputation to carry the documents to Santa Anna. San Antonio's influential elder, Erasmo Seguín, was to have accompanied him, but there were funds for one passage only, and Austin departed at once.

Santa Anna, however, was a master of intrigue. He was installed as President on April 1, 1833 (the same day that the San Felipe Convention assembled). Immediately, he took a leave of absence, leaving Vice President Farías to implement the reforms—and also take the heat from Mexico City's powerful upper class. Austin arrived in July, and for three months Farías would not make a decision. When Santa Anna returned, he pronounced Farías and the reforms a disaster, and consolidated his power into a Centralist dictatorship that made Bustamante look like a liberal. Austin saw through it all in a minute. In exasperation he wrote the ayuntamiento of San Antonio that Texas might as well organize a state government on their own, as the central government would not act. For a man of Austin's usual tact and patience it was an appalling blunder. San Antonio's ayuntamiento was dominated by Mexican nationals, who folded the letter back up and sent it to Santa Anna.

WILLIAM BARRET TRAVIS, a native of South Carolina, was a married lawyer relocated in Alabama by age twenty. A turbulent romantic, in 1831 at the age of twenty-two he deserted his infant son and pregnant wife, Rosanna, to come to Texas. Rumor had it that he had killed the man he suspected of being her paramour. After the trouble at Anahuac in 1832, Travis moved to San Felipe and occupied his time practicing law, dallying with ladies, and reading Sir Walter Scott's novels. Rosanna showed up in 1835 to try to save her marriage, but they divorced in November. This sketch of Travis was made a month later by one of the scouts in his volunteer company.

Austin meanwhile had been granted an audience with Santa Anna. Statehood was still refused, but the President agreed to soften the more hateful provisions of the Law of April 6. Austin was well on his way home when the treasonable letter came to Santa Anna. Austin was arrested as he paid his respects to the commandant general in Saltillo, returned to Mexico City, and imprisoned. He was held incommunicado, in solitary, for three months, before getting a larger cell and permission to write home.

Austin counseled patience and quiet to his colonists, and blamed no one but himself for his troubles. Still, most Texas Anglos were outraged. The "unruly frontier republicans" had often slighted and abused Austin, but they respected him. He was fair, scrupulous, honest, and patient with even the least of them. For Santa Anna to have imprisoned this gentle paragon of citizenship had immeasurable effect on the colonists. It fixed in their minds that if there were ever to be an end to the indignities and abuses, they would have to fight for it themselves.

ANTONIO LÓPEZ DE SANTA ANNA's life was a series of ambitious intrigues. "If I were God," he once said, "I would wish to be more."

He first gained appointment as an infantry cadet in 1810, at the age of sixteen, and fought in campaigns against Indians. An able mover, he rose steadily in rank after distinguishing himself at the Battle of the Medina River against the Gutiérrez-Magee army in 1813. He declared for Iturbide and courted the emperor's daughter—among many other dalliances—but turned on him in 1822. The machinations that brought him to dictatorship, his brutal methods, and the loss of Texas all cost him popularity.

Santa Anna's defeat of the French in 1838, and his loss of a leg in battle, restored him to power, but again his despotism caused his downfall and exile to Cuba in 1845. Back in Mexico to lead the war against the United States, he lost the battles of Buena Vista, Cerro Gordo, and finally for the capital itself. He spent another five years in exile before returning to head a conservative government in 1853. Two years later he was deposed and banished once more, again for ruthlessness, and for raising money by selling some northern territory, the "Gadsden Purchase," to the United States.

Subsequent conspiracies with Maximilian and the French, and the Americans, to return to power all failed. His return was not allowed until 1874, after which he lived quietly in Veracruz until his death in June of 1876.

Revolution

By mid-1835 Santa Anna's Centralist legislative program had rendered the Constitution of 1824 a nullity, and once entrenched in power he turned his attention to two states that still clung to their Federalist precepts, Zacatecas and her neighbor, Coahuila y Texas. When the government of Zacatecas declined Santa Anna's directive to discharge their militia, he sent a Centralist army that ravaged the capital into subjection. He sent a second force under his brother-in-law, General Martín Perfecto de Cós, to suspend the government of Coahuila y Texas. The governor and his council fled Saltillo for Texas, but were overtaken and arrested.

All the Anglos in Texas viewed the political changes with alarm, but the peace faction, believing that some accommodation might still be reached with Santa Anna and armed with Austin's letter from prison counseling patience, held sway. In June of 1835, however, the customs house was reopened at Anahuac, with a new garrison of army regulars. Two local men railed publicly against the reimposition of duties, and the customs collector, an impolitic and unpopular fortune hunter named Antonio Tenorio, had them arrested. That encouraged a number of men to gather in San Felipe on June 21 to discuss what to do. The affair might have passed without violence, but as the meeting continued an official courier arrived. The disgruntled colonists lightened him of his dispatches, and they learned three shocking bits of news. Two of the messages were from Cós himself—one to the alcalde of San Felipe, announcing the suspension of the government of Coahuila y Texas and Cós' own installation as military chief, and the second to Tenorio at Anahuac, calming him that a troop column was even then on the road to strengthen his garrison. The third dispatch announced that after the Federalists at Zacatecas had been humbled, His Excellency the President would personally lead a punitive expedition into the colonies of Texas. The reaction of the men in San Felipe was indignant enough for Bill Travis, a veteran of the first Anahuac troubles, to round up twenty-five men and a cannon and head for Anahuac to drive out the garrison before Cós' reinforcements could make them a threat. They arrived on June 29 and fired one shot from their cannon; the forty-five-man garrison surrendered on the morning of June 30, without resistance, and promised to leave.

If Travis expected for his effort a hero's welcome back in San Felipe, he got a surprise. Calmer heads had prevailed again, and wrote a lowly apology to the garrison commander, regretting and disavowing Travis' "outrage upon the supreme government." Taken aback, Travis composed his own explanation, concluding that "there only wants a good understanding between the Government and the people of Texas to set all things right."

When General Cós heard of the assault on the Anahuac garrison, he issued papers for Travis' arrest, but he was not delivered up, out of fear of the Mexican army's reputation for summary justice. More angry than ever, Cós prepared to move a large force into the recalcitrant colonies to establish his authority.

In the middle of August, William H. Wharton, without Austin now to stay his hand, called a consultation to assemble on October 15, but on September 1 the unexpected happened: Austin returned, released from his dungeon in a general amnesty. His cousin Henry wrote Mary Austin Holley a few days later describing reaction in the colonies. "Brasoria, 10 Sept. 1835, My Dear Sister: Stephen has at last arrived. I rode all night through the swamp and rain to meet him at Perry's. His arrival unites all parties. . . .

A Grand Dinner and Ball were got up for the occasion on two days' notice in a manner very creditable to the committee—the only thing I did not like was 7$ a head for ball and supper and $30 more for a decent suit of clothes which I had not and could have done without. Despite the short notice, the table was filled three times by men alone. In the evening the long room was filled to a Jam. [There were] at least sixty or eighty ladies who danced the sun up, and the Oyster Creek girls would not have quit then had not the room been wanted for breakfast. You never saw such enthusiasm."

The Austin who returned from prison was significantly changed from the Austin who had departed more than two years before, bearing the petitions asking Mexican statehood for Texas. Now he was weak and pale, nagged by a cough; and his political outlook was altered as well. Though he still was not a radical of Wharton's uncompromising stridence, he made it clear in a conservatively argued address to the welcoming crowd at Perry's Point that Wharton's Consultation was necessary. He framed his own call for a representative meeting, however, in terms of "inform[ing] the general government, and especially General Santa Anna . . . of the evils that are likely to result from [his] mistaken and most impolitic policy." Glumly, he went on:

"My friends, I can truly say that no one has been, or is now, more anxious than myself to keep trouble away from this country. No one has been, or is now more faithful to his duty as a Mexican citizen, and no one has personally sacrificed or suffered more in the discharge of this duty. I have uniformly been opposed to have anything to do with the family political quarrels of the Mexicans. Texas needs peace, and a local government; its inhabitants are farmers, and they need a calm and quiet life. . . .

"[But] my efforts to serve Texas involved me in the labyrinth of Mexican politics. I was arrested, and have suffered a long persecution and imprisonment. . . . I fully hoped to have found Texas at peace and in tranquillity, but regret to find it in commotion; all disorganized, all in anarchy, and threatened with immediate hostilities. . . . Can this state of things exist without precipitating the country into a war? I think it cannot. . . . The crisis is such as to bring it home to every man that something must be done, and that without delay. Let a general consultation of the people of Texas be convened as speedily as possible, to be composed of the best, and most calm, and intelligent, and firm men in the country, and let them decide what representations ought to be made to the general government, and what ought to be done in the future."

Irrespective of most Texans' misunderstanding of a Mexican culture that accepted imposed regimes as legitimate—if only because they were a fact of life about which they had never had power to do anything—the basis of Austin's argument remained the law of May 7, 1824, by which the Constituent Congress joined Texas to Coahuila only provisionally, with Texas to be advanced to full statehood in the Mexican Republic when conditions became apparent that it was necessary. What Austin now realized was that no legal structure, neither the law nor the Congress nor the Constitution, had survived Santa Anna's rise to power with any virility. Austin had now dealt with Santa Anna face-to-face and seen what power had done to him. The self-styled Hero of Tampico was now the self-styled Napoleon of the West. He had become self-indulgent to an extreme, addicted to country girls and opium. His fabulous uniforms sagged under medals and braids and epaulets and sashes, admired by the obsequious courtiers with which he surrounded himself. The political liberalism by which he came to power had been a feint. He was a despot, a duplicitous lizard whom Austin now characterized as a "base, unprincipled bloody monster." When word came of the fate of Zacatecas, he proved himself as well a butcher of Gothic heritage. The only cause that Austin had sought to advance was the Mexican statehood that Texas had been pledged, and for this he had been dungeoned up, and for this the dictator was organizing a punitive expedition. Austin directed that his address be published, and left his cousin Henry to correct the printer's proofs, while he went on to San Felipe to prepare for the Consultation. He would have liked to rest, but there was no time. And as hurriedly as he moved, events moved faster.

In 1831 the ayuntamiento of Gonzales had received from San Antonio de Béxar a small iron cannon, perhaps originally a swivel gun, as protection against Indians. Late in September 1835 Domingo de Ugartechea, now the colonel commanding the garrison at San Antonio, sent an order to the alcalde of Gonzales, Andrew Ponton, recalling the piece on the pretext that it was again required in Béxar. It seems possible that the order was unrelated to General Cós' approach at the head of an army of fourteen hundred regulars, but the timing was very suspect, and all the Texans knew that San Antonio was amply stocked with artillery. The gun, moreover, had little contribution to make as a weapon, "having been spiked," wrote one observer, "and the spike driven out, leaving a touch-hole the size of a man's thumb. Its principal merit as a weapon of defense, therefore, lay in its presence and the noise it could make, the Indians being very much afraid of cannon." To the colonists' thinking, Ugartechea was attempting to disarm them in the face of Cós' arrival, and they had to submit or fight.

Ponton, with the support of the ayuntamiento, had the cannon buried in a peach orchard and plowed over, and sent messages throughout the colonies for assistance. Then he tried to stall the small detachment that Ugartechea had sent for the cannon, writing the *jefe político* of San Antonio, "Gonzales Sept 26th 1835, Excellent Sir, I received an order purporting to have come from you for a certain piece of Ordnance which is in this place. It happened that I was absent and so was the remainder part of the Ayuntamiento when your dispatch arrived[.] [I]n consequence the men who bore sd dispatch were necessarily detained untill to day for an answer. This is a matter of delicasy to me nor do I know without further information how to act[.] [T]his cannon was as I have always been informed given in perpetuity to this Town for its defense against the Indians. The dangers which existed at the time we received this cannon still exist and for the same purposes it is still needed here—our common enemy is still to be dreaded or prepared against.

"How or in what manner such arms are appropriated throughout the country I am as yet ignorant at least as long as the procuring cause exists. I must therefore be excused

ANDREW BRISCOE, a twenty-four-year-old Anahuac merchant, would probably have opposed the reimposition of customs on American goods even if their collection had not been irregular and corrupt. His attempt to sell unlevied goods to his brother-in-law resulted in the arrest of both men, an event that helped spark the Revolution.

from delivering up the sd cannon untill I have obtained more information on the subject matter[.] At least untill I have an opportunity of consulting the chief of this department on the subject—as well as to act without precipitation—as to perform clearly and strictly my duty, and I assure you, that if, after a mature deliberation on the subject, I find it to be my duty & in justice to your self—I obligate my self to comply with your demands—and will without delay send the cannon to you." He closed the letter with the common, sloganistic subscription "God & Liberty-/Andrew Ponton, *Alcalde.*"

Word of Cós' approach to San Antonio with his army was now widespread, and volunteer regiments were forming in virtually every major town. All was transpiring as Austin had warned Santa Anna, "in all my conversation . . . I advised that no troops should be sent to Texas, and no cruisers along the coast. I gave it as my decided opinion, that the inevitable consequence of sending an armed force would be war. I stated that there was a sound and correct moral principle in the people of Texas, that was abundantly sufficient to restrain or put down all turbulent or seditious movements, but that this moral principle could not, and would not unite with any armed force sent against the country; on the contrary, it would resist and repel it, and ought to do so."

The year's crops had mostly been gathered in; there was no shortage of volunteers, and many of these units were, however haphazardly, on the march to San Antonio to oppose Cós when couriers brought Ponton's news that the first test was to be in Gonzales instead. At that place they began to assemble. A more motley crew would be hard to imagine; there was no uniformity of clothing, arms, command, or even ideals. "Some were for independence," wrote new volunteer Noah Smithwick, "some for the constitution of 1824, and some for anything, just so it was a row." Each company was headed by its own organizer or popular favorite, and even then the men sometimes voted on whether to obey an order. Still, they had the presence of mind to dig up the cannon, which was rendered as serviceable as it could be and mounted on "trucks," two ungreased axles inserted into coarsely rounded cross sections of tree trunk. They were having a grand time. Some of them began hammering crude balls out of sections of iron bars, their only ammunition for what they joked was their "flying artillery." Others cut cane poles from the river bottom and beat files into blades to equip a company of lancers. Still others undertook to design a flag: six feet of white cotton cloth, at the top of which was a single star—the first image of the Lone Star. In the middle was a painting of the contested cannon, and across the bottom the legend Come and Take It. About four in the afternoon of September 28 a dozen or so volunteers crossed the river and took captive the Mexican corporal, his small escort, and the cart drivers whom Ugartechea had sent to fetch the cannon. They were held overnight and then let go, hustled off down the road toward San Antonio. Revolution could be fun.

By this time Ugartechea had received Ponton's thinly disguised stall, and sent a reply in the form of one hundred dragoons under command of a Lieutenant Castañeda and a demand to give over the cannon or be taken in arrest to San Antonio.

The Mexicans freed from Gonzales had gone only a few miles when they encountered Castañeda and told all they knew of the Anglo colonists' strength—about 150—and equipage. The officer prudently sent a courier ahead with Ugartechea's demand and a message of his own asking for a talk with the alcalde. Castañeda reached the Guadalupe River later in the day, but the colonists refused to let him cross. Instead, a secondary official of the ayuntamiento, the *regidor,* advised that Ponton was temporarily absent, but would return within a few hours and speak to Castañeda. The alcalde failed to show up, however, and Castañeda spent the evening writing a report to Ugartechea.

In the morning he walked to the riverbank, but was again met by the *regidor,* who shouted across the river the text of a paper in his hand: "In the absence of the alcalde it has fallen to my lot to reply to the communication sent to him asking a second time for the cannon. . . . The right of consulting our political chief seems to be denied us. Therefore my reply reduces itself to this: I can not nor do I desire to deliver up the cannon. . . . This is the sentiment of all the members of the ayuntamiento now present. The cannon is in the town, and only through force will we yield. We are weak and few in number, nevertheless we are contending for what we believe to be just principles."

Castañeda argued but it did him no good, and he returned to his camp to consider the situation. The ferry was on the Gonzales side of the river, which could not be safely forded here. That evening he removed his camp some three hundred yards upstream, and a little later, to a defensible prominence seven miles further. The Texan colonists guessed his motive was to await reinforcements, and on the evening of October 1 they crossed the river in force—with the cannon—and headed up after him, intending to rout him before he could be strengthened. In a war council John H. Moore, at the head of a volunteer company from La Grange, was selected colonel, and J. W. E. Wallace as lieutenant colonel. Other volunteers to cross the river included James Walker Fannin of Georgia at the head of his "Brazos Guards."

At about 4 A.M. on October 2 the Anglos formed into a battle line and advanced until fired on by Mexican sentries. A wet fog as thick as cotton prevented the colonists from engaging, and they held their position. When it was light enough to see, they advanced in formation. Three hundred and fifty yards from the Mexican line a flare was touched to the little iron gun. Much of the muzzle blast was lost through the once spiked touchhole, and the disfigured, shrieking boom that began the Texas Revolution was clearly heard by the people in Gonzales.

The Mexicans fell back and asked for a talk. The two forces could now see one another plainly; Moore and Castañeda strode to the center of the field and engaged in one of those baroque little exchanges of principles that no longer grace an advent of hostility. When the two officers returned to their commands, the Texans attacked again, quickly routing the Mexicans from the field; they abandoned their baggage and fled, leaving one dead. One Texan had been injured.

The volunteers were still celebrating their victory when word was received that a Mexican force was marching on Guadalupe Victoria, and about one hundred men were sent south to defend it. The information seems to have stemmed from the fact that as Cós approached San Antonio, he diverted a small detachment of his army not to Victoria but to Goliad just southwest of there, the town that grew up around the old Mission La Bahía. Cós intended them to garrison the old church that was now an armory and ammunition dump, which also commanded the road to his main source of supply, the port of Cópano.

From Victoria the captain of volunteers, George Collinsworth, sent a hurried note to Stephen F. Austin—addressing him as "Colonel"—that he intended to take Goliad the following day, October 9. Thickly anglicizing La Bahía to "Laberdee," (others tried it "Labaher") he estimated there were between sixty and a hundred Mexicans there. "I have under My charge 47 Good and Effective men which I think all Sufficient to take that place, from whence if I have No advice I Shall direct My March to Bexar." His next communication, from the morning of the tenth, gave a succinct account of the fight: "Goliad 8 oclock A.M. Octr 10th 1835, Dear Sir: I arrived here last night at 11 Oclock and marched into the fort, by forcing the Church doors and after a small fight they surrendered with 3 officers and 21 soldiers, together with three wounded and one killed —I had one of my men wounded in the shoulder. . . ."

Collinsworth's tally of captured matériel included some two hundred stands of muskets and carbines—mostly in poor repair—a half dozen saddles, a barrel of musket cartridges, a hundred 4-pounder balls, forty-four lance heads and one hundred to two hundred bayonets. A parenthetical note drew particular attention to these last two items and their usefulness in case of a charge. While he was making his foray into Goliad, the remainder of the volunteers stayed around Gonzales, drilling. They had little enthusiasm for it, but even they understood that they had to learn to maneuver and fire by companies, for if a Mexican force should catch them all reloading at the same time they would be charged and overwhelmed. After a brush with ever present Comanches, the Gonzales volunteers began their march to San Antonio on October 13, though they did so warily in the knowledge of Cós' numerical advantage. Austin, who by now had joined his army, had doubts about the venture, but was carried along almost as a captive figurehead. The lauded "flying artillery," commanded by Captain Almeron Dickinson, rumbled and creaked on its ungreased trucks behind two yokes of oxen. Although wetted and tallowed to keep the axles from bursting into flame, the giddy contraption broke down less than halfway to San Antonio, and the historic iron gun was sunk in Sandies Creek. "I never saw nor heard of it again," wrote Smithwick, "and am unable to ascertain what became of it."

The first approach to Béxar was against the old Mission San José, about eight miles south of the city. They advanced as far as Cibolo Creek, where word was received of a strong Mexican picket guard on the Salado, just beyond. Under cover of night a small scouting force was sent ahead, among them the ubiquitous Smithwick: "We knew not how many of the enemy there were, but we knew there were just twenty-five of us and no reinforcements at hand. At length, when we were nearing the site . . . one fellow began to weaken. 'Boys,' he said in a shaky whisper, 'I don't like this. Ef thar's a big force of 'em they'll whop us.' Thereupon Conrad Rohrer, a big Pennsylvania Dutchman who never realized the meaning of the word fear, hissed half under breath: 'Shet up, damn you; don't say they'll weep us; you're weeped already!' "

The report of a Mexican camp proved to be bogus, and the men returned to their comrades. A prominent volunteer joined them on the Cibolo, Jim Bowie, the legendary knife fighter and pioneer figure, and son-in-law of the late Governor Veramendi. He was placed on Austin's staff, and with the San José Mission secured, Bowie was selected to lead a reconnaissance in force to the Concepción Mission, only two miles below the

The carriage bearing the GONZALES CANNON broke down less than halfway to San Antonio, and the gun was buried in Sandies Creek. It remained there until exposed by a flood in 1936, and was stored for a time in the Gonzales Post Office. X rays of the barrel and fiber-optic examination of the inside plug and bushings established its identity in 1980.

city. Bowie took with him ninety men from two companies (one of them Fannin's Brazos Guards) and had a light brush with the Mexicans before camping at a bend in the San Jacinto River about a quarter mile from the mission, expecting the main army to follow shortly. During the night they came under desultory bombardment from a heavy gun that Cós had mounted in a cathedral tower in San Antonio. At dawn they received musket fire and discovered that they had been "more or less surrounded" by about four hundred Mexicans, and the rest of their volunteers were nowhere in sight. As Bowie cautioned the men to stay low and hold their fire, the Mexicans wheeled up a little field gun and peppered the Texan position with shot, but as Smithwick recorded, "We lay low and their grape and canister crashed through the pecan trees overhead, raining a shower of ripe nuts down on us, and I saw men picking them up and eating them with as little apparent concern as if they were being shaken down by a norther."

The Mexicans moved up until they were well within range of the Texan long rifles, and when the volunteers opened their accurate fire the enemy began to drop by the dozens. The Mexicans charged three different times, each one being met by a line of muzzle blasts, and three different crews were picked off as they serviced the cannon.

Mission San José began operation in 1720, the second of the missions of San Antonio de Béxar. By the time of its secularization in 1794, it was the largest and most successful, called the Queen of the Missions for its exquisitely carved portal and rose window. The roofless ruin shown here was later restored to its former splendor.

After losing about sixty dead the Mexicans broke ranks and fled for San Antonio, being sent off by a final shot from their cannon, which the volunteers had captured and turned round on them. One Texan had been killed, a fellow named Richard Andrews and known as Big Dick, who had foolishly exposed himself to enemy fire for a better shot; the first casualty of the Revolution was buried at the foot of a pecan tree, the grave unmarked.

The Mexicans had left a number of wounded on the field, many of whom began to beg for their lives. To the Texans this was bizarre behavior, as they hadn't thought for a moment of slaughtering wounded prisoners. But then they hadn't yet experienced Santanista warfare. The volunteers had no medical supplies, but the prisoners were made comfortable until a priest came out from San Antonio with carts to take in the wounded, to which Austin gave his assent.

In twelve days the Texan volunteers had routed units of the Mexican army three times, and inevitably in the context of the time, many of the Anglo settlers took a racially disparaging attitude toward their adversary. Noah Smithwick wrote that he did not support a war for absolute independence, "yet it is not in the nature of things for the superior race to long remain under the domination of the inferior."

Orceneth Fisher, a traveling Methodist minister, wrote more expansively that "had Mexico been wise, she would have fostered those [democratic] principles" introduced by American colonists. "She would have retained her identity as a nation, but she would have exchanged her low, grovelling, and worthless character, for one truly great and elevated.

"But," he lamented, "this was too high for her to reach."

Still, the Texan Revolution was not a race war. The constitutional considerations were large, and many Mexicans opposed the dictatorship of Santa Anna. The state of Zacatecas had to be forcibly crushed, and Lieutenant Castañeda, before he was run off the field at Gonzales, averred that perhaps two thirds of the Mexicans were republicans. And, as General Cós neared San Antonio with his army, Juan Seguín, the son of the liberal alcalde who had greeted Stephen F. Austin in 1821, recruited a company of volunteers to fight with the colonials.

At San Antonio General Cós tightened his defensive perimeter. The Texans, knowing they had no chance of dislodging him, settled down to a siege, and as attention on the military slackened, political activity increased. The Consultation that William Wharton had called for mid-October did not meet for lack of a quorum; most of the men who had been elected representatives were with the army. One delegate who did show up in San Felipe, a Nacogdoches lawyer, went out to fetch the rest. As Smithwick recalled, "At the Cibolo, Sam Houston came up with us. . . . I have a vivid picture of him before my mind's eye as he rode into our camp alone, mounted on a little yellow Spanish stallion so diminutive that old Sam's long legs, incased in the conventional buckskin, almost touched the ground."

Sam Houston

SAM HOUSTON always dressed for effect, whether in Indian blankets or in one of his splendid suits. At Lamar's inauguration in December of 1838, Houston, the outgoing President of the Republic, mortified his opponents by showing up in federal knee breeches. This rare early view of him may date from that time.

AT the time he first entered Texas on a presidential mission in December of 1832, Sam Houston was already a frontier legend. Born in Virginia on March 2, 1793, he was transplanted to a Tennessee farm in 1807 when his mother was widowed. He was a youth of enormous contradictions. He loathed school and later admitted that he stood it for less than a year, yet he devoured his father's library of classics. He was vaguely ambitious for himself, but hated chores so much he deserted the family and took up with a group of Tennessee Cherokees under Chief John Jolly. Houston reveled in Indian life, not least because it gave him freedom to indulge his prodigious appetites for liquor and sex. For three years he lived a stunningly eclectic idyll, walking wild stream banks with Indian girls and—as he phrased it—"making love and reading Homer's *Iliad.*"

Still, Houston would not dodge responsibility. At nineteen he went on a drinking spree and ran up a debt that he paid off by teaching school for six months. At twenty-one, big boned and six feet four, he enlisted in the Tennessee Regulars to fight in the Creek Indian War, soon gaining an officer's billet and the notice of Andrew Jackson. At the climactic battle of the war, at Horseshoe Bend, Alabama, Houston was wounded three times, musket shots in the right arm and shoulder, and an arrow puncture above his right kidney that penetrated the intestine. They never healed properly, and for the rest of his life the bandages had to be changed. General Jackson took him on as a political protégé, and in 1817 Houston became subagent to his Cherokees. In 1818 he became a lawyer; 1819, attorney general of Tennessee; 1821, major general of the state militia; 1823, congressman; and 1827, governor. A terrible reverse struck in 1829; he married the handsome and well-connected Eliza Allen. He left her after three months, refusing a word of explanation to even his closest friends, and the scandal caused him to resign the governorship. He returned to the Cherokees, and the name they once gave him in honor, Raven, was supplanted by one more descriptive: Big Drunk.

Houston reemerged in 1832 in Washington, at the head of a Cherokee delegation, and in Congress a representative from Ohio accused him of making his living by defrauding the Indians. Houston caned the culprit in a dark alley, and the House tried him for assaulting a member. It was the moment of his comeback. If they had buried the case and fined him ten dollars, he was later heard to say, it would have killed him. Instead, they gave him a national platform, and his thundering defense summation won his case and restored the self-confidence lost with Eliza.

Houston's political ambitions were unknown, but he had been mentioned in connection with the American colonies in Texas. He was acquainted with William and John Wharton, two of Austin's most prominent—and difficult—colonists, and he had legal ties to the Galveston Bay and Texas Land Company, two of whose principals were New Jersey lawyer David G. Burnet and a prominent Mexican political liberal, Lorenzo de Zavala. President Jackson, in the last year of his first term, helped him get to Texas by appointing him to deliver a message to the Comanche Indians.

He entered Texas on December 2, 1832, at the northeastern border and went to San Felipe, via Nacogdoches. At Austin's capital Houston crossed paths with his old drink-

Houston occasionally modified his signature more to resemble "I am Houston."
The coolly imperial gesture was one of a hundred small tortures he inflicted on his enemies.

ing buddy, Jim Bowie, whose own life had settled down considerably since his marriage to María Ursula de Veramendi, the governor's daughter. Bowie escorted Houston to San Antonio, and the Tennessee governor was received at the Veramendi Palace. Conveniently, a group of Comanche Indians were also in the town, so Jackson's business was completed straightaway, and Houston turned his attention to the surroundings.

"Jack!" he wrote his cousin, "Texas is the finest portion of the Globe that has ever blessed my vision." Houston had a long interview with Stephen F. Austin when he returned to San Felipe, and was granted a headright on Karankawa Bay. He settled, however, in Nacogdoches, living with another Tennessee acquaintance, Mayor Adolphus Sterne, and his wife, the latter standing as his godmother when he was baptized a Catholic in the front room of their house. The substance of Houston's mysterious political maneuvers along the Arkansas and Louisiana borders never surfaced, but enough troubling stories of his fomenting unrest reached Jackson that he sent him a cautionary letter. Both Sterne and Houston were delegates to the 1833 Convention, where Houston chaired the committee that drafted a state constitution which Austin took to Mexico. In the meantime he had lost the Galveston Bay and Texas Land Company business, filed for divorce from Eliza, and set to courting the very beautiful (and very young) daughter of Henry Raguet, Anna. Through 1834 and 1835 he lay low, confident in the belief that a Texas revolution was inevitable, and that when it came, his time would come as well.

After the fighting began on October 2, 1835, Houston had within four days written to an Arkansas contact for volunteers, raised a company of local men and been named commander of troops from Nacogdoches, and was on the march west.

When Houston resided in Nacogdoches, he stayed with the town's mayor, ADOLPHUS STERNE (left). A native of Cologne, Germany, Sterne made Houston's acquaintance while living in Tennessee.

During the Fredonian Rebellion of 1826, Sterne had smuggled munitions to the rebels, for which he was imprisoned in the Old Stone Fort and sentenced to death. He was paroled on the influence of a Masonic connection. He married EVA CATHERINE ROSINE RUFF (right) in Natchitoches in June of 1828; the STERNE HOUSE shown here (center) was built upon their return. During the Revolution Sterne was Texas' agent in New Orleans and raised a company of volunteers that helped capture San Antonio in late 1835. He also fought in the Cherokee War; after statehood he served two terms in the legislature, and was a state senator at the time of his death in March 1852.

Like all landowners in Mexican Texas, Houston was required to become a Catholic. The baptism took place in the left front room of the Sterne home. Eva stood as godmother.

The Battle of San Antonio

AUSTIN offered command of the army to Houston, but he declined, on the grounds that the pending political matters required his attention. At first the volunteers refused to let the leaders go, but reluctantly changed their minds, insisting only that Austin, Wharton, and a few others stay on. This was done, although Austin's intellect, particularly, was needed at San Felipe.

The Consultation finally convened on November 3, 1835 (Austin's forty-second birthday), and the Austin-Wharton conflict—whether to declare independence or adhere to the Mexican Constitution of 1824—was fully aired. With the principals absent, Austin's more conservative stance was argued by Houston; Wharton's brother John argued for independence. By a vote of 33 to 15 a declaration of independence was rejected, although everyone agreed that separation from Mexico was only a matter of time, and timing. They published instead a "Declaration of Causes" for resorting to arms. The government set up was intended as a provisional state within the Mexican Republic, with Henry Smith of Matamoros as governor, with legislative authority in a Permanent Council. The arrangement was anything but workable, as Smith was of the Wharton minority and the Council favored statehood. Relations between the two branches of government soon degenerated into some creative name-calling. When Smith tried to suspend the Council, he was impeached and replaced, although he continued to exercise his authority over those who recognized it. Among the latter was Houston, who had been named commander-in-chief of the army.

The volunteers besieging San Antonio de Béxar had meanwhile become restive, disgusted with the political wrangling in San Felipe. Their lark had now become tedious, winter weather had turned foul—many volunteers who went home for warmer clothes failed to return—and the difficulty of supply led to short rations. All resulted in loud grumbling to fall back to Gonzales or Goliad. After the first of December the problem became critical; Ed Burleson, who had succeeded Austin in command when the latter was permitted to return to San Felipe, ordered his army to stand pat, but junior officers took a mutinous vote and decided to withdraw. Just at the same time news arrived, from three colonists who had escaped jail in the city, that Cós' forces were becoming demoralized under the pressure of the siege. The same message was brought by a Mexican deserter. One old Texas hand and one of the most respected volunteers, forty-seven-year-old Ben Milam of Kentucky, drew the men's attention and delivered a blistering lecture on the thought of pulling back when the Mexicans were ready to collapse. Mentioning the abundant supplies and comforts within the city —including, reportedly, the warmth to be found in the brothels—he marked a line in the dirt, yelling, "Who will go with old Ben Milam into San Antonio? Who will follow old Ben Milam?"

Three hundred colonists divided themselves into two columns, one under Milam and the other under Francis W. Johnson, and roared into the city early on the morning of December 5, 1835. Colonel Burleson had little choice but to consent, and he commanded the reserves. The first news of the action, signed by both Burleson and Milam, admitted that they "have so far had a fierce contest, the enemy offering a strong and obstinate resistance. It is difficult to determine what damage has been done him; many killed, certainly, but how many cannot be told. On our side, ten or twelve wounded, two killed."

BEN MILAM. During the 150 years since the Texas Revolution, its popular appeal has rendered irresistible the temptation to romanticize it, with the result that its heroes have been depicted as ever more rakish, posturing, and youthful.

This very early, partly obliterated photo image, however, shows an older and more dyspeptic-looking Milam, who was forty-seven at the time of his death. The star that appears on his tunic here was probably added by a later hand.

Little is known of Milam's early life, except that he was born in Kentucky in 1788 and was a veteran of the War of 1812. In 1815 he and three other adventurers chartered a ship to South America in connection with some flour speculation. Yellow fever broke out on board, killing most of the crew, and the rest were nearly lost in a storm. Milam made his way back home, and 1818 found him trading goods to Comanche Indians on the upper Colorado River. There, incidentally, he made the ac-

quaintance of David G. Burnet, later Provisional President of the Republic, who was living with the Comanches while they cured him of consumption.

Milam involved himself in James Long's filibustering activities in 1819, and after Long's suspicious demise in 1822, Milam and some others resolved to avenge themselves on those responsible—presumably Governor Trespalacios. They were themselves betrayed instead, and imprisoned until the American consul could get them freed. From that time Milam was active in land and mining schemes in North Texas; he became a Mexican citizen and joined the army.

The Revolution broke out while he was in Monclova, Mexico, on land business. Cós' army, ordered by Santa Anna to suspend the state government of Coahuila y Texas, captured its officials as they tried to reach San Antonio. Milam, however, escaped to join the Texan volunteers shortly before the attack on La Bahía.

Cós gave up the city one block at a time, covering his withdrawal with artillery that screened him effectively but was too poorly aimed to do much damage to the volunteers. At Military Plaza the Texans captured the important buildings, including the Veramendi Palace. On the third day of the battle Ben Milam was shot through the head before the great house. That he should have been the third (and as it happened, the last) Texan fatality enraged the men who followed him, and they fought with a fierce purpose that took Cós by surprise. The Mexican general's army now numbered only eleven hundred thanks mostly to desertion, and he pulled them into the Alamo, the fortified compound of the abandoned Mission San Antonio de Valero, and held out two days more before surrendering. Rather than hold Cós or any of his army as prisoners of war, Burleson paroled them to return home, on Cós' oath that he would not again enter Texas under arms.

After San Antonio was secured, most of the volunteers, whom Burleson now discharged with thanks, decided it would be a good idea to march against the Mexican border city of Matamoros. The Council, taken with the highly improbable notion that the many Federalist liberals there would welcome Texans as liberators, endorsed the idea, and then in an even sillier blunder authorized both Fannin and Johnson to head the expedition. Left at San Antonio was J. C. Neill with a stripped garrison at the

THE VERAMENDI PALACE, in a photograph taken before the structure was razed in 1902. The only part saved was the ten-foot-high entrance portal before which Ben Milam was killed.

Alamo that would have fallen to any force to come along. Houston was disgusted: "I was a General without an army, serving under a pretended government, that had no head, and no loyal subjects to obey its commands." Governor Smith, if he was still governor, backed Houston in his opposition to the Matamoros idiocy, and left him open to assert control over the military however he could.

Houston had information that Santa Anna had begun marshaling his forces to storm through Texas, and issued orders to all men in the field to fall back to Goliad and Gonzales to prepare. On January 8, 1836, he left San Felipe for Goliad, where he lobbied and politicked to his formidable utmost, and finally convinced most of the volunteers to accept his authority. On January 17 he sent Jim Bowie and about thirty men to Neill at the Alamo with orders to blow up the fortress and fall back. Then on January 20 Johnson trumped him with new orders from the Council authorizing the Matamoros invasion. Houston gave up and returned to San Felipe. He then undertook a mission to the large group of Cherokee Indians living in East Texas to ensure their neutrality in the upcoming war. The Council cooperated to the extent of passing a resolution recognizing the land claims that the Cherokees had been pressing on the Mexican Government. Houston's background as a friend to Cherokees was well known to them, and with the Indians pacified Houston turned his attention to the imperative reorganization of the government.

THREE VIEWS OF THE ALAMO. The painting depicts the church, Long Barracks, and Low Barracks as they appeared shortly after the battle.

By the time the photograph *(above)* was taken in 1849, a new pediment and roof had been built over the church. After annexation the Alamo was occupied as the first federal military installation in Texas; in this image, covered wagons enter and leave the church, which was used as a supply depot.

The 1880 stereograph *(below)* shows the church building much as it appears today. The ornate, scroll-topped pediment now familiar to millions as the outline of the Alamo bears little resemblance to the original structure. When the limestone building was raised about 1770, it had a crenellated upper story with a rose window over the portal, and a high belfry over the south wing of the transept. A restoration architect who saw the new facade in the 1890s groused that a great monument to American freedom had been made over to look like a bedstead.

The Alamo Falls

IN December of 1835 the General Council had issued, over Governor Smith's veto, a call for a new convention. As a further measure of Stephen Austin's decline, of the fifty-nine delegates elected on February 1, only ten had been in Texas before 1830. The new group met not at Austin's San Felipe, but at a new, ad hoc capital named, tellingly, Washington-on-the-Brazos. Convening in an unfinished house during a frigid "norther" on March 1, they wasted no time, adopting a declaration of independence the next day. They barely had time to appoint New Jersey empresario David Burnet Provisional President, and prominent Mexican liberal Lorenzo de Zavala Provisional Vice-President, before clearing out eastward before Santa Anna's northern column could snag them.

Meanwhile, bizarre things had been happening at the Alamo. Jim Bowie had arrived with Houston's orders to blow up the place and fall back, but Colonel Neill refused to do it, saying he had no transport with which to withdraw the artillery. The volunteers, as during the autumn battles, also did as they pleased, and passed resolutions refusing to budge. Bowie fell under their spell. The people of San Antonio were fond of him for his reputation and for his marriage into the Veramendi family. When he arrived, they offered supplies to the Anglos holding the fort, which they had withheld before, and which made the situation seem less grim. Then one of Bowie's own men, James Butler Bonham, staged a rally for the volunteers on January 26 at which they resolved that "we cannot be driven from the post of honor." Bowie explained in a letter to Governor Smith that "the salvation of Texas depends in great measure in keeping Bexar out of the hands of the enemy. . . . If it were in the possession of Santa Anna, there is no stronghold from which to repel him in his march toward the Sabine. . . . Colonel Neill and myself have come to the solemn resolution that we will rather die in these ditches than give it up to the enemy."

The situation complicated itself even more when Bill Travis, never far from the action, arrived at the beginning of February. Armed with an ego that would have been formidable in a man twice his age, he had convinced Governor Smith to give him a commission. Old Texas hands thought his new signature, William Barret Travis, Lieutenant Colonel of Cavalry, was piffle. He was to have raised one hundred recruits, but managed only thirty before setting out for San Antonio.

Neill took a leave of absence to tend a sick relative, assigning temporary command to Travis, but after taking a vote the volunteers decided they would take orders only from Bowie. Travis was furious. "Bowie was elected by two small companies;" he wrote to Governor Smith, "& since his election he has been roaring drunk all the time; has assumed all command—& is proceeding in a most disorderly & irregular manner . . . & turning everything topsy turvey." The volunteers' preference for Bowie was understandable. He was forty, a legendary fighter, and a good storyteller. He was a favorite with the Mexican community; he was a capital drinking companion and was welcomed into all the best cantinas. Travis was twenty-six and full of himself. On February 14, the day after Travis' tattling letter, he and Bowie wisely agreed to share command. However, Bowie's drinking bouts had weakened him; when he caught what was probably diphtheria, he fell into death's grip, only sporadically coherent and seldom able to rise from his cot.

Unchallenged by Bowie, Travis did able service as the post's commander, and selected capable men to improve their defenses. Green Jameson, a twenty-nine-year-old lawyer, shored up breeches in the twelve-foot-high walls around the three-acre plaza and directed the construction of palisades from which to fight. Almeron Dickinson, who had pulled the Gonzales cannon halfway to San Antonio, now had formidable artillery to work with. Working with Jameson, he positioned and mounted no fewer than eighteen guns around the perimeter of the compound.

Other volunteers straggled in, adding a few more to the Alamo's number. A dozen from Tennessee came in on February 8, followers of disaffected Jacksonian congressman David Crockett. Travis offered the legendary fighter and frontiersman a position of authority, but the fifty-year-old Crockett pronounced himself satisfied to serve as a "high private." "Assign me some place," he told Travis, "and I and my Tennessee boys will defend it all right."

On February 23, as Santa Anna's huge army—more than five thousand men, with artillery, ammunition, baggage, and supplies—creaked and rumbled into San Antonio, Travis sent a message to the alcalde of Gonzales: "The enemy in large force is in sight. We want men and provisions. Send them to us. We have 150 men and are determined to defend the Alamo to the last. Give us assistance." The difference in the two forces was

THE CAPITOL AT COLUMBIA. The approach of Gaona's division precipitated the abandonment of Washington-on-the-Brazos within days after independence was declared. After the war, until a permanent seat of government could be selected, Texas' affairs were run from Columbia, on the Brazos River west of Harrisburg. This is the house in which the First Congress met.

appalling. Within the past year Santa Anna had spent the equivalent of $7,500,000 on his armed forces. "If there has ever been a dollar here," Colonel Neill had written of the Alamo, "I have no knowledge of it."

At first sight of the Mexican thousands, which took Travis by surprise because he didn't expect them for three more weeks and had repeatedly ignored scouting reports of their approach, an alarm bell was rung. Last-minute supplies and refugees were hustled in. Dickinson raced into town and snatched his wife, Susanna, and infant daughter up onto his horse, demanding "Ask me no questions!" Bowie left his sick bed long enough to bring in some of his wife's relatives.

The first of Santa Anna's twenty or more guns were in place by dawn of February 24, and the siege began in earnest. After hours of bombardment Travis wrote his most famous plea for assistance, a letter "To the People of Texas and All Americans in the World," that has frequently been called the most heroic document in American history. But both Bowie and Travis sent inquiries to the Mexican camp to learn whether terms could be discussed. They were answered that any surrender would be "at discretion," which in Santanista warfare meant summary execution. Travis sent a number of messages calling for reinforcements to Goliad, where Colonel Fannin had more than four hundred men. Fannin, however, was still planning to invade Matamoros, and would not submit to serve under Travis.

For days the Mexican cannon pounded the limestone walls around the plaza, every day a little closer. Feints and bugle calls at all hours kept the Texans awake and preyed on their nerves. Atop the tower of San Fernando Cathedral they could see the bloodred flag of no quarter.

SAN FERNANDO CATHEDRAL. From their positions on the walls of the Alamo, its defenders could see clearly the cathedral tower in the middle of the city. When Santa Anna made the church his headquarters, he unfurled from the belfry not the red, white, and green Mexican tricolor, but a chilling, solid dark red flag: no quarter for anyone taken alive. In response, Travis fired a shot at it from his largest gun, the 18-pounder on the southwest parapet.

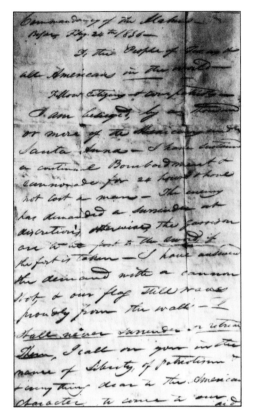 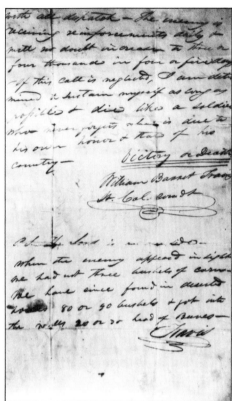

TRAVIS' LETTER FROM THE ALAMO.

Commandancy of the Alamo—.
Bejar, Feb'y 24th 1836—

To the People of Texas and all Americans *in the World*—

Fellow Citizens and Compatriots—I am besieged, by a thousand or more of
the Mexicans under Santa Anna—I have sustained a continual bombardment & cannonade for 24 hours & have not lost a man—The enemy has
demanded a surrender at discretion, otherwise, the garrison are to be put to
the sword, if the fort is taken—I have answered the demand with a cannon
shot, and our flag still waves proudly from the walls—*I shall never surrender or
retreat. Then,* I call on you in the name of Liberty, of patriotism & everything
dear to the American character, to come to our aid with all dispatch—The
enemy is receiving reinforcements daily & will no doubt increase to three or
four thousand in four or five days. If this call is neglected, I am determined
to sustain myself as long as possible & die like a soldier who never forgets
what is due to his own honor & that of his country—VICTORY OR DEATH.

William Barret Travis
Lt. Col. Comdt.

P.S. The Lord is on our side—When the enemy appeared in sight we had not
three bushels of corn—We have since found in deserted houses 80 or 90
bushels & got into the walls 20 or 30 head of beeves—

Travis

DAVID CROCKETT was a legend long before he entered Texas, famed for his skill at hunting, fighting, and frontiersmanship. Like most Tennesseeans a protégé of Andrew Jackson, Crockett learned to read and write but was ousted after three terms in Congress for his independent attitude. He gained wide notice for his remark that the Jacksonians could go to hell and he would go to Texas, which he did, after rounding up an inebriated entourage. He was nearly fifty at the time the Alamo fell, one of the oldest men present.

It was a trying time, through which Davy Crockett's wit, fiddle, and courage did much to keep the garrison's spirits up. Don Rafael Saldana, a captain in Santa Anna's Tampico Battalion, became quite familiar with the distant figure atop the plaza walls:

"He wore a buckskin suit and a cap all of a pattern entirely different from the suits worn by his comrades. This man would kneel or lie down behind the low parapet, rest his long gun and fire and we all learned to keep at a good distance when he was seen to make ready to shoot. He rarely missed his mark and when he fired he always rose to his feet and calmly reloaded his gun, seemingly indifferent to the shots fired at him by our men. He had a strong resonant voice and often railed at us, but as we did not understand English we could not comprehend the import of his words further than that they were defiant. This man I later learned was known as *Kwockey.*"

On March 1 Travis' letter to Gonzales bore results, as 32 more volunteers from that place slipped through the Mexican lines and into the fort. There were now 182 men to face Santa Anna's 5,000. Travis on that date reported that none of his men had been killed by the more than two hundred shells that had landed within his fort.

The incessant cannonade took its toll on his nerves, though. "Let the Convention go on and make a declaration of independence," he wrote, "and the world will understand what we are fighting for." With Travis unaware that independence was declared on March 2, the flag over the Alamo was the Mexican tricolor, with "1824," the year of the liberal Constitution, sewn into the white stripe. Again he pleaded for reinforcements, that his men should not be "sacrificed to the vengeance of a Gothic enemy."

But, if they were killed, he consoled himself that "the victory will cost the enemy so dear, that it will be worse for him than a defeat."

Daybreak of March 5 revealed that the siege guns had been lugged to within two hundred yards of the walls and new breastworks thrown up to protect the crews. After a fearsome, daylong pummeling, Travis assembled his men. It was unspoken knowledge that no more help could get through. If any of them wished to attempt an escape, said Travis, he would not stop them. Only one, one of Bowie's men, Louis Rose, a mercenary and Napoleonic veteran who knew a losing scenario when he saw it, deserted, and made good his escape. All the others stayed.

Before dawn on Sunday, March 6, the Texans were awakened by the chilling fanfare of the *Degüello*—Fire and Death—a bugle call of no quarter. Francisco Ruíz, the alcalde of San Antonio de Béxar, was a witness:

"On the 6th of March at 3 a.m., General Santa Anna at the head of 4000 men advanced against the Alamo. The infantry, artillery and cavalry had formed about 1000 yards from the walls. . . . The Mexican army charged and were twice repulsed by the deadly fire of Travis's artillery which resembled a constant thunder. At the third charge the Toluca battalion commenced to scale the walls and suffered severely. Out of 830 men only 130 were left alive."

In the cold, predawn light the Texans began to make out Santa Anna's plan of attack—one column to assault the battered south palisade next to the church, another to assault the rear of the church and adjoining courtyard, and the main thrust, two columns to swarm the north wall on the left and right sides. From the outset it was apparent that Santa Anna was unprepared for the skill with which Dickinson had arranged his cannon. On the south palisade, whose defense was led by Crockett and his Tennesseeans, were mounted four 4-pounders, each primed with grapeshot that whipped into the onrushing Mexicans. Within the ruined church, Dickinson had piled rubble up to the rear wall, mounting three 12-pounders there that now butchered Santa Anna's eastern column. The bulk of Travis' men received the attack on the north wall, supported by a battery of 8-pounders. The slaughter was horrible. Mexicans who reached the relative safety of the base of the wall began to pick off Texans who exposed themselves. Travis, directing artillery fire at the middle of the wall, was felled by a musket ball in the forehead.

A KENTUCKY LONG RIFLE. Some five feet in overall length, this gun's range and accuracy were determined by its 45-inch barrel length and powerful .58-caliber charge. This specimen was crafted by J. Dickert, a German immigrant who opened his gunsmith shop in Lancaster, Pennsylvania, in 1762. It is now on display in the Alamo it defended.

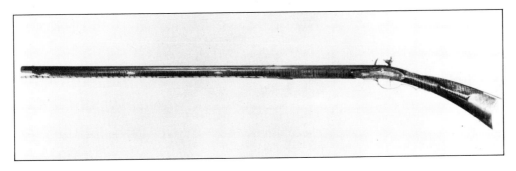

After two attacks were beaten back, the eastern column, seeking to escape the scorching fire from the 12-pounders atop the church, shifted to the northeast. With Mexican officers behind him literally whipping their men forward into the bloody maelstrom, General Juan Amador climbed up bodies and wreckage to gain the top of the short palisade in the eastern part of the wall. Texan gunners could not reload fast enough, and moments later other Mexicans succeeded in swarming the northwest parapet and opened the postern gate below.

With the enemy pouring in, the Texans fell back on a signal to the two-story Long Barracks. They wheeled their guns around—two 8-pounders in the courtyard and a swivel gun atop the hospital and boomed charge after charge of grapeshot at point-blank range until the crews were overwhelmed.

The outer walls and plaza were now in Mexican hands. As some of them turned the great 18-pounder around and blasted chunks out of the barricaded church, others charged room by room through the Long Barracks, exterminating the Texans at their last stand. Bowie, by most accounts, was bayoneted to death in his room. When the door of the church was forced open the Mexicans found one Texan crawling, torch in hand, to the powder magazine. He was killed before he could blow them all to shreds, and the battle was substantially over.

As the firing died away, the door crashed open to the chapel anteroom where the noncombatants were huddled. One of Dickinson's artillerymen ran in, followed by four Mexican soldiers who shot him and hefted his corpse aloft on their bayonets. The women, children, and servants sat there horrified when an officer strode in and demanded that Susanna Dickinson come forward. Friends of hers in the city had interceded with Santa Anna to spare her, and he decided to send her eastward with news of the slaughter—that it would happen to anyone who dared to oppose him. Clutching her baby, Susanna followed the officer across the plaza; a shot rang out and she fell,

THE WIDOW OF THE ALAMO. SUSANNA DICKINSON, wife of Travis' artillery commander, recovered from her wounds. She later married J. W. Hannig of Austin and lived a long life celebrated as the only Anglo survivor of the Alamo.

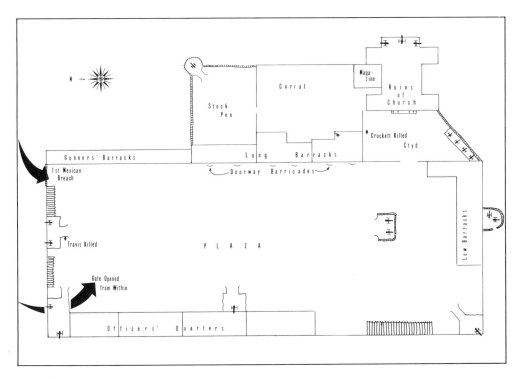

GROUNDS PLAN OF
THE ALAMO

wounded in the leg. Soldiers picked her up and carried her out of the compound, but not before she saw "Colonel Crockett lying dead and mutilated between the church and the two-story barracks. I even remember seeing his peculiar cap by his side."

Susanna Dickinson's account lent credence to the story of the last moments of a man who was probably Crockett. According to Sergeant Félix Nuñez, he "had on a long buckskin coat and a round cap without any bill, made out of fox skin with the long tail hanging down his back . . . of the many soldiers who took deliberate aim at him and fired, not one ever hit him. On the contrary, he never missed a shot. He killed at least eight of our men, besides wounding several others. This being observed by a lieutenant who had come in over the wall, he sprang at him and dealt him a deadly blow with his sword, just over the right eye, which felled him to the ground, and in an instant he was pierced by not less than 20 bayonets."

When the fighting was over, Santa Anna undertook an inspection of the Alamo compound. One in his retinue was Apolinario Saldigua, his sixteen-year-old fifer. The dictator "had ordered that no corpse should be disturbed, till after he should have looked upon them all, & seen how every man had fallen. He had employed three or four citizens of San Antonio to enter with him, & to point out to him the bodies of several distinguished Texians. . . .

"The bodies of the Texians lay as they had fallen; & many of them were covered by those of Mexicans who had fallen upon them. The close of the struggle seemed to have been a hand to hand engagement; & the number of slain Mexicans exceeded that of the Texians. The ground was covered. . . ."

In recent years it has become fashionable for revisionist debunkers to publish accounts of the fall of the Alamo, depicting its defenders—Davy Crockett in particular—as having surrendered and begged for their lives before being executed. Such accounts are usually traceable to Mexican officers, such as General Cós, trying to present themselves in a favorable light to offset their having reentered Texas in violation of the parole granted them after the first battle at San Antonio, or for some other ingratiation. Crockett's own final posture was described by Saldigua. Santa Anna, he said, "was then conducted to the body of [Crockett]. This man lay with his face upward; & his body was covered by those of many Mexicans who had fallen upon him. His face was florid, like that of a living man; & he looked like a healthy man asleep. Santa Anna viewed him for a few moments, thrust his sword through him & turned away."

It is possible that five or six Texans were taken alive and killed, but according to alcalde Ruíz, "The gallantry of the few Texans, who defended the Alamo, was really wondered at by the Mexican army. Even the generals were astonished at their vigorous resistance and how dearly victory was bought."

Smoke still billowed from the blasted church as Santa Anna dictated his own report for the Secretary of War and Navy.

> Most Excellent Sir:
>
> Victory belongs to the army, which, at this very moment, 8 o'clock a.m., achieved a complete and glorious triumph that will render its memory imperishable. . . .
>
> [T]he force at my disposal, recruits excluded [numbered] 1400 infantry. This force, divided into four columns of attack, and a reserve, commenced the attack at 5 o'clock a.m. They met with a stubborn resistance, the combat lasting more than an hour and a half, and the reserve having to be brought into action. . . .
>
> The Fortress is now in our power, with its artillery, stores, etc. More than 600 corpses of foreigners were buried in the ditches and intrenchments, and a great many, who had escaped the bayonet of the infantry, fell in the vicinity under the sabres of the cavalry. . . .
>
> Among the corpses are those of Bowie and Travis, who styled themselves Colonels, and also that of Crockett, and several leading men. . . . We lost about 70 men killed and 300 wounded, among whom are 25 officers. . . .
>
> The bearer takes with him one of the flags of the enemy's battalions, captured today. The inspection of it will show plainly the true intention of the treacherous colonists, and of their abettors, who came from the ports of the United States of the North.
>
> God and Liberty!
>
> Antonio López de Santa Anna
>
> Headquarters, Béxar, March 6, 1836

Most of the lies of the Santa Anna report speak for themselves; when he congratulated his surviving officers on their victory, one grumbled that another like it would ruin them. Out of a total force and reserve of about fifty-four hundred, perhaps fifteen hundred by the best estimate were dead. According to Ruíz, "Santa Anna . . . directed me to call on some of the neighbors to come with carts to carry the [Mexican] dead to the cemetery . . . but not having sufficient room for them, I ordered some to be thrown into the river, which was done on the same day."

JIM BOWIE, like Crockett, was from Tennessee, but his career was even less conventional. Renowned throughout the South as a knife fighter, the weapon that bears his name was tailored for him after he was wounded in a duel.

In Louisiana he partnered his brother Rezin trading in shady land certificates and smuggling slaves, often with the connivance of Jean Lafitte.

After coming to Texas in 1828 he spent most of his time searching for a fabled Spanish mine on the San Saba River. He married into the Mexican aristocracy via María Ursula de Veramendi in 1831. When cholera swept San Antonio two years later, Bowie sent her and their two children to Monclova for safety. The deaths of all three there, of cholera, sent him into an alcoholic depression that lasted, off and on, until his death.

Other details of soldiers, recalled Saldigua, "began to take up the Texians, & to bring them together, & lay them in a pile . . . four soldiers walked around it; each carrying a can of camphine, from which he spurted the liquid onto the pile," which was then torched.

From a military standpoint the only thing more foolish than defending the Alamo at all costs was Santa Anna's decision to take it at all costs. The Texans' suicidal, two-week struggle bought time for Houston to organize a defense of the country, but Houston needed men more than he needed time. Santa Anna could have easily left enough troops in Béxar to pin Travis down, and continued on his path of destruction across Texas.

But the Alamo had become a symbol, a ground of spiritual contention whose importance transcended its military advantage. It was an object lesson that some dictators are willing to squander whole armies in the oppression of their people, and conversely, that some men are able to look destruction in the face and accept it as the cost of freedom. "If we fail," wrote twenty-two-year-old Daniel Cloud before entering the walls, "death in the cause of Liberty and humanity is not a cause for shuddering."

It was because of the widespread perception that this was what the Alamo was all about that news of the siege and its grisly ending electrified people in the United States and gained the respectful notice of the world.

Declaration of Independence of the Republic of Texas

WHEN a government has ceased to protect the lives, liberty and property of the people from whom its legitimate powers are derived, and for the advancement of whose happiness it was instituted; and so far from being a guarantee for the enjoyment of those inestimable and inalienable rights, becomes an instrument in the hands of evil rulers for their oppression; when the Federal Republican Constitution of the country, which they have sworn to support, no longer has a substantial existence, and the whole nature of their government has been forcibly changed without their consent, from a restricted federative republic, composed of sovereign states, to a consolidated central military despotism, in which every interest is disregarded but that of the army and the priesthood—both the eternal enemies of civil liberty, and the ever-ready minions of power, and the usual instruments of tyrants; When, long after the spirit of the constitution has departed, moderation is at length, so far lost, by those in power that even the semblance of freedom is removed, and the forms, themselves, of the constitution discontinued; and so far from their petitions and remonstrances being regarded, the agents who bear them are thrown into dungeons; and mercenary armies sent forth to force a new government upon them at the point of the bayonet; When in consequence of such acts of malfeasance and abdication, on the part of the government, anarchy prevails, and civil society is dissolved into its original elements; In such a crisis, the first law of nature, the right of self-preservation—the inherent and inalienable right of the people to appeal to first principles and take their political affairs into their own hands in extreme cases—enjoins it as a right towards themselves and a sacred obligation to their posterity, to abolish such government and create another in its stead, calculated to rescue them from impending dangers, and to secure their future welfare and happiness.

Nations, as well as individuals, are amenable for their acts to the public opinion of mankind. A statement of a part of our grievances is, therefore, submitted to an impartial world, in justification of the hazardous but unavoidable step now taken of severing our political connection with the Mexican people, and assuming an independent attitude among the nations of the earth.

The Mexican government, by its colonization laws, invited and induced the Anglo-American population of Texas to colonize its wilderness under the pledged faith of a written constitution, that they should continue to enjoy that constitutional liberty and republican government to which they had been habituated in the land of their birth, the United States of America. In this expectation they have been cruelly disappointed, inasmuch as the Mexican nation has acquiesced in the late changes made in the government by General Antonio Lopez de Santa Anna, who, having overturned the constitution of his country, now offers us the cruel alternative either to abandon our homes, acquired by so many privations, or submit to the most intolerable of all tyranny, the combined despotism of the sword and the priesthood.

It has sacrificed our welfare to the state of Coahuila, by which our interests have been continually depressed, through a jealous and partial course of legislation carried on at a far distant seat of government, by a hostile majority, in an unknown tongue; and this too, notwithstanding we have petitioned in the humblest terms, for the establishment of a separate state government, and have, in accordance with the provisions of the national constitution, presented to the general Congress, a republican constitution which was without just cause contemptuously rejected.

It incarcerated in a dungeon, for a long time, one of our citizens, for no other cause but a zealous endeavor to procure the acceptance of our constitution and the establishment of a state government.

It has failed and refused to secure on a firm basis, the right of trial by jury; that palladium of civil liberty, and only safe guarantee for the life, liberty, and property of the citizen.

It has failed to establish any public system of education, although possessed of almost boundless resources (the public domain) and although, it is an axiom, in political science, that unless a people are educated and enlightened it is idle to expect the continuance of civil liberty, or the capacity for self-government.

It has suffered the military commandants stationed among us to exercise arbitrary acts of oppression and tyranny; thus trampling upon the most sacred rights of the citizen and rendering the military superior to the civil power.

It has dissolved by force of arms, the state Congress of Coahuila and Texas, and obliged our representatives to fly for their lives from the seat of government; thus depriving us of the fundamental political right of representation.

It has demanded the surrender of a number of our citizens, and ordered military detachments to seize and carry them into the interior for trial; in contempt of the civil authorities, and in defiance of the laws and the constitution.

It has made piratical attacks upon our commerce; by commissioning foreign desperadoes, and authorizing them to seize our vessels, and convey the property of our citizens to far distant ports of confiscation.

It denies us the right of worshipping the Almighty according to the dictates of our own consciences, by the support of a national religion calculated to promote the temporal interests of its human functionaries rather than the glory of the true and living God.

It has demanded us to deliver up our arms; which are essential to our defense, the rightful property of freemen, and formidable only to tyrannical governments.

It has invaded our country, both by sea and land, with intent to lay waste our territory and drive us from our homes; and has now a large mercenary army advancing to carry on against us a war of extermination.

It has, through its emissaries, incited the merciless savage, with the tomahawk and scalping knife, to massacre the inhabitants of our defenseless frontiers.

It hath been, during the whole time of our connection with it, the contemptible sport and victim of successive military revolutions and hath continually exhibited every characteristic of a weak, corrupt, and tyrannical government.

These, and other grievances, were patiently borne by the people of Texas until they reached that point at which forbearance ceases to be a virtue. We then took up arms in defense of the national constitution. We appealed to our Mexican brethren for assistance. Our appeal has been made in vain. Though months have lapsed, no sympathetic response has yet been heard from the Interior. We are, therefore, forced to the melancholy conclusion that the Mexican people have acquiesced in the destruction of their liberty, and the substitution therefor of a military government—that they are unfit to be free and incapable of self-government.

The necessity of self-preservation, therefore, now decrees our eternal political separation.

We, therefore, the delegates, with plenary powers, of the people of Texas, in solemn convention assembled, appealing to a candid world for the necessities of our condition, do hereby resolve and declare that our political connection with the Mexican nation has forever ended; and that the people of Texas do now constitute a free, sovereign and independent republic, and are fully invested with all the rights and attributes which properly belong to the independent nations; and conscious of the rectitudes of our intentions, we fearlessly and confidently commit the issue to the decision of the Supreme Arbiter of the destinies of nations.

RICHARD ELLIS, president of the convention
and Delegate from Red River.

Charles B. Stewart
Thos. Barnet
John S. D. Byrom
Franco Ruiz
J. Antonio Navarro
Jesse B. Badgett
Wm. D. Lacey
William Menefee
Jno. Fisher
Mathew Caldwell
William Mottley
Lorenzo de Zavala
Stephen H. Everitt
Geo W Smyth
Elijah Stapp
Claiborne West
Wm. B Scates
M. B. Menard
A. B. Hardin
J. W. Bunton
Thos. J. Gazley
R M Coleman
Sterling C. Robertson
Jas Collinswor'h
Edwin Waller
Asa Brigham
Geo. C. Childress
Bailey Hardeman
Rob. Potter

J B Woods
Thomas Jefferson Rusk
Chas. S. Taylor
John S. Roberts
Robert Hamilton
Collin McKinney
Albert H Latimer
James Power
Sam Houston
David Thomas
Edwd. Conrad
Martin Parmer
Edwin O. LeGrand
Stephen W. Blount
Jas. Gaines
Wm. Clark, Jr
Sydney O. Penington
Wm. Carrol Crawford
Jno Turner
Benj. Briggs Goodrich
G. M. Barnett
James G. Swisher
Jesse Grimes
S Rhoads Fisher
John W. Moore
John W. Bower
Saml. A Maverick
(from Bejar)
Sam P. Carson
A. Briscoe

Test. H. S. Kemble, Secretary

Goliad

DURING middle to late February, as Travis was laboring to make his Alamo defensible, James W. Fannin and his volunteers, largely from Georgia, were working to improve the Mission La Bahía at Goliad, which had been quickly captured from the Mexicans the previous October. Travis' first appeal for aid reached Fannin on February 19, but Fannin, authorized by the Permanent Council itself to head the invasion of Matamoros, was unwilling to submit to Travis' command. On February 25 another plea arrived from Travis, this one desperate in tone, and the next morning Fannin started for Béxar with four pieces of artillery and nearly all his men. They camped the night on the San Antonio River, but then in the morning suddenly returned to Goliad. The change of heart sparked a bitter controversy whether Fannin was displaying cowardice or good sense. In his own report he gave cogent enough reasons for the action: "Our baggage wagons and artillery were all drawn by oxen (no broken horses could be obtained) and there were but a few yokes of them. In attempting to cross the San Antonio River, three of our wagons broke down and it was with the utmost labor and personal hazard, that our four pieces of cannon were conveyed safely across. We remained there during the day, with our ammunition wagon on the other side of the River. During the night, some of the oxen strayed off and could not be found the next morning. Our situation became delicate and embarrassing in the extreme. . . . The country between us and Bexar is entirely unsettled, and there would be but little hope of obtaining provisions on the route and we would be able only to carry 12 rounds of cartridges each. . . . Intelligence also reached us that the advance of [General José Urrea] had surprised San Patricio about 50 miles in front of our position and put the entire garrison . . . to the sword. Five of them have reached this place. Col. Johnson is one of them, and they are probably all that have escaped. . . . It was apparent to all that the evacuation of Goliad . . . would leave the whole frontier from Bexar to the coast open to the incursions of the enemy. . . . Everyone felt an anxiety to relieve our friends . . . yet everyone saw the impropriety, if not the impossibility of our proceeding under existing circumstances."

Back at La Bahía, orders arrived from Houston to link up with him on Cibolo Creek and march to Travis' aid, but after news of the Alamo reached Houston in Gonzales on March 11, fresh orders went out. Now Fannin was to blow up his fort, which he had named Defiance, and fall back to Victoria as soon as he could. Fannin's transportation problems—and probably his own reluctance—prevented him from starting his retreat until March 19, but by then Urrea was upon him. Only six miles east of town Fannin found himself closely pursued by two Mexican divisions, perhaps fourteen hundred men. Fannin's men were within sight of the thick woods bordering Coleto Creek, from which he could have made an effective stand. But, inexplicably, he halted on the prairie, forming a square barricade with his baggage wagons as his European gunnery officer positioned the cannon to their best advantage. Urrea surrounded him easily and the outcome was only a matter of time.

JOHANNA TROUTMAN, often called the Betsy Ross of Texas, was only eighteen when she helped organize the Georgia Battalion of volunteers that left for Texas late in 1835. On their departure she presented them with her "Lone Star" flag of silk, blue on white, with a single, five-pointed star subscribed Liberty or Death. Most of the Georgia Battalion drew death, having become attached to Fannin's command and massacred at Goliad. Her flag was ripped to pieces after the battle, but by then the imagery of the Lone Star had gained irresistible currency among the rebels.

The Battle of Coleto: General Urrea's Diary

MARCH 19

After marching two leagues, I was informed by my spies, whose activity is truly marvelous, that we were near the enemy, and that it seemed that they were not taking all the force that had garrisoned Goliad. I ordered 100 infantry to return, therefore, to protect the artillery and munitions which were being brought up, and redoubled the vigilance of the rest of my forces. At half past one in the afternoon, I overtook the enemy and succeeded in cutting off their retreat with our cavalry, just as they were going to enter a heavy woods from where it would have been difficult, if not impossible, to dislodge them. They were marching in column formation and carried nine pieces of artillery. Seeing themselves forced to fight, they decided to make the best of it and awaited our advance with firmness, arranging their force in battle formation with the artillery in the center. . . .

Expecting the artillery and our munitions to reach us soon, agreeable to instructions given, I decided to engage the enemy at once. Our fire was immediately returned by their rifles and cannon. I ordered the brave Col. Morales to charge the left with the rifle companies; the grenadiers and the first regiment of San Luís, under my immediate command, to charge the right; the remainder of the battalion of Jiménez to form itself into a column and charge the front, while the cavalry was to surprise the enemy's rear. These instructions having been issued, the orders were immediately carried out and a determined charge was made on the right and left flanks.

In order to obtain a quick victory, I ordered my troops to charge with their bayonets at the same time that Col. Morales did likewise on the opposite flank; and, according to previous instructions, the central column advanced in battle formation, sustaining a steady fire in order to detract the attention of the enemy while we surprised the flanks. Though our soldiers showed resolution, the enemy was likewise unflinching. Thus, without being intimidated by our impetuous charge, it maneuvered in order to meet it; and, assuming a hammer formation on the right, they quickly placed three pieces of artillery on this side, pouring a deadly shower of shot upon my reduced column. A similar movement was executed on the left, while our front attack was met with the same courage and coolness. . . .

While defending themselves from our determined attack, they built up defences with their baggage and wagons, forming a square. . . . Realizing the importance of preventing the enemy from finishing its fortifications, especially in the form in which they were doing it, I tried to disconcert them with a cavalry charge on their rear, and placed myself at the head. . . . Although disposing of very little time, they had foreseen my operation and received me with a scorching fire from their cannons and rifles. Our horses were in very poor condition and ill-suited for the purpose, but the circumstances were urgent and extraordinary efforts were necessary. My efforts, however, were all in vain, for after repeatedly trying to make the dragoons effect an opening in the enemy's ranks, I was forced to retire—not without indignation. I placed the cavalry in a position where it could continuously threaten the enemy, avoiding, as far as possible, their fire.

Seeing that our artillery and munitions did not arrive, my anxiety was great. In the midst of our trials and in proportion as they increased I cast furtive glances towards the point by which they were to come. . . . The sun was going down and our munitions would soon give out. They were exhausted sooner than I expected. Though I had given instructions for the infantry to be provided with four rounds to the man, this order had been neglected, [for] they had counted on the early arrival of what was coming up on our rear. The party conducting it, however, lost its way and did not arrive until the following day.

I decided to make a new and simultaneous charge on all fronts to see if I could disconcert the enemy before the sad moment arrived when we would be entirely without munitions. I gave the necessary orders and, as the bugler gave the signal agreed upon, all our forces advanced with firm step and in the best order. I placed myself again at the head of the cavalry and led the charge on one of the fronts. All our troops advanced to within fifty and even forty paces from the square. So brave an effort on the part of our courageous soldiers deserved to have been crowned with victory; but . . . the enemy redoubled its resistance with new vigor. They placed their artillery on the corners, flanking, in this way, our weakened columns. The fire from the cannon, as well as from the rifles, was very lively, making itself all the more noticeable in proportion as ours died out for lack of ammunition. In these circumstances, I ordered all our infantry to fix bayonets and to maintain a slow fire with whatever powder remained.

For almost an hour, this unequal contest was kept up, then I finally gave the order to retire.

The enemy spent the night digging a ditch all around the square. My aides . . . were with me, all harassing the enemy and keeping it awake with false bugle calls. The enemy's cavalry, which was small in number, had escaped the moment we overtook them, thanks to their good horses. Some there were who, choosing the fate of their brave companions, dismounted and abandoned their horses. I took advantage of this to replace the worst mounts of our dragoons.

MARCH 20

At daybreak I inspected the position of the enemy, which I found to be the same as that of the day before, with the exception of the trenches formed by their baggage and wagons, now reenforced by the piling up of the dead horses and oxen, and by the digging of a ditch. . . .

The troops having taken up their respective positions, rations were issued consisting of hard tack and roast meat. The latter was furnished by the teams of oxen that had been taken from the enemy the night before. Those that remained to the enemy were killed by sharpshooters detailed for the purpose.

At half past six in the morning the ammunition arrived . . . [and] one hundred infantry, two four-pounders, and a howitzer were added to my force. I placed these as a battery about 160 paces from the enemy protected by the rifle companies. I ordered the rest of the infantry to form a column that was to advance along the left of our battery when it opened fire. As soon as we did this and began our movement as planned, the enemy, without answering our fire, raised a white flag.

After raising their token of surrender, Fannin and some officers were received in the Mexican camp, where they tried to bargain for terms. For many years controversy raged whether Fannin turned over his men "at discretion," as the saying went, or received from Urrea a promise to be treated as prisoners of war. When the documents were finally uncovered, it became apparent that he surrendered to the mercy of the government, although with Urrea's spoken commitment to intercede for them with Santa Anna. Fannin was unable to bring himself to tell his men they were surrendering at discretion, and assured them of fair treatment.

Urrea was as suspicious of Santa Anna's harshness as Fannin, and sent dispatches making good on his word to Fannin. When he moved on with his army, Urrea took with him as many of the Americans as he could to serve as nurses and attendants to his wounded. The others—somewhat over four hundred—were locked in the mission compound at Goliad.

The conditions in which they were kept were harsh and primitive, but for a week the commander left at Goliad, Lieutenant Colonel Portilla, obeyed Urrea's orders to treat Fannin and his men reasonably well. However, at seven in the evening of March 26 he received a dispatch from President-General Santa Anna ordering him to execute his prisoners without delay. Enclosed with it was a copy of a message from Santa Anna to Urrea, a stinging rebuke for the maneuvering to try to save them. On March 27— Palm Sunday—Portilla had his men awaken the prisoners early. Some of the Mexican guard started the rumor, whether out of pity or derision one cannot tell, that the Texans were to be marched to the coast and sent to America.

As they were escorted out of the mission complex, one of the prisoners, Dick

José Nicolás de la Portilla, the lieutenant colonel commanding the La Bahía garrison, found himself in a verbal cross fire between General Urrea, who would have spared Fannin and his men, and President-General Santa Anna, whose order he obeyed to shoot down the four hundred Anglo prisoners.

Ehrenberg, whose later merciless criticism of Fannin managed to impeach his own credibility, was clear in his recollection of what happened next: "The Mexican soldiers were unbearably silent . . . the atmosphere was hot and close. Mexican soldiers were drawn up in two lines, so we were closely guarded on both sides. . . . I noticed for the first time their parade uniforms and lack of baggage."

The Texans were marched in this fashion about half a mile down to the river; two more groups went out in other directions. Near the San Antonio River the guard detail formed into a single line. "A command to halt given in Spanish struck our ears like the voice of doom. The Mexican officer shouted at us to kneel. A man who spoke Spanish cried out, and a fearful crash interrupted him, then all was quiet; thick clouds of smoke rolled slowly toward the river. The blood of my lieutenant spurted on my clothes. I saw no more; quickly making up my mind, I sprang up and took advantage of the thick smoke which hid me to make for the river."

Ehrenberg and perhaps thirty others made good their escapes. About 370 men—the exact figure cannot be known—were either killed in first volleys or were momentarily shot, lanced, or put to the sword. The forty Texans at Goliad who were injured and unable to be marched out, Fannin among them, were executed inside the fort.

Urrea had advanced as far as Victoria when a courier brought news of the mass killing, received within a few hours of its occurrence. Outraged and mortified, he divorced himself from the episode as far as he dared without provoking Santa Anna further. He had held a particularly high regard for the "much esteemed and fearless Fannin," and fumed to his diary the dishonor of the event: "I never thought that the

horrible spectacle of that massacre could take place in cold blood . . . a deed pro-
scribed by the laws of war and condemned by the civilization of our country. . . .
[The Texans] surrendered confident that Mexican generosity would not make their
sacrifice useless, for under any other circumstances they would have sold their lives
dearly, fighting to the last."

The fate of the victims' bodies was described by Private Zuber of Houston's army:
"Mr. Abel Morgan, who belonged to Fannin's command, & who was one of the men
who were spared as nurses for the sick & wounded Mexicans, said that, in going to the
river for water, & while hunting near its bank for fuel, he came upon the bodies of his
butchered countrymen; & that they had been stripped of the last article of clothing. He
also found a large number of Mexican soldiers in the river, washing the clothes which
they had stripped from the murdered men: & the river was tinged red with the blood
which they wrung from the clothes. . . .

"Some of [the bodies], those nearest to the town & fort, were thrown together; &
piles of green mesquit brush were built upon them, & fired, with intent to burn them.
But the green brush did not burn well; & the fire performed its duty but in part. The
bodies were partly burned, & partly roasted. But the burning was adopted only as a
sanitary measure. They that were shot furthest from the town & fort, were left to
satisfy the appetites of wolves & vultures."

The dead Texans remained where they lay until June 3, when General Thomas J.
Rusk had the remains gathered and interred in a mass grave close beside the mission
chapel.

MISSION LA BAHÍA. Originally established in
1722 near the site of La Salle's fort, Mission La
Bahía del Espíritu Santo was moved to its present location, and the new compound begun, in
1746. Although now a considerable distance
from the Gulf, it retained the general designa-
tion "La Bahía." The surrounding settlement
was named Goliad in 1829. The mission was
largely spoiled during and after the Revolution. One visitor in 1854 found a man living in
one corner of the chapel: "He was a man of
forty years, thin, and dark-complexioned. 'I
am glad to see you here. Ah, it's a poor old
ruin; come in and you shall see. It was once a
very fine church, but the Americans destroyed
it as much as they could. See, there we had a
gallery, with the oriel over it; they burned it.
All the pictures they burned; the carvings they
cut with knives—ah it is all ruins.'" A massive
belfry, crumbled in this view from the near
corner of the chapel, was rebuilt during later
restoration.

The Runaway Scrape

SINCE his arrival at Gonzales on March 11, General Houston had endured one headache after another. First came news of the Alamo, and then lack of news from Fannin that he would fall back to Victoria as ordered. Santa Anna had already left San Antonio and was now marching on Gonzales, Houston noting with alarm that the dictator had advanced twenty-four miles in one day. Houston, with 374 effectives in his command, knew he was no match for him, and in the dark early hours of March 14 he and his volunteers sunk two precious cannon in the Guadalupe for want of transport, and pulled out. They had virtually all the local citizenry in tow, leaving behind them the receding red horizon of the town they had set afire. It was the beginning of the "Runaway Scrape," a pell-mell depopulation of the entire frontier—the very object that Santa Anna meant to accomplish.

Houston reached Jesse Burnham's crossing on the Colorado on March 17, now with 600 men, of whom he rated 420 as effective. He sent word to Fannin, again ordering him to the defense of Victoria and the crucial supply link of Lavaca Bay. Then, fearing to be trapped by waters rising in spring flood, Houston crossed his men to the east bank of the river and burned the ferry. The army marched southeast along the Colorado to Beason's Crossing, near Columbus, where they camped the week of March 19 to 26, resting, drilling, and assimilating new volunteers. It was on the twentieth Houston learned that Fannin had been trapped, but concealed the news from his men.

From Santa Anna's viewpoint, his expedition—aside from his fearful losses at the Alamo—was succeeding splendidly. He had left General Andrade in San Antonio with fifteen hundred troops, and was himself now in Gonzales with a thousand. Urrea was in Goliad with two thousand, and his northern column of one thousand under General Antonio Gaona had entered Bastrop. The pandemonium that spread before them was complete. In his retreat Houston had deployed rear guards to round up stragglers, and Noah Smithwick was among the scouts sent to Bastrop to try to get livestock across the rising river. They failed, retiring in the face of Gaona's sudden appearance, but he left a telling picture of the countryside: "Houses were standing open, the beds unmade, the breakfast things still on the tables, pans of milk moulding in the dairies. There were cribs full of corn, smoke houses full of bacon, yards full of chickens that ran after us for food, nests of eggs in every fence corner, young corn and garden truck rejoicing in the rain, cattle cropping the luxuriant grass, hogs, fat and lazy, wallowing in the mud, all abandoned. . . . Hungry cats ran mewing out to meet us, rubbing their sides on our legs. Wagons were so scarce that it was impossible to remove household goods, many of the women and children, even, had to walk. Some had no conveyance but trucks [carts] . . . one young lady said she walked with a bucket in hand to keep the trucks on which her mother rode from taking fire.

"It was a time to try the souls of all, even the little children realizing something of the situation, which must have left such a vivid impression on their minds that time has not effaced it."

Smithwick did not know how right he was. Dr. Pleasant W. Rose of St. Louis and his family had been settled at Stafford's Point near the lower Brazos only since December of 1833. Rose's ten-year-old daughter, Dilue, was quite aware of the circumstances: "We left home at sunset, hauling clothes, bedding, and provisions on the sleigh with one yoke of oxen. Mother and I were walking, she with an infant in her arms." They were soon able to exchange their sledge for a cart, and continued eastward. "We arrived at the San Jacinto in the night. There were fully five thousand people at the ferry."

With a steady stream of soldiers deserting to help their families escape—most came back as soon as they could—and almost simultaneously with learning of Fannin's predicament, Houston was shocked to find himself staring across the swollen Colorado at a Mexican division of six or seven hundred under Joaquín Ramírez y Sesma, an advance unit of Gaona's column. His army now demanded a fight, but Houston knew that Sesma's force was only one tine of a massive assault, and that anything short of a victory for the Texans would lose their cause forever. A couple of hundred more volunteers arrived, including Colonel Sidney Sherman with fifty-two Kentuckians and a battle flag sewn for him by a group of Kentucky women; it depicted a bare-breasted Liberty surging forward, saber aloft holding the banner Liberty or Death. Houston, the size of his army fluctuating with daily enlistments and desertions, for the moment outnumbered Sesma by perhaps as many as two to one, so to quiet the army he allowed some of them to engage. Sherman led a unit within the Mexicans' firing range, hoping to draw Sesma's cavalry into an ambuscade, but it didn't work.

After treating his men to their little taste of action, Houston assembled them and sprung the news of Fannin's capture, that those present were "the only army in Texas. . . . There are but few of us, and if we are beaten, the fate of Texas is sealed. The salvation of the country depends upon the first battle. . . . For this reason I intend to retreat and I shall continue to retreat" until the Mexicans could be engaged with a guarantee of success.

On the twenty-seventh he removed his camp to the neighborhood of San Felipe on the Brazos. He was forced to deny rumors that he was seeking safety in Louisiana, but the next day retreated farther north up the Brazos to Groce's plantation, "to a position where," he assured his men, "you can whip the enemy ten to one, and where we can get an abundant supply of corn." While still along the Brazos, recalled one of Houston's soldiers, "a Mexican prisoner was brought into camp. He was a copper colored boy, eighteen years old. I was present when Gen Houston questioned him, through an interpreter; & heard him state that he was one of the men who handled the 'Gaut-dam-yees,' in the Alamo; that every butcher knife, pocket knife, pistol, handkerchief, watch, & every dollar, upon the bodies of the slain Texians, was appropriated by the soldiers, & that he obtained an excellent pocket knife, which he took from the pocket of a dead man."

Masterfully, Houston was building his men's emotional readiness for battle to a pitch, but it was opposite Groce's that he endured the worst storm of abuse. The provisional government had fled Washington-on-the-Brazos on March 17, and on April 4, no less a messenger than the Secretary of War, Thomas Jefferson Rusk, arrived with a strident message from President Burnet: "Sir: The Enemy are laughing you to scorn. You must fight them. You must retreat no farther. The country expects you to fight. The salvation of the country depends on your doing so."

Houston growled against the propriety of Burnet's sending such a communiqué when it had been the President himself who ran farther and faster than anybody, but Rusk countered that he was authorized to relieve Houston if he deemed it necessary. Houston, who had revealed his strategy to no one, relented, and Rusk, seeing the wisdom of drawing the Mexicans into some more vulnerable situation, stayed on to assist. They grew to be intimate friends.

The Texan army continued to receive new volunteers both domestic and from America; most were serviceable, some merely ridiculous. Among the latter was a

SIDNEY SHERMAN was thirty-five when he came to Texas at the head of fifty-two Kentucky volunteers. A native of Massachusetts, orphaned at twelve, he failed in business at seventeen and moved to New York.

He went west in 1831 and in Newport, Kentucky (across the Ohio River from Cincinnati), he opened the first sheet-lead smelter west of New York and founded the first plant for producing cotton bagging by machine. Already a captain in the Kentucky militia, he sold the latter business to outfit his volunteer company and embark them for Texas. One of the officers always pressuring Sam Houston to stand and fight, Sherman was said to have been the first to cry "Remember the Alamo!" as the charge began across the plain at San Jacinto.

Sherman took his land grant in Harris County, which he represented in the Seventh Congress of the Republic, and was Major General of Militia at the time of statehood. After annexation he relocated in Harrisburg, which he organized anew by buying all the remaining town lots. He became part owner of a sawmill, and formed a company that built the Buffalo Bayou, Brazos and Colorado Railroad, the first in Texas.

Shown here as the Confederate general in charge of the defense of Galveston, the ill health that always dogged him forced his retirement before the Union invasion in October of 1862. His son and namesake died in the battle there three months later. First his sawmill and then his house and railroad office burned down, and his wife and second son died. An impoverished invalid, he resided with a married daughter until his death in 1873.

painter and poet and journalist named Mirabeau Buonaparte Lamar. Upon hearing of the democratic struggle in Texas, he had deserted his newspaper and stormed out of Georgia, his head full, one supposes, of visions of Byron and Missolonghi. He was ready for action, and when he arrived at Groce's and saw that the only activities were drilling and grumbling, the first thing he did was attempt to depose Houston and ride off with himself at the head of the army. Coolly, Houston ordered some graves dug and announced that they would be filled by anybody who attempted to draw volunteers from his command. Lamar backed down and enlisted as a corporal of cavalry.

Houston formed his army into two regiments, one under Sherman and one under Ed Burleson, who had commanded the siege of San Antonio the previous winter. Houston pulled out of Groce's on April 15, retreating still eastward. To the south Santa Anna was now ahead of him, having advanced as far as Harrisburg. The dictator had learned that the Texan Government was there for the moment. Believing that if he could capture and execute the ringleaders the war would be over with one more stroke, he left most of his troops at Fort Bend under his second-in-command, General Vicente Filisola, and raced ahead with only 750 men—about the size of Houston's army.

Santa Anna found Harrisburg empty and burned it. The government had fled to New Washington, on Galveston Bay, and the dictator pursued. There President Burnet and his cabinet had scant seconds to run for the dock, clamber into a rowboat and pull for their lives. They were still within musket shot when the first Mexican dragoons pulled up, but their colonel, Juan Almonte, refused to open fire when he saw there was a woman—Mrs. Burnet—in the boat.

Houston was aware of Santa Anna's whereabouts, thanks to captured dispatches. (One courier using saddlebags stamped "William Barret Travis" was saved from hanging only by the general's intervention.) Santa Anna had finally made the mistake Houston had been praying for. Houston whipped his men fifty-five miles in less than three days. On April 17 they came to a fork in the road, one trail heading southeast to Harrisburg, and one northeast to Nacogdoches; the army had been openly muttering mutiny if he took the latter. Houston had already made up his mind, and at the "Which-way Tree" ordered "Columns right."

A few miles down the Harrisburg fork the army came to a halt as a certain Mrs. Pamela Mann came storming and cursing up to Houston. By her account he had borrowed her ox team on the assurance he was marching to Nacogdoches, and now in language that left the volunteers grinning she demanded the stock back. As the team was not at that moment hitched to anything, Mrs. Mann got hold of them and led them away. The incident gave momentary new fuel to the speculation whether Houston really intended to take the Harrisburg fork or was forced into it by the certainty of insurrection if he didn't. But just then Houston's wagonmaster came up, who happened to be Conrad Rohrer, the Dutchman whose colorful anglicisms had won him Smithwick's respect during the San Antonio campaign. He arrived grumbling that one of the Twin Sisters—two 6-pounder cannon that Sherman brought from Kentucky— had bogged in the mud, and he had come up for the ox team to pull it out. On finding them gone, he matched Mrs. Mann oath for oath and set off up the Nacogdoches fork after her.

Houston turned in his saddle to view the commotion. "Rohrer," he called out after him, "that woman will fight!" While he was gone, a number of men, including the general, slogged through the muck to free the gun, and the column continued its march. Rohrer rejoined them that night, clothes torn and mad as a fighting cock, but without the oxen.

The Runaway Scrape, meanwhile, continued apace. Dr. Rose's family, after crossing the San Jacinto, had wanted to stop and rest. Word came, however, that the Trinity River was already several miles wide and still increasing, so they and the long cart train of other refugees they traveled with hurried on. Ten-year-old Dilue sometimes rode, sometimes walked, until they reached the Trinity: "The river was rising and there was a struggle to see who would cross first. Measles, sore eyes, whooping cough, and every other disease that man, woman, or child is heir to, broke out among us. . . . One of my little sisters was very sick, and the ferryman said that those families with sick

THOMAS JEFFERSON RUSK, when he first came to Texas in 1832, was a twenty-nine-year-old Georgia lawyer in pursuit of business associates who had "G. T. T." (Gone to Texas) with money embezzled from their ventures. Being a capable speculator himself, Rusk recognized Texas' possibilities and settled in Nacogdoches.

At the start of the Revolution he raised a company of volunteers, but was soon made a contractor; by the end of 1835 he was Inspector General of the Army. After independence was declared, he was named Secretary of War, the capacity in which he relayed President Burnet's strident orders to General Houston to turn and fight Santa Anna.

Rusk's strong and emotional friendship with Houston suffered when, as Chief Justice of the Texas Supreme Court, he led rangers and militia against Cherokee Indians at the Battle of the Neches in 1839. As president of the Convention of 1845, Rusk was crucial to annexation, and after guiding the organization of the state government was elected, along with Houston, to the federal Senate. In Washington he was an effective advocate for war with Mexico and of Texas' positions in the Compromise of 1850; he voted against Houston, however, in favor of the Kansas-Nebraska Bill in 1854. By the time he became president pro tempore of the Senate in 1857, Rusk was considered presidential timber in some quarters. The death of his wife and other personal reverses left him desolate; he took his own life in Nacogdoches in July of 1857, a few weeks after making his peace with Houston.

children should cross first. When our party got to the boat the water broke over the banks above where we were and ran around us. We were several hours surrounded by water. . . . The sick child was in convulsions.

"At the Trinity men from the army began to join their families. I know they have been blamed for this, but what could they have done? The Texas army was retreating and the Mexicans were [advancing], Col. Fannin and his men were prisoners, there were more negroes than whites among us and many of them were wild Africans, there was a large tribe of Indians on the Trinity, and there were tories, both Mexican and American, in the country. It was the intention of our men to see their families across the Sabine, and then to return and fight the Mexicans. I must say for the negroes that there was no insubordination among them. . . .

DAVID G. BURNET demonstrated his liberal idealism as early as age seventeen, when he spent his inheritance in an unsuccessful attempt to save his employer from bankruptcy. The following year he joined the insurgent forces of Francisco de Miranda; off the coast of Venezuela he fired the first shot for independence in that part of the world. Before Moses Austin ever left Missouri, Burnet, having failed as a trader in Natchitoches and contracted tuberculosis, rode deep into Spanish Texas. He collapsed from his horse near the upper Colorado River, but was saved by Comanche Indians who took him in. Burnet lived with the Comanches for two years before settling in Ohio to practice law.

After Mexican independence from Spain he became an empresario, securing part of a land grant along the Louisiana border; title rested in the Galveston Bay and Texas Land Company, whose legal counsel, for a time, was Sam Houston. Burnet nurtured a hearty dislike for the hard-drinking, hard-swearing Houston, who in turn thought of Burnet as a stuffed shirt and a phony.

Burnet's two great acts of statesmanship as Provisional President, however—facing down a military near-rebellion and resigning immediately after Houston's election—possibly saved Texas from a period of anarchy. The two men sniped at each other off and on for a quarter century before finding themselves allies in the struggle to prevent Texas from seceding.

His last surviving son was killed in the war, and Burnet was elected to the United States Senate in 1866. With military rule imposed after the Civil War, however, he never served. He died in Galveston in 1870 at the age of eighty-two.

"When we landed the lowlands were under water, and everybody was rushing for the prairie. . . . The night was very dark. We crossed a bridge that was under water. As soon as we crossed, a man with a cart and oxen drove on the bridge, and broke it down, drowning the oxen. That prevented the other people from crossing, as the bridge was over a slough that looked like a river.

"Father and mother hurried on, and we got to the prairie and found a great many families camped there. A Mrs. Foster invited mother to her camp, and furnished us with supper, a bed, and dry clothes.

"The other families stayed all night in the bottom without fire or anything to eat, and the water up in the carts."

Santa Anna could not possibly have appreciated the hatred welling up in people whose lives he had so disrupted. Five days after crossing the Trinity the Rose family came to the town of Liberty, where the sick infant died. Mrs. Rose was inconsolable; they and many other refugees camped just outside the town to await developments. Then it started again: "One Thursday evening all of a sudden we heard a sound like distant thunder. When it was repeated father said it was cannon, and that the Texans and Mexicans were fighting. The cannonading lasted only a few minutes, and father said the Texans must have been defeated, or the cannon would not have ceased firing so quickly."

The Roses and the other families again cast their belongings into carts and lit out for Louisiana, certain that they would never see their Texas homes again.

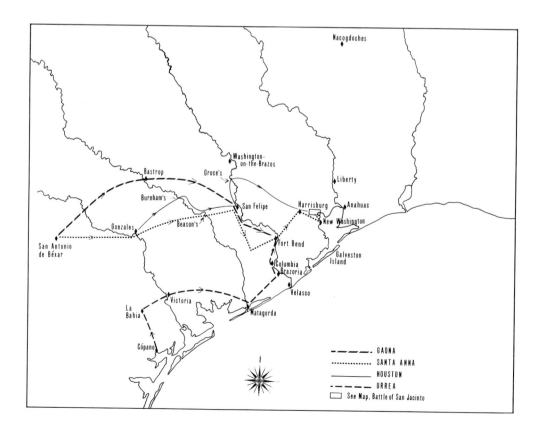

THE RUNAWAY SCRAPE

San Jacinto: Independence Baptized in a Bloodbath

THE SAN JACINTO BATTLE FLAG. A ladies' auxiliary in Kentucky stitched together the banner that Sidney Sherman's volunteers brought with them to Texas. It was the only flag that waved over the Texan army at San Jacinto. Once reduced to a wooden chest, full of tatters, the flag was restored for the Texas Centennial celebration in 1936. At that time the figure of Liberty, which had originally been draped in a way to keep the soldiers' interest up, was clad in a somewhat more chaste manner.

AFTER leading his men down the road to Harrisburg, Houston let them get a good look at the smoldering ruins of the town, never missing a chance to stoke up their hatred for the Mexican enemy. On the morning of April 19 he dashed off a letter to his friend Henry Raguet, whose fifteen-year-old daughter Houston still hoped to marry. "This morning we are in preparation to meet Santa Anna. It is the only chance of saving Texas. We will only have about seven hundred to march with, besides the camp guard. We go to conquer. It is wisdom growing out of necessity to meet the enemy now; every consideration enforces it. No previous occasion would justify it."

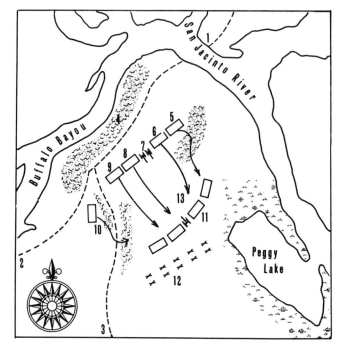

1._Lynchburg – Town & Ferry
2._Road to Vince's Crossing
3._Road to New Washington
4._Texan Camp
5._Sherman's Infantry
6._Burleson's Infantry
7._Hockley's Artillery
8._Rusk's Infantry
9._Millard's Infantry
10._Lamar's Cavalry
11._Mexican Line
12._Mexican Camp
13._Houston Wounded

THE BATTLE OF SAN JACINTO
APRIL 21, 1836

Captured dispatches told him where Santa Anna was and in what strength. As his army prepared to raft over to the south bank of Buffalo Bayou, Houston mounted his white stallion, Saracen, and addressed them: "The army will cross and we will meet the enemy. Some of us may be killed and must be killed. But soldiers, remember the Alamo! the Alamo! the Alamo! Victory is certain! Trust in God and fear not! The victims of the Alamo and the names of those who were murdered at Goliad cry out for vengeance!"

After crossing Buffalo Bayou the Texans waited in the woods for nightfall, then headed downstream, crossed a wooden bridge over flooded Vince's Bayou, the only road to the San Jacinto plain. At 2 A.M. they slept for an hour before continuing to the end of the road, at Lynch's Ferry on the San Jacinto River, just below the mouth of Buffalo Bayou. Thick woods bordered the south bank of the latter stream, and here Houston hid his army to wait.

Santa Anna had heard what he probably could have surmised anyway, that a Texan force would try to stop his march at Lynch's Ferry. The dictator wrote back to his base at Fort Bend for reinforcements to join him for battle at Lynch's; he would go there himself as soon as he captured the upstart government at New Washington. (These were the dispatches Houston had captured.) When Burnet and his cabinet escaped, Santa Anna led his 750 troops the eight miles north to Lynch's. Seeing Texan patrols across the San Jacinto plain the Mexicans went into a defensive encampment to decide the best way to proceed. His artillerymen wheeled up the only ordnance, a 6-pounder, that Santa Anna had brought with him. The Twin Sisters, set out on the plain just in front of the woods, roared back; a Texan cavalry company galloped out for a skirmish, mainly to look over Santa Anna's positions and test his strength. The Mexicans did not engage them in force. The dictator himself, in his glittering uniform, appeared at the Mexican cannon, apparently hoping to lure the Texans out for an open fight. Incredibly, he did not know he was facing Houston's whole army, that behind the distant tree line, 750 dirty, bearded, boiling-mad Texans were watching him prance around his artillery.

Houston's men were rearing to swarm out, but the general forbade it. Again he had disappointed them, but in his own mind forcing them to pen up their wrath just a little longer. When no attack came, Santa Anna prepared to receive a dawn assault, keeping his men up all night digging breastworks. The Texans indeed were up at dawn, staggered to discover that Houston had left strict orders not to be disturbed until eight o'clock.

Shortly after the general awoke, word came that Santa Anna had received the expected reinforcements: five hundred more men under General Cós had clattered across Vince's Bridge and joined him. Secretly, Houston sent out his best scout, Erastus (Deaf) Smith, to destroy it before any more could cross. With the bridge down, there would be no escape for either army. "Unless you hasten," Houston told him, "you will find the prairie changed from green to red on your return."

Houston then whiled away the day. At noon he conferred with his officers on how the battle should be waged—a courtesy only, for he had already made up his mind. They argued and wrangled, concluding to wait for Santa Anna to attack. Houston strolled among his men like a cook poking at embers to see if they were hot enough, asking almost casually if they wanted to fight. They cursed and swore the affirmative.

GENERAL VICENTE FILISOLA was Santa Anna's second-in-command, and was responsible for conducting the Mexican forces out of Texas after their cause was lost.

JOHN WHEELER BUNTON signed the Declaration of Independence, helped draft the Constitution, and fought with the Mina Volunteers at San Jacinto, but his revolutionary adventures were not over. After serving in the First Congress of the Republic, he returned to his native Tennessee to marry. Sailing back to Texas, their vessel, the *Julius Caesar,* was ambushed and captured by a Mexican warship; the couple spent their honeymoon in a Matamoros prison. After their release Bunton served in the Third Congress and was a charter member of the Philosophical Society of Texas. He died in August of 1879.

"Very well," said the general, "get your dinners and I will lead you into the fight, and if you whip them every one of you shall be a captain."

Across the mile-wide plain of knee-high grass, the Mexicans were baffled. Cós' men had marched all night; those with Santa Anna had built defenses all night. Dawn had brought no attack, nor noon, and after dinner it seemed as if nothing would happen then, either. The exhausted Mexicans slept, their arms stacked, the dictator himself possibly with help from his opium box. Texans up in the live oaks could not even locate sentries.

Quietly, Houston formed his men into two lines, one behind the other, nearly a thousand yards from end to end. Corporal Lamar from Georgia was sent with cavalry to the right side of the field to cut off the only Mexican escape possible, to the southwest. At 4:30 P.M., in beautiful weather, Houston mounted Saracen and ordered, "Trail arms; forward!" Three infantry companies marched out across the plain; the fourth, under Colonel Sherman, held back in reserve. No sound issued from the Mexican camp.

Only two hundred yards from the breastworks, Houston gave the signal. The Twin Sisters were wheeled and fired, their double booms ripping the quiet afternoon. The Texan band, a drummer and four fifers, struck into the only tune they all knew, a raunchy barroom ballad, "Will You Come to the Bower?"

Houston had spent most of the previous month drilling his men to fire by companies, so they would not become vulnerable by all reloading at the same time. But now the Texans were moving on hate and adrenaline. With Houston bellowing, "Halt! Now is the critical time! Fire away! God damn you, fire! Aren't you going to fire at all?" his soldiers loped forward, not shooting until certain of a target. Those who fired continued forward, most not reloading, but holding their guns like clubs and drawing their Bowie knives.

The Mexican defense was brief. Saracen was hit by five balls simultaneously and fell. One of the general's men ran up with a riderless Mexican cavalry horse, and he rode on. A minié ball shattered Houston's right ankle; the second horse fell and he found another on which to leap the barricade. Just as the Texan line reached the barricade, Sherman charged into the fray from the left side with his reserve, and from the right, as Houston had arranged, Deaf Smith galloped onto the field, shouting that Vince's Bridge was down; the case now was literally win or perish.

No Texans thought of perishing, however; the surprise was complete and the rout was pathetic. Stephen F. Austin's eighteen-year-old nephew, Moses Austin Bryan, remembered it as "the most awful slaughter I ever saw. . . . Texans pursued the retreating Mexicans, killing on all sides, even the wounded." A drummer boy with two broken legs clutched one of Sherman's men around the knees, begging for his life; the volunteer pulled out his pistol and shot him through the head.

A proud old general, Manuel Castrillon, stood on an ammunition box to rally his soldiers. When they paid him no attention and ran hell-for-leather to get away, Castrillon folded his arms across his chest and scowled at the onrushing Texans. War Secretary Rusk saw him and ordered his men not to shoot, and deflected as many guns as he could before Castrillon was blown from his defiant perch. San Jacinto was a battle in which neither the winning nor losing generals had much say.

After a quarter hour of orgiastic slaughter Houston tried to regroup his forces, knowing that the struggle might not be over at all. Santa Anna had escaped, and if he reached Fort Bend, the united commands now there would be upon him before any plans could be made. One junior officer, however, in relaying Houston's orders to take prisoners, told his men, "Boys . . . you know how to take prisoners, take them with the butt of yor guns, club guns, & remember the Alamo, remember Labaher, & club guns right & left, & nock their god damn brains out."

Many of the Mexican soldiers had sought to escape by plunging into Peggy Lake, a boggy, marsh-bordered inlet of the San Jacinto River. A number of volunteers were engaged in picking them off as they surfaced to breathe. Colonel John Wharton rode up and ordered them to stop, but the crazed volunteers defied him. Said one, "Colonel Wharton, if Jesus Christ were to come down from heaven and order me to quit shooting Santanistas, I wouldn't do it, sir!" Moses Bryan saw Wharton start to draw his saber, but when one of the men "took a few steps back and cocked his rifle, Wharton, very discreetly (I always thought), turned his horse and left."

So obsessed was Houston with the fear that Sesma, or Gaona, or Urrea, or all three would materialize while his men were so completely vulnerable, that when he saw a column of Mexicans marching across the prairie, he thought it had actually happened and despaired that all was lost. Momentarily, he learned that the men were prisoners that Rusk had managed to form up, and he was moving them to the rear.

That night Houston's wound caused him much pain, but his mind was eased the next day when the President-General of Mexico was led before him. Santa Anna had fled the field at the first firing—intending, as he later defended himself, to reach the army at Fort Bend and return. He became lost during the night and changed into ragged clothing he found in a deserted house, but neglecting to remove his silk blouse with diamond studs. That had given him away. With the dictator a prisoner, Texas' immediate safety was secure.

What has been listed as one of the decisive battles in history, for paving American expansion to the Pacific, had lasted some eighteen minutes. Houston's report of the losses was as close to true as anyone knew:

"In the battle our loss was two killed and twenty-three wounded, six of them mortally. The enemy's loss was six hundred and thirty killed . . . prisoners seven hundred and thirty. . . . Santa Anna and General Cos are included in the number.

"—Our success in action is conclusive proof of daring intrepidity and courage. . . . Nor should we withhold the tribute of our grateful thanks from that Being who rules the destinies of nations."

Noah Smithwick had been delayed by flooded streams and, to his disgust, missed the fight. He did arrive at the battlefield, however, in time to observe "rifles broken off at the breech, the stocks besmeared with blood and brains. . . . The dead Mexicans lay in piles, the survivors not even asking permission to bury them, thinking, perhaps, that, in return for the butchery they had practiced, they would soon be lying dead themselves." At least one Mexican prisoner held a different opinion. Colonel Don Pedro Delgado wrote of their confinement: "I will only say, to the ever-lasting shame of our conquerors, that they kept us starving, sleeping in the mud, & exposed to frequent & heavy showers. Still more intolerable was the stench arising from the corpses on the field of San Jacinto; which they had not the generosity to burn or bury, after the time-honored custom." ·

On their way home at last, the Rose family had to cross the grisly plain at San Jacinto, the most direct route having been destroyed with Vince's Bridge. It was April 26, two days before Dilue's eleventh birthday. "We left the battle field late in the evening. We had to pass among the dead Mexicans, and father pulled one out of the road, so we could get by without driving over the body, since we could not go around it the prairie [being] very boggy. It was getting dark, and there were now twenty or thirty families with us. We were glad to leave the battle field, for it was a grewsome sight. We camped that night on the prairie, and could hear the wolves howl and bark as they devoured the dead." Smithwick's recollection was slightly different. "The buzzards and coyotes were gathering to the feast, but it is a singular fact that they singled out the dead horses, refusing to touch the Mexicans, presumably because of the peppery condition of the flesh. They lay there unmolested and dried up, the cattle got to chewing the bones, which so affected the milk that residents in the vicinity had to dig trenches and bury them."

By May first the Rose family was almost home. They were unsure of what to expect, but learned that their house had not been spared when they were told by a relative that the Mexicans had torn up the floor in a search for eggs.

"As soon as it was light enough for us to see we went to the house, and the first thing we saw was the hogs running out. Father's bookcase lay on the ground broken open, his books, medicines, and other things scattered on the ground, and the hogs sleeping on them. When sister and I got to the door, there was one big hog that would not go out till father shot at him. Then we children began picking up the books. We could not find those that Colonel Travis gave us, but did find broken toys that belonged to our dear little sister that died. . . .

"Mother was very despondent, but father was hopeful. He said Texas would gain her independence and become a great nation. . . .

"Father had hid some of our things in the [river] bottom, among them a big chest. Mother had packed it with bedding, clothes, and other things we could not take when we left home. After a few days, Uncle and brother hauled it to the house, and that old blue chest proved a treasure. When we left home we wore our best clothes. Now our best clothes were in the chest, among them my old sunbonnet. . . .

"There was no prospect for a cotton crop in our neighborhood. The people had been very short of provisions, and there would have been suffering among them if the citizens of New Orleans had not sent a schooner load to Harrisburg. The provisions were distributed without cost."

The talk of the day turned to two brothers named Allen who had tried to buy out the Harris holdings in Harrisburg, were rebuffed, and so determined to start their own

SAM HIGHSMITH. After the Battle of San Jacinto and capture of the Mexican camp, one of Houston's volunteers, Sam Highsmith of Kentucky, tried Santa Anna's uniform on for size. It is probable though not certain that he was one of the men who took the dictator prisoner.

Highsmith had followed Milam into San Antonio, and briefly had deserted Houston's army to help his family flee the Mexican advance in the Runaway Scrape. He later had an active career in the Texas Rangers and served two sessions as sergeant at arms in the House of Representatives of the Republic.

town, about ten miles up Buffalo Bayou from Harrisburg. Dilue Rose recalled that "the new town . . . was named Houston, in honor of General Houston. There were circulars and drawings sent out, which represented a large city, showing churches, a courthouse, a market house and a square of ground set aside for a building for Congress, if the seat of government should be located there."

Sam Houston was, predictably, enchanted with the idea of a capital city named after himself. When the Allens sweetened the offer with word that they would construct a capitol building at their own expense, Houston City was designated the new seat of government late in 1836.

The Allens' 2,200-acre site hived with carpenters and workmen, and the first boatload of goods came up Buffalo Bayou in January 1837, the enterprise of New Orleans merchant FRANK LUBBOCK *(left)*. He missed the site entirely and continued upstream until he ran out of bayou.

He then backed downstream, keeping a sharper lookout for the landing, which proved to be a thread of a path leading up from the bank. Lubbock later gained more familiarity with Texas and served a term as governor during the first half of the Civil War.

When the government convened in Houston in May 1837, the spacious CAPITOL *(above)* was unfinished, and carpenters hurriedly lashed tree boughs in the rafters for shade. The PRESIDENT'S HOUSE *(top)* was decidedly less commodious. Houston shared the residence with the surgeon general, Ashbel Smith.

The Republic of Texas

BY early May the ankle wound that Houston took at San Jacinto was so infected his doctors thought he would die without expert treatment. He left for New Orleans on May 5, and missed the signing one week later of the Treaty of Velasco, ending the war with Mexico.

He returned with his foot still attached, although he would limp for the rest of his life, and people's attention turned to the national election which had been called for September 5. Houston and Stephen F. Austin had accepted nominations for President, and as the votes were counted, it became clear that Austin had been buried by popular acclamation for the hero of San Jacinto. As Austin had written his cousin Mary, with insight that was sad and a little bitter, "a successful military chieftain is hailed with admiration and applause and monuments perpetuate his fame. But the bloodless pioneer of the wilderness, like the corn and cotton he causes to spring where it never grew before, attracts no notice. No slaughtered thousands or smoking cities attest his devotion to the cause of human happiness, and he is regarded by the mass of the world as an humble instrument to pave the way for others."

Houston, who still held Austin in high esteem and needed his diplomatic abilities, named him Secretary of State, but the Great Empresario had nothing left to give. His health shattered by years of overwork, he died two days after Christmas 1836.

Houston had not neglected to send his "laurels" from San Jacinto—a swatch of magnolia leaves—to his coveted Miss Anna, but still she would not encourage his affections. Sober and abstemious during the war, he returned to heavy drinking, and concentrated on the myriad details of establishing an independent government. There were positions to create and fill, a great seal to devise for affixing to documents of the Republic, and currency to design and print. There was no bullion in the treasury from which to strike coins; the most abundant resource of the new country was land, nearly 380,000 square miles by claiming the Rio Grande to its headwaters, and the government used it voraciously. Veterans of the Revolution were paid off with it, and homesteaders from the United States were attracted with it. Texas' population of thirty thousand surged upward with newcomers.

It was Houston's wish for America to annex Texas as a gigantic state, but when the United States responded with diplomatic recognition in March of 1837, there were trade agreements to negotiate with European governments, ministers to appoint and dispatch, bonds to issue and sell, and tariffs to levy and collect at port towns that had to be built. Galveston, Jean Lafitte's old pirate's cove, was finally organized as a town in 1836.

The greatest national problem was the army. The Revolution had ended so suddenly that peace caught numerous volunteer regiments disembarking in Texas with nobody to fight. Felix (Longshanks) Huston had arrived only weeks after San Jacinto with five hundred Kentucky and Mississippi volunteers in his entourage alone. The army was large, growing, restive, and unruly. The troops voted overwhelmingly to spurn Mirabeau Lamar as their commanding general, and passed resolutions demanding that Santa Anna be hanged. Against this, however, both Provisional President Burnet and elected President Houston stood firm. The dictator should be held long enough to guarantee Texas' safety, and then released. He could be counted on, said Houston, to keep Mexico "in commotion for years," but it was with no little maneuvering that the President-General of Mexico was spirited out of the country. No sooner was the dictator free than Mexico denounced the Treaty of Velasco, the peace document recognizing Texas' freedom that the captive Santa Anna had signed, threatened reinvasion, and massed a new army in Matamoros.

The Texas army made their choice of Felix Huston as their commanding officer; his headquarters, with twenty-five hundred clamoring troops, was twenty-five miles east of Victoria at "Camp Independence." Houston knew perfectly well that Mexico was far too chaotic to mount a new offensive, but Huston and his army were demanding, loudly, permission to strike south of the border. It was the Matamoros madness all over again. Houston relieved Huston of command and turned the army over to another promising young officer, Albert Sidney Johnston. When Johnston arrived at Camp Independence, Huston trumped up an argument and in a duel dangerously wounded Johnston in the thigh. President Houston was not to be outdone, however. The army burden was crushing the treasury, Mexico could be let alone, and if the military were needed anywhere, it was at home, as protection against the Indians. When General Huston grew impatient waiting for orders to Matamoros, he showed up in Houston to plead his case to the Congress, and the President handled it in a typical way. He sent a loyal aide to Camp Independence, thanking the army for their service and putting them on indefinite furlough. They were given their choice between land grants as Texas veterans, or paid transportation back to the United States. Huston dashed back to his headquarters, livid to discover that his army had dissolved like sugar into water.

Houston's disbanding the army did not leave the frontier unprotected. He had already seen to the organization of a militia, and took a month's leave of absence to regroup the Texas Rangers into a potent six-hundred-man force.

The second great headache of the Republic of Texas was Indian pacification. The Cherokees were getting impatient for the secure land titles that the provisional government had promised them, but were for the most part peaceable. Raids by Comanche and Kiowa Indians from the Red River country to the north were another matter entirely. One of the most savage depredations occurred less than a month after San Jacinto, at "Parker's Fort" on the Navasota River in central Texas. There a religious settlement of thirty "Hardshell" Baptists was wiped out. Elder John Parker and his wife, known as Granny, were taken alive. He was stripped, staked out, scalped, and castrated before his wife's eyes, and then dispatched. Granny was then pinned to the ground by a lance and gang-raped, but she survived. Several of the other men were killed, and two women and four children were whisked into bondage. The survivors walked for days through uninhabited country before reaching safety, where one more horror story became known and Texan rage against the natives increased a little more. Solutions to both the Indian problems, however, awaited the next administration.

Among Texans, who snorted at military regulations and were accustomed to fighting "on their own hook" in small ad hoc groups, the ascendance of paramilitary ranging companies was probably inevitable. It also made sense in a country whose needs for defense were continuous, localized, and often arose with no more warning than the spread of an Indian alarm.

This organization's inception, however, is indistinct. In 1823 Stephen Austin hired ten "Rangers" for protection against Indians, and three years later increased the force to vary between twenty and thirty. But it was only in 1835, at the Consultation, that Texas Rangers were legally formulated. During the Revolution these companies served Houston as scouts, reconnaissance "spies," and as a rear guard to round up citizen stragglers during the Runaway Scrape. There were 150 men in this battalion, required to furnish their own horses and weapons, for daily pay of $1.25. They would have nothing to do with uniforms, and on the trail were as mobile as Indians, living mostly on wild game.

From the beginning the Rangers developed a tradition of following officers of their own choosing, and Ranger captains like W. A. A. (Bigfoot) Wallace, John H. Moore, and Ben McCulloch became frontier legends. The greatest of them, however, was John Coffee (Captain Jack) Hays of Tennessee, a born leader who gained command of the San Antonio station when only twenty-three.

It was Hays who began to get the upper hand on Comanche Indian raiders by his institution of Samuel Colt's repeating pistol. Previous to this the warriors had kept the Rangers at a respectful distance because, although the Indians' guns were inferior, a warrior could charge forward and loose a half dozen arrows in the time it took a Ranger to reload his single-shot side arm. The American Army scoffed at the 5-shot repeater, which nearly ruined Colt, but Hays recognized its potential instantly and made sure his men were outfitted with them.

Early in 1840 Hays was at the head of fourteen Rangers by the Pedernales River, far northwest of San Antonio, when he was pounced on by not less than seventy Comanches. Instead of reaching cover and holding the Indians at bay with their rifles, Hays led his men charging straight through, pistols blazing. The Comanches fled in terror, leaving thirty dead. Hays quickly refined his tactics. Only days later he engaged another war party, letting the Comanches fight their own way. Every time they charged the whites, certain this time they must have empty guns, they were met by another

HAYS' TEXAS RANGERS IN 1844.

CAPTAIN JACK HAYS, whose prescient recognition of the importance of repeating pistols revolutionized Indian warfare. In society he had a reputation for wit and charm, but when in the field with his men, as in this rare 1844 photograph, his cool bravery made him a peerless Ranger. Hays and his wife later moved to California, where he achieved some political prominence.

fusillade. First one and suddenly the rest of the Comanches threw their lances and bows to the ground and pounded away whooping and gobbling. Never had they encountered such evil medicine as inexhaustible guns, and war in Texas would never be the same.

Sam Houston's message to the public after San Jacinto, "Tell them to come on, and let the people plant corn," was taken to heart, and Texas' roads were soon clogged with westbound traffic of all descriptions. Towns in the new Republic were widely separated; night frequently overtook travelers in the middle of the countryside. However, virtually every farmhouse within hailing distance of a road accepted strangers as overnight guests, and thus began the tradition of Texan informal hospitality that became legendary. One properly bred Yankee from Connecticut was a little put off by it, noting dubiously in her journal, "There is a peculiar feeling among them about game. No one will receive payment for any thing taken by his gun, but will cheerfully give you as much as you will take, and feel insulted, if you offer him money in return. . . . It would be better for the public if this feeling did not prevail, as provisions of this sort, could be furnished at so easy and cheap a rate.

"[But] the people are universally kind and hospitable, which are redeeming qualities. Every body's house is open, and table spread, to accommodate the traveller. . . ."

Another American unused to this unwritten law admitted to his journal that "to be received at the house of strangers with cheerfulness and pleasure, and welcomed with every favor in their power, is doubly agreeable when you feel that your society is regarded as a rich reward for all you receive."

Not all households, of course, lived up to the ethic as graciously as they might, and at such times it was a point of embarrassment whether to offer money or not. One experienced traveler, when it was obvious that his needs had been an imposition, developed the habit of discreetly offering some money to his hosts' children, if they had any. If they were allowed to keep it, he knew he had acted properly.

Some families took advantage of their locations on the most heavily traveled routes by becoming full-time innkeepers. The house shown here was one of the most successful operations.

By the time Stephen F. Austin reported the completion of his three-hundred-family empresario contract in December of 1830, ten of the headrights had been abandoned. The following month two eligible young brothers from South Carolina, John and William Townsend, arrived and filed for adjoining grants of a quarter league each, near the junction of the Upper La Bahía road and the Gotier Trace from San Felipe to Bastrop. William married a daughter of Jesse Burnham, and probably began the house, in 1834, utilizing sawed lumber from two new mills nearby, instead of the conventional hewn logs.

Later the property passed to surveyor and congressman of the Republic, Samuel K. Lewis, who expanded the house to its spacious eight-room proportions, with deep verandas, exterior stairway, and center halls upstairs and down. The Sam Lewis Stopping Place was the most popular inn in the area for years.

Some time after Sam Lewis' death in 1867, the stopping place was bought by Joseph George Wagner, a Silesian shoemaker, who converted the inn into his family farmstead. It is Wagner's family spaced here along the front porches.

SAM LEWIS STOPPING PLACE.

One of the first tasks to which Houston applied himself after his inauguration was the settlement of the Cherokee land question. To the Senate he presented the treaty that he and other emissaries had concluded with the Indians, with the message "that it is just and equitable and perhaps the best which could be made at the present time."

The Senate spurned the document, however, with excuses that were nothing if not creative. They resented the fact that the Cherokees had contributed no warriors to help fight in the Revolution, although the treaty had made no such requirement. Moreover, the "said treaty was based on premises that did not exist and . . . the operation of it would not only be detrimental to the interests of the Republic but would also be a violation of the vested rights of many citizens." One of those many citizens was Provisional President Burnet, whose old empresario grant overbounded lands once assigned to the Cherokees, and whose settlers might be displaced if the treaty went into effect.

"My Brother," Houston wrote the Cherokees' Chief Bowles, "Do not be disturbed by the troubles which are around you, but be at peace—Remember my words, and listen to no bad talks of any one! I have never told you a lie, nor do I intend to."

If it was military service that the Senate required, the Cherokees seemed willing. In the spring of 1837 Houston dispatched Bowles to negotiate some kind of peace with the plains tribes, and when they turned him away, Bowles offered the services of his men to fight them. Their title was still not secured, and although Bowles remained fast in his friendship with Houston, his responsibility was to his people. When Mexico entered the quarrel with a whisper of secure Cherokee land title in exchange for assistance in the reconquest of Texas, Bowles—fatally—listened.

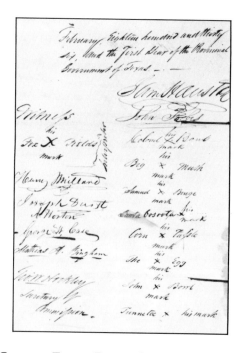

SIGNATURE PAGE, CHEROKEE TREATY. During the Revolution Texas curried Cherokee favor with a treaty promising land titles, but reneged in a way that made Sam Houston, a signatory, boil.

The Talented Amateur

HOUSTON'S Vice President was Mirabeau Lamar, the Georgia poet who had tried to unhorse Houston as army commander but settled for corporal. Lamar had distinguished himself at San Jacinto, for which Houston promoted him to colonel, but as they became better acquainted and Lamar formed around himself a political nucleus to rival Houston's, the two became bitterest enemies. They could not have been more different, politically or personally. Houston's fondest wish was to see Texas annexed to the United States, with himself leading her into the fold; Lamar's vision was of a mighty mid-continent empire, with himself at the head. Houston laid complex plans and worked practically at them; Lamar was a pipe dreamer with no patience. Houston exulted in his own nickname, the Talleyrand of the Brazos, while Lamar spent much time trying to live down the sobriquet Houston gave him: the Talented Amateur. Houston was a swaggering alcoholic with a mighty soul; Lamar a man whose delicate sensibilities were so wrapped in self-righteousness that he couldn't recognize his own meanness of spirit—especially where it concerned the Indians of whom Houston was so solicitous.

Houston was constitutionally barred from succeeding himself, and Lamar was nominated by the faction held together chiefly by their one common sentiment: the anti-Houstons. When Lamar's two principal opponents both died, suicides, Lamar's elevation to the presidency was inevitable. At the inauguration on December 10, 1838, Houston showed up dressed in knee breeches and powdered wig, and spoke for hours about his administration. Lamar's rage rendered him literally speechless—his secretary had to read the address for him. Houston then took a vacation to tend to personal affairs and make a long trip to the United States. He spent most of the summer with his now retired idol, Andrew Jackson, at the Hermitage in Tennessee.

Lamar moved with jarring swiftness to efface Houston's imprint upon the government. Within weeks of taking office he abolished the Texas flag Houston cherished— royal blue with a single golden star—and replaced it with the present tricolor, a vertical blue stripe with a white star, and two horizontal stripes of white over red. Then he gave attention to reversing Houston's Indian policy. Addressing the Congress about the "impudent and hostile Cherokee," Lamar declared:

"As long as we continue to exhibit our mercy without showing our strength, so long will the Indian continue to bloody the edge of the tomahawk, and move onward in the work of rapacity and slaughter. . . . How long shall this cruel humanity, this murderous sensibility for the sanguinary savage be practised? Until other oceans of blood, the blood of our wives and children, shall glut their voracious appetite? . . .

"The white man and the red man cannot dwell in harmony together. Nature forbids it."

It was true that some of the Cherokees had not been in Texas much longer than some of the Anglos—Bowles had brought them in the winter of 1817–18. But what sparked Lamar against them was a minor rebellion led by one Vicente Córdova, aiming for the reconquest of Texas by Mexico. Córdova suggested an alliance to Bowles: Cherokee help against the Texans in exchange for secure land title from the Mexican Government. Before the revolution Bowles had traveled as far as Mexico City in search of land title for his people, and gotten nowhere. There was never any evidence that Bowles agreed to the Córdova scheme, but he failed to boot Córdova's men off Cherokee land. Lamar, after Córdova was defeated, ordered the army to erect a fort in Cherokee country, but Bowles' warriors made such a show of force that the troops withdrew. The President then wrote Bowles angrily that the Cherokees would, in any event, be expelled from Texas. If they pledged and proved their friendship, they would be removed gently and be given generous compensation. If they made trouble, "the violence of war must depend upon the Cherokee themselves."

One of the delegation who delivered the letter was John H. Reagan, a twenty-year-old Tennessean, new in Texas and performing the first service of a long career. Bowles

MIRABEAU LAMAR was a visionary spendthrift, but not all his programs were expansionist disasters. His measures to devote part of the public domain to the funding of a public school and university system led to his being honored as the "Father of Education" in Texas. Lamar opposed annexation until his fear that Texas as a British protectorate would endanger slavery prompted him to switch sides. Back in uniform he fought under Zachary Taylor in the Mexican War, and subsequently served in the state legislature. Lamar went into partial retirement in 1848 to travel and to follow his historical, philosophical, and literary interests. He was a founder of the Philosophical Society of Texas, and spent much time writing poetry —an example of which is shown (right) in hand. Lamar died in 1859, shortly after returning from a tour as United States Minister to Nicaragua and Costa Rica.

was then eighty-three, showing "dignity of bearing which could hardly have been exceeded by the most enlightened diplomats," and made a profound impression on Reagan. "If he fought, the whites would kill him; and if he refused to fight, his own people would kill him." Although Bowles saw the war as hopeless, the Cherokee decision was to fight. Neither side, however, was just then prepared. Bowles sent runners to other woodland tribes in Texas for help, and suggested to Lamar's delegation that, if fighting were postponed until after the harvest, they might settle things peaceably before then. Lamar, needing time to hurry up volunteers under General Rusk and army regulars under General Burleson to the area, appointed a commission to negotiate removal terms.

The Cherokee camp was near the Neches River below the present city of Tyler; that of the Texas commissioners, including former Provisional President and now Vice President Burnet, War Secretary Johnston and Adjutant General Hugh McLeod, was a short distance off, separated from the Indians by a neutral strip.

By mid-July of 1839, Rusk and Burleson had united their commands with other units, to a total of about nine hundred men. The troops, inevitably, bickered over which officer to follow before compromising on General Kelsey Douglas. Bowles, with help from Delaware, Shawnee, and small Caddoan tribes, had perhaps eight hundred warriors behind him. The spark flashed on July 14, in the neutral ground, when a Texan patrol collided with an Indian party led by Bowles' son John. The excited Cherokees dashed into their camp and, finding the commission busily negotiating, tried without success to have the delegation killed.

The next morning, Bowles decamped and started to leave the area, and the army gave pursuit. While some Texans accused that the Cherokees were deserting the place in violation of an agreement to stay until the negotiations were settled, there was also evidence that, with the Texan army in place, it would have imposed a "settlement"

The Heart to Friendship true.

O, Sarah Ann, sweet morning rose,
I soon shall bid thy smiles adieu!
And take my farewell leave of those,
Whose hearts have been to Friendship true.

As chance directs, I widely stray;
Yet oft will memory call to view,
Thy cheerful mien, thy pleasant ways,
Thy guileless heart, to Friendship true.

Bright lassie, ever gay and mild,
As thou shalt grow in beauty's hue
O, may the woman, like the child,
Still boast a heart to Friendship true.

When Youth's bright light no longer glows,
And Beauty dies like morning dew,
Their loss is scarcely felt by those,
Who keep their hearts to Friendship true.

Then Sarah Ann, sweet child of light,
The paths of virtue still pursue;
And keep that gem forever bright
Thy guileless heart to Friendship true.

And if my prayers can aught avail,
Thy joys shall not, like mine, be few;
And no rude care shall e'er assail
The generous heart to Friendship true.

within a day or so had not the Indians given it an excuse to pursue and attack. Bowles crossed the Neches and headed north; about five hundred of the Texans rode to cut him off but couldn't catch him. Later in the day Bowles' group crossed a small creek, the far side of which was a high dirt bank like a natural redoubt. Sending his women and children on ahead, Bowles spread his men along the bank and waited, intending to fight a holding action to give them time to reach safety. The warriors held the Texans off until dark. They were not dislodged by simultaneous assaults from Rusk on their front and Burleson from their right rear, but lost nearly twenty dead to the whites' mere two.

During the night Bowles slipped away and continued north, abandoning stock and camp stores which the Texans captured when they took up the chase again in the morning. The soldiers found and torched a Delaware village, but before going much farther arrived at a brushy ravine where Bowles had concealed his men. A three-sided attack of an hour and a half failed to drive them out; Bowles was often seen within the thicket, wearing an elegant waistcoat, sash and sword—gifts from President Houston— riding up and down the line on a paint horse, energetically encouraging his warriors. When their attack failed, the Texans tried three times by feints to lure the Indians out into battle, with the result that several Cherokees slipped behind the Texan lines and nearly succeeded in stampeding their horses.

Reorganizing from the disarray this caused, the Texans charged vigorously on all fronts and finally drove the Indians from their thicket. Once this was accomplished the battle became a rout, and Cherokees fell by the score. Bowles fought gallantly; by the time his horse collapsed after being shot several times, the old chief was the last Indian on the field. Already wounded in the thigh, he limped after his retreating warriors when he was shot in the back and fell. In much pain he rolled over and sat up, facing the enemies he never wanted. John Reagan was moved to pity by the scene: "I had witnessed [Bowles'] dignity and manliness in council, his devotion to his tribe in sustaining their decision for war against his judgment, and his courage in battle, and, wishing to save his life, ran towards him, and, as I approached him from one direction, [Captain Smith] approached him from another, with his pistol drawn. As we got to him I said, 'Captain, don't shoot him.' but as I spoke he fired, shooting the chief in the head, which caused instant death."

Bowles' body was scalped and mutilated by different Texans who came across it; one cut a strip from his back and tanned it as a razor strap. The Texas army followed the Indians' trail for several days, and although opportunities presented themselves to renew the fight, the Cherokees were running so hard and the trail splitting into so many directions, seeking another engagement seemed not worth the trouble. The soldiers had lost only two killed and about thirty wounded, against as many as a hundred casualties among their enemy.

The troops did, however, raid and burn a number of villages of Delaware and Shawnee Indians who had not been involved in the Neches battle. This was against their orders, but no complaint was ever filed for their having seized the opportunity to drive all Indians out of East Texas. With the exception of two small tribes north of Houston (and far from the battle), the Alabamas and Coushattas, they succeeded. President Lamar was then free to turn his army on the great Indian menace to the northwest, the Comanches.

Raids by that tribe had been voracious, and increased as more whites moved farther north and west. Men were killed, blockhouses and ranches overrun and burned, stock and merchandise stolen—but the most dolorous statistic, and cause of the greatest distress to the Texans, were the some two hundred white women and children who had been carried off into captivity. Most of the Comanche bands lived far to the northwest of the line of settlement; of main concern now were the Southern Comanches—the Penatekas, or Honey Eaters—of the Hill Country west and north of San Antonio. Jack Hays had surprised and mauled them with his men's use from horseback of the new repeating pistols, and now the Texas Rangers, with President Lamar's blessing, were raiding into the Hill Country strongholds and gunning down Indians at least as frequently as the Penatekas swooped down onto the settlements. It was probably no coincidence that, almost simultaneously with the appearance of repeating pistols and iron-nerved officers like Hays, the Comanches modified their attitude. They were not whipped, but they were willing to bargain.

In January of 1840 three headmen of the Southern Comanches showed up in San Antonio and requested a peace talk, a result that had always eluded the conciliatory Houston. Henry Karnes, the Ranger officer in charge of the San Antonio office, agreed, reluctantly, and instructed the Indians to return in March, bringing with them all the white prisoners they held. Karnes then began to lay a trap for the Comanches, in the

Virtually all political questions of note in the late thirties and early forties became webbed in the Houston-Lamar rivalry. The settlement of a boundary between Texas and the United States was no exception.

Houston's man for boundary commissioner was CHARLES STANFIELD TAYLOR (left), who was only twenty when he arrived in Nacogdoches from England. Like Houston, he boarded with Mayor Sterne, and later married Mrs. Sterne's sister. He served in public office in San Augustine before returning to Nacogdoches, for whom he signed the Declaration of

Independence. Houston's first term expired before Taylor could be confirmed, leaving his nomination to languish in the Congress before Lamar withdrew it.

Lamar's commissioner was GEORGE WASHINGTON SMYTH of Alabama (right). He also had signed the Declaration, on behalf of Bevil's Settlement, where he was surveyor and judge; it was Smyth who ran the boundary. After annexation he served as land commissioner and went to Washington as a congressman. He opposed secession and died serving in the Constitutional Convention of 1866.

expected event that they would prove faithless. His ambush plan was endorsed by Secretary of War Johnston, and when it came time for Lamar to choose commissioners to treat with the Indians, he picked Adjutant General McLeod to head the group.

The Comanches came timely in on March 19, clearly not expecting any trouble. As savage as their warfare was, they lived by a strict code of honor. Hospitality was sacred to them, and once it was offered, even to one's bitterest enemy, he could not be harmed while a guest. As it never occurred to them that the Texans felt differently, when the sixty-five Comanches came into San Antonio their number included a dozen chiefs and many women and children. But they had with them only one white captive, a fifteen-year-old girl named Matilda Lockhart, who had been in bondage for two years.

When the assembled citizens gaped and gasped at her condition, Matilda hid her face and begged to be taken away. She was given over to some of San Antonio's prominent ladies to be cared for, among whom was Mary Adams Maverick, wife of a leading merchant and former mayor of the city. Mrs. Maverick recorded that Matilda's "head, arms, and face were full of bruises, and sores." As the women bathed her and dressed the wounds, she sobbed that she had been sexually debased and daily beaten, and that the Indians "would wake her from sleep by sticking a chunk of fire to her flesh, especially to her nose, and . . . shout and laugh like fiends when she cried." Matilda was not lying; only charred meat and bone protruded where her nose should have been. "Both nostrils were wide open," wrote Mary Maverick, "and denuded of flesh."

JOHN H. REAGAN of Tennessee was a newcomer to Texas when he fought the Cherokees in 1839. He then spent three years as an itinerant surveyor before embarking on a legal career as county and district judge and member of the legislature. Reagan was elected to Congress in 1856; he was also a delegate to the Secession Convention, and during the war Jefferson Davis tapped Reagan's superior ability, first as Postmaster General and then as Treasury Secretary of the Confederacy. He was immensely popular in his home district of Palestine, but fell from favor when, writing from a federal prison after the war, he urged his constituents to grant civil rights to freedmen.

Reagan was returned to Congress in 1875 and served twelve years before the legislature elevated him to the Senate. An expert on trade matters and a creator of the Interstate Commerce Commission, he reluctantly resigned from the Senate in 1891 to serve four terms on the Texas Railroad Commission. He finally retired from public life in 1903, two years before his death.

This treatment was typical for Comanche captives, and the Indians could not fathom the effect on the Texans of knowing that as many as two hundred other white women and children were suffering this horror.

Matilda Lockhart told the commissioners of some fifteen other whites she had seen herself in these Indians' camp, and further that in her two years with the Comanches she had learned enough of their language to know their strategy was to get the most ransom by bringing them in one at a time. When the Texans demanded answers from the chiefs about this, their principal civil headman, Muk-warra, acknowledged that there were indeed other captives, but they were held by bands who did not follow him. He was sure, however, that they could be ransomed for large tributes of weapons and trade goods. In the immunity of a council, Muk-warra finished, "How do you like this answer?" The commissioners saw their duty as simple. Rangers awaiting the signal filed quickly into the Council House, and the translator was directed to inform the Comanches they would be held hostage until all the whites were returned.

The interpreter, a former Comanche captive who knew the result of making such a statement to a roomful of heavily armed warriors, edged toward the door as he spoke. As he feared, the Indians made a break for freedom; a guard at the door was knifed, and the order was given the Rangers to fire. By the time the shooting was over, seven Texans and some thirty-five Comanches were dead, including two children, three women, and all of the chiefs. The deaths of the children were not in cold blood; after the fighting spread outside, one of them shot a circuit judge through the heart with his toy bow and arrow. The remaining Indians were captured and locked in the San José Mission.

To the Comanches the Council House Fight was the rankest sort of treachery, news of which was brought to them by one of the chiefs' widows. She was released from San José to deliver an ultimatum to the Indians, giving them a twelve-day truce to bring in all their captives, or else the ones still held in San Antonio would be executed. The loss of their chiefs was an unprecedented disaster for the Penatekas, and they went mad with grief, gashing themselves horribly, some even to death, in the mourning custom of self-mutilation. The Council House Fight was also the death warrant for the white captives. Two escaped when the wailing Indians were not watching, and two had been adopted by Comanche families and could not be harmed. The rest, numbering ten to twelve, including Matilda Lockhart's six-year-old sister, were stripped, staked out by the campfire, and skinned alive.

The whole frontier sector braced for a firestorm of raids, but for a week nothing happened. The Penatekas were not only without leadership, but the dead chiefs had possessed the strongest war medicine; the remaining warriors were in confusion. Nine days after the fight about three hundred of them pounded down to the San José Mission and demanded a fight. The Ranger officer in command was under strict orders to observe the twelve-day truce, and did so, at the expense of being branded a coward by most of his men, who preferred the leadership of another officer. The Indians rode away frustrated, while the two Ranger officers killed each other in a duel. Texas officials, unwilling to implement their threat, eventually allowed the Comanche prisoners to escape.

Few raids were experienced during the spring and summer of 1840, but not, as the whites hoped, because the Comanches were whipped and gone away. The Penatekas had only one chief left, Pochinaw-quoheep. The whites came to know him as Buffalo Hump, being delicately unwilling to acknowledge the more accurate translation, Hard Penis. It took time for the warriors, factious individualists even in the best times, to accept his leadership. By the end of August, however, the Penateka warriors had rested their horses, prepared their weapons, and were ready to follow Hard Penis in what would be the largest raid ever mounted by their band. Estimates of their number have run as high as a thousand, a figure that includes the warriors' families, who followed along to make camps and gather in plunder. The number of men was most likely between four hundred and five hundred.

The wide trail they made as they forged down the Guadalupe Valley was discovered on August 5, sixty miles southeast of San Antonio. The first intended victims were two Texans pounced on near the present site of Hallettsville. One escaped, but the other was taken alive, and the Comanches amused themselves by cutting away the soles of his feet, then they tied him to one of their horses and forced him to run behind them for miles before they tired of the game and killed him.

Moving fast, they surrounded the town of Victoria on the afternoon of August 6, cutting down a number of slaves in their fields and killing some whites as well who were slow to reach fortified buildings. Driving with them a large herd of stock captured around the town, the Comanches thundered south all the way to the Gulf coast, storming the small port of Linnville early on August 8. This was far beyond the usual Penateka range; residents, some jarred bleary-eyed from their beds, were totally unprepared. Two slaves and three whites were killed in their race to jump into boats and pull to safety in the bay. The only reason most escaped was that, after killing customs officer H. O. Watts, a number of warriors either attempted to ravish his wife or looked on with amusement as her attackers were defeated by her bristling whalebone corset. Taken aback, they tied her half dressed to a horse to deal with later.

As residents watched from their rowboats, the Indians sacked and looted stores and warehouses, tying ribbons and bolts of red cloth to their ponies' tails, trying on formal suits and top hats, whooping with delight as they opened and shut dainty parasols. The Comanche women soon fell upon the bonanza—cookware, cloth, utensils, ornaments, even books to roll cigarettes from the pages—and loaded them onto pack mules. The greed proved to be their undoing; what began as a revenge raid was now laden with plunder that had to be gotten home through two hundred miles of angry tejanos. With tons of booty, three thousand horses, and various captives, they turned north again.

It was Texas Ranger Ben McCulloch who first cut their trail on August 5, and since then had been preparing to engage them, gathering volunteers himself and joining with other groups that formed all over the frontier. By August 8 his exhausted group was at Victoria, where it became clear that, instead of returning to Comanchería by going west through the dry brush country, the Indians were returning—foolishly, arrogantly—the way they had come. McCulloch knew that route, and sent riders out in all directions with the message for every available man to rendezvous at the "Big Prairie" by Plum Creek, near the San Marcos River. The Comanches would have to cross it. An army unit dogged the Comanches' rear, but the warriors avoided open battle, only grudgingly abandoning the most cumbersome plunder. Most of the warriors were occupied in keeping the captured horses in the middle of their formation.

By August 12, when the Comanches approached Plum Creek, a small army of

SAM MAVERICK was an unpredictable, independent nonconformist who never ran for political office. Yet his forthright honesty led the citizens of San Antonio to draft him into a variety of important posts, including mayor and state representative. His peculiar style of politics left a new word in the dictionary, but its origin was less flattering. While he was an able administrator, Maverick was an inattentive rancher and seldom got around to branding his herd's annual increase. Rustlers had such an easy time stealing his calves that in time, any unbranded yearling on the range became known as a "maverick."

For ten years, 1839 to 1849, the Maverick family lived in a three-room house on the Main Plaza, a square they shared with such notable structures as the Town Hall, San Fernando Cathedral, and Madame Bustamente's Fandango Hall. As the family grew, they moved into a larger house *(below)* on Alamo Plaza.

Cheerful and sociable, MARY ADAMS MAVERICK reared ten children and still found time to be active in civic affairs, and was one of the women entrusted with the care of the reclaimed Comanche captive, Matilda Lockhart.

regulars, militia, volunteers, and locals was ready. More than a dozen Tonkawa Indians had jogged some thirty miles from their camp, eager to help fight their traditional enemies. The Comanches, singing, bantering, dressed in their Linnville finery, were taken by surprise to see the long line of white men advance out onto the Big Prairie. Still trying to dodge a fight, the available warriors took up a position to hold them off while the rest tried to steer their laden pack mules and captured remuda to safety. Their guards put up a tremendous show of warfare Comanche-style, individuals proving their bravery with whooping, lance-brandishing charges at the Texan line. Comanche warriors were challenging targets, for they fought not from horseback, but rather riding clinging to its side, using it for a shield, and shooting from beneath its throat while holding onto a loop braided into its mane. One such warrior who took a leading part wore above his breechcloth an elegant black dress coat, backwards, and stovepipe hat, his gun in one hand and a parasol in the other.

The more experienced Rangers saw perfectly that this was all a delaying tactic, and urged the overall commander, militia General Felix Huston, to order a charge. Finally, another leading warrior "wearing a tremendous headdress, who had been exceedingly daring, approached so near that several shots struck him and he fell forward on the pommel of his saddle, but was caught by a comrade on either side and borne away, evidently either dead or dying, for as soon as he was led among his people in the oaks they set up a peculiar howl, when Capt. Caldwell sang out: 'Now General, is the time to charge them; they are whipped.' "

The Texans came on at a gallop and the Comanches, in the style of their warfare, broke and ran, thinking to reassemble and harass them at another place. Only this time it did not work. Their heavily laden pack mules had become mired in a boggy section of creek bottom; the Texans' charge stampeded the captive horse herd straight into them. Comanches who were not trampled in the melee of plunging animals were shot down by Rangers who rode up and down the edge of the bog. At last the Penatekas abandoned stock and booty both and just tried to get away with their lives. They did find time to execute their captives, including a Mrs. Crosby, granddaughter of Daniel Boone, captured at Nine Mile Point. Mrs. Watts was also tied to a tree and shot, but her corset deflected the arrow. She suffered a painful breast wound, but lived to tell of the adventure.

Rangers and militia pursued the routed Indians for ten and twelve miles before returning to divide the spoils of lances and buffalo horn headdresses. Against a loss of one dead and seven wounded, as many as 130 Indians had been killed. Numerous women and children were taken prisoner to San Antonio, where they were given out as servants to various families until they escaped to rejoin their people.

The Tonkawa Indian scouts had acquitted themselves well in the fight. They had arrived on foot, but were fully mounted and equipped from the spoils. The night after the battle they celebrated; ritualistic cannibals, they dismembered and roasted their choice of the dead enemy.

The loss of so many warriors in the Plum Creek Fight reinforced the Comanches' belief that they had lost their war medicine with their chiefs killed in the Council House. The following October these losses were compounded by fifty more dead men, women, and children, killed in a sleeping village deep in their own territory by a Ranger expedition. After these clashes the Penateka threat in central Texas was dramatically diminished.

A New Capital

EDWIN WALLER, born in Virginia in 1800, agitated for Texan independence almost from the moment he received his land grant in 1831. He was involved in the Velasco Fight in 1832, elected to the Consultation and signed the Declaration of Independence. After Lamar's election to the presidency, Waller refused to serve as his postmaster, and became instead first mayor of Austin. He resigned that post before his term was up and returned to his farm in southeast Texas, serving there three terms as chief justice of the county. In 1861 he voted with the majority of the Secession Convention to pull out of the Union.

DURING the revolution and the early years of the Republic, the seat of government had been located at various places, as necessity or convenience demanded. In 1839 a commission was established to select the site of a permanent capital city. They desired a location where they believed the north-south and east-west trade routes would intersect, which suggested a location then at the edge of inhabited country. The commission therefore visited the little outpost of Waterloo, on the Colorado River about fifty miles west-northwest of La Grange and eighty miles northeast of San Antonio. From there they traveled a short distance further upriver, to where the rolling gulf prairie broke against the limestone escarpment of the Hill Country. The location was mild, elevated, healthful, and scenic, and massive volumes of excellent water poured from nearby springs. President Lamar approved the selection, and the new capital was to be named in honor of Stephen F. Austin.

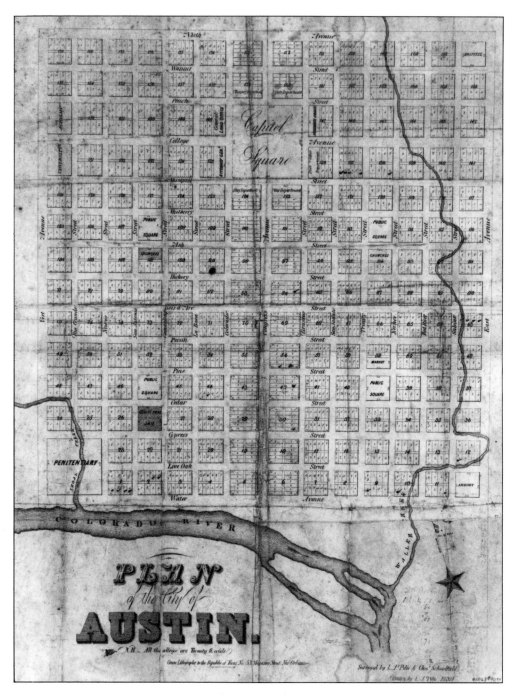

JUDGE WALLER'S PLAN for the city of Austin, laid out in 1839, featured cabinet offices surrounding Capitol Square. The first capitol, however, a log stockade, was located in the southwest part of the city. Blocks elsewhere provided for an armory, hospital, university, academy, penitentiary and four public squares.

WILLIAM MENEFEE was one of the commissioners who selected the site of Austin to be capital of the Republic. Born in Tennessee when George Washington was President of the United States, he entered public life soon after arriving in Texas in 1830. He sat in five of the nine congresses of the Republic and was defeated by General Burleson for Vice President in 1841.

The planning and construction were entrusted to Judge Edwin Waller, a signer of the Declaration of Independence. With $113,000 in Republic scrip and two hundred laborers of questionable energy, Waller toiled from May until November. Lamar and some of the cabinet arrived for an inspection in mid-October to be greeted by Waller, at the head of a large crowd, "In the name of the citizens of Austin, I cordially welcome you and your cabinet to the new metropolis." The last word may have been a bit extravagant to describe the wooded crosshatch of streets and cabins; but Waller's visionary plan for the mile-square city of parks and boulevards virtually ensured that Austin would, in his words, "aided by its salubrity of climate and its beauty of situation, become famous among the cities of the New World."

With an oratorical style like that, it was no surprise when Judge Waller was elected the first mayor.

During Sam Houston's American sojourn, he was elected *in absentia* to a seat in the Texas Congress from San Augustine, one of many East Texas towns where he lived at least briefly during his career. He came home blistering mad at the fate of his Cherokees, who were guilty of nothing more, he thundered to the Congress, than being "dupes enough to believe" in the treaty they had made with the government. He opposed Lamar's other policies at every turn, laying plans as he did so to recapture the presidency in the next election and set things right.

Houston also used his influence to oppose the location of the new capital, seizing upon the issues of its exposed position and the impracticability of either defending it or conducting government business from it. Then, too, it was probably not just a coincidence that by opposing it he could bedevil Lamar, and also humor his understandable partiality toward maintaining the capital in the booming little city that bore his own name.

Houston lost the day, however, and the seat of government was removed to Austin in 1840. An itinerant Methodist minister who visited the place was taken with its picturesque character. Its hills, he wrote, "commence with a high peak, called *Mount Bonnell,* about four miles above Austin city. This bold eminence overlooks the Colorado River, with a perpendicular front seven hundred feet high, affording a most enchanting prospect."

THE VIEW FROM MOUNT BONNELL. When Sam Houston finally arrived in the new capital, he sought to make his peace with its citizens by taking the popular buggy pilgrimage to the Mount Bonnell overlook. The locals seemed appeased when, after a few minutes' reverence, Houston proclaimed that this must have been the high place where the devil tempted Jesus with the riches of the world.

The Santa Fe Pioneers

WHEN Representative Houston growled about Austin City's exposed position, that there "is not a house between this and Santa Fe," the prescience of the remark would have surprised even him. Lamar's Indian wars had plunged the country deeply into debt, and when he began casting about for quick and ready cash his eye fell on the Santa Fe Trail.

The profitable trade route ran from the western United States through unorganized territory to Santa Fe, since 1610 the capital of the interior province that became New Mexico. While an act of the Texas Congress asserted dominion west to the Pacific Ocean, most Texans accepted their western boundary to be the Rio Grande, from mouth to source—a vast country extending as far north as the present state of Wyoming. By either measure Santa Fe was now in Texas and, Lamar reasoned, its inhabitants would surely prefer enlightened Texan government to Mexican despotism. Then sorely needed revenue would be gained by levying tariffs on goods brought over the trail.

His mind set, Lamar went to work. He talked one William Dryden, a Santa Fe citizen in Austin, into representing Texas there as a commissioner. He provided Dryden with two other commissions for Santa Fe men who could be counted on, and a letter "To the People of Santa Fe" describing the virtues of life under Texas rule, and giving a promise to send up civil commissioners to consummate the union. Lamar then went to the Congress. He thought he was presenting them with a *fait accompli,* but when that body turned him down cold, Lamar backwatered, reformulating the scheme as a trade mission. On his own authority the President recruited volunteers, and an expedition formed up. Lamar convinced four men to serve as commissioners; one of them, José Antonio Navarro, the late Stephen Austin's good friend whose own life was now forfeit in Mexico, went, against his better judgment. Texas merchants filled twenty-one large wagons with trade goods valued at some two hundred thousand dollars, a mammoth investment for a country of such modest means. To protect the expedition, five volunteer companies supported by artillery were entrusted to the command of Hugh McLeod, the same who had prosecuted the Council House Fight in San Antonio.

Calling themselves the Santa Fe Pioneers, they set out from Austin on June 19, 1841. A month of travel brought them to the Cross Timbers region of the upper Brazos, by which time it was apparent that they had not allowed themselves sufficient provisions. Then they mistook the Wichita River for the Red, and lost two weeks following it westward before their guide, a Mexican, deserted. No path could be found to get the wagons over the thousand-foot-high rim of the Cap Rock, and from surrounding buttes the Comanche and Kiowa Indians could scarcely believe their good fortune to have so much plunder to attack so close to home. A number of Texans were killed fighting off incessant pillaging and horse-stealing raids.

HUGH MCLEOD.

With streams dwindling in the late summer heat and the men reduced to eating stray Indian dogs, McLeod divided his force, himself staying with the wagons while sending some volunteers west to find the Mexican settlements. Contact was made on September 12, when it was discovered that, far from being welcomed, New Mexico's Governor Manuel Armijo had learned all, and his troops were waiting for them. A couple of the first Texans to surrender were stood up to a wall and shot before one William Lewis turned coat and offered to help capture the rest. During the latter part of September McLeod had found a trail up to the Staked Plains, and was approaching the New Mexico towns. The capture was effected on October 5, without resistance; the Santa Fe Pioneers were too worn down and too far from help to resist. The officers were separated from the men, and all were chained and marched southward under the most brutal conditions. As one wrote later: "One of our men died . . . from exhaustion and fatigue; and we had not proceeded far when some of the guard were sent to the rear and shot one of the men who was lame. . . . We had two of our own wagons with us, in one of which he might have been permitted to rest himself, and there was nothing to justify the act. The ears of these men were cut off to be kept . . . as evidence that they had not escaped."

By the time the humiliated Texans were clapped into prison in Mexico City, at least sixty of the original number were dead, killed either by Indians or exhaustion, or shot by roadsides. Navarro had been surrendered on a particular pledge of humane treatment; sentenced to death and thrown into San Juan de Ullóa dungeon, he later escaped on a British vessel and made his way home.

The fate of the Santa Fe Pioneers was not learned for months, but from the floor of the House, Sam Houston predicted that no good would come of it, nor from any of Lamar's follies. Politically, Houston was feistier than ever, but his personal life was undergoing a dramatic transformation.

He had given up courting Anna Raguet, who spurned him even though the Eliza

Allen divorce was long since final, and his Cherokee wife, Tiana Rogers, had died in 1838. During his rest in America, Houston met, wooed, and won the lovely Margaret Moffette Lea of Marion, Alabama. A belle of delicate health and formidable character, she arrived in Galveston, followed by her mother and *grand boudoir* rosewood piano. She was twenty-one and he was forty-seven. Those who knew him best predicted a calamity as she settled at the house in San Augustine and he continued on to the log stockade that served as a capitol in Austin. Back in the seat of power, Houston by day bellowed against Lamar's idiocy, by night writing home meekly about his drinking: "My Love, I do sincerely hope that you will hear no more slanders of me . . . if you hear the truth you never shall hear of my being on a 'spree.' "

The marriage was blissful; children began to appear one after another, but the state was in trouble. "I might have been happy," wrote Houston to a friend, "had I not known the full extent of Lamar's stupidity." To another he asserted, "He wou'd no doubt be impeached, but the poor soul is too contemptible to incur hatred."

The days of Lamar's three-year term were now numbered, though, and his chosen replacement, Vice President Burnet, and Houston opposed each other in a campaign of spectacular mudslinging.

Aside from helping himself to trade on the Santa Fe Trail, President Lamar seized upon another scheme for raising cash for the Republic, not less incendiary than the Santa Fe Expedition.

From the time he took office in 1836 President Houston had been required to give much of his attention to the Texas navy. Neither San Jacinto nor the Treaty of Velasco, which Mexico promptly repudiated, ended hostility between Texas and Mexico. Out in the Gulf, the war for independence continued apace as thundering broadsides were traded under tall canvas and battle pennants. Only two months after San Jacinto the Mexican schooner *Watchman* arrived at the tiny Texas port of Cópano, unaware that Santa Anna had been beaten. Captain Isaac W. Burton hid his men along the shore and

REPUBLIC OF TEXAS $100 NOTE. Another of Lamar's solutions to the national debt was as artless as his poetry: print more money. He printed so much that by the end of his term Texas currency, such as this hundred-dollar bill bearing his signature, traded at only three cents on the dollar.

SLOOP-OF-WAR AUSTIN.

captured the vessel by ruse. Two other schooners followed, which Burton and his celebrated "Horse Marines" also captured, netting twenty-five thousand dollars worth of badly needed supplies.

But not all the news was good. In 1837 the Texan warship *Independence,* bringing news of Texas' recognition by the United States, was captured by the *Vencedor del Alamo,* and Texas' commissioner of long experience, William H. Wharton, was predictably dungeoned up in Mexico. Texas' *Invincible* dueled the *Bravo* and took the *Pocket* before being lost at sea, along with another Texan vessel, the *Brutus.* When the *Liberty,* which had captured the *Pelicano* and put in at New Orleans for repairs, was seized by the yard and auctioned off for debt, the Texas navy was depleted.

Sometimes during his tenure Houston had to pledge his personal credit to back that of his Republic, but by one means or another, eight new ships were ordered from American yards and began sliding down the ways.

The new vessels, among them a 600-ton sloop of war, 130 feet long and mounting twenty guns, christened the *Austin,* were not delivered until Lamar had taken office. For an initial payment of twenty-five thousand dollars (of which, after paying the crews and provisioning the ships, nearly eighty-five hundred dollars remained as profit for the government), Lamar rented out the Republic's navy to Mexican rebels based in Yucatán. Under command of Edwin W. Moore, a Virginian not yet thirty years old, but a sailor for fifteen of them, the venture proved profitable in preying upon Mexican shipping. Only two days before leaving office Lamar signed an agreement with the Yucatán rebel chief to continue the arrangement for eight thousand dollars per month, plus half the take. Lamar's archenemy Houston was to replace him, but the fleet sortied from Galveston before new orders could be issued, embroiling Moore and Houston in a bitter struggle that survived the existence of the navy itself.

Mier and the Black Beans

IN the election of September 1841, Sam Houston triumphed over the Lamar-Burnet faction and took office as President for the second time. While his first order of business after arriving was to call off Lamar's holy war against the Indians, other business snatched his attention.

On March 6, 1842, six years to the day after the fall of the Alamo, Lamar's expansionist mischief bore fruit, as a Mexican army pounced across the boundary and quickly captured Goliad, Refugio, Victoria, and San Antonio, spreading general terror across the countryside. The Texan forces mobilized as rapidly as possible, but before any action could be taken, the Mexicans retired, as suddenly as they had come, beyond the Rio Grande.

There was no shortage of public opinion favoring a retaliatory invasion, but Houston, sensing a disaster to Texas' fragile economy and citing that fighting Mexicans in Mexico would be a vastly different proposition than merely defending the home soil, passed it over. "Fools only pursue phantoms," he soothed, "and children will chase butterflies." Privately, he knew he had not heard the last from Santa Anna, and made certain that channels were open to import volunteers from New Orleans.

In September a larger force, about fourteen hundred under General Adrian Woll, a French soldier of fortune frequently in Mexican service, recaptured San Antonio. This time there was more fighting, and Woll's army took a serious—but indecisive—licking by six hundred Rangers under John Coffee Hays. He had managed to bait the Mexicans into leaving the safety of the city, and in a furious ambuscade on Salado Creek the Rangers killed about sixty while losing only one. (With Woll, incidentally, was an unhappy Juan Seguín. As Stephen Austin had foreseen, the swelling tide of "leatherstockings" he deplored soon outnumbered and began browbeating the Mexican population even in their center of San Antonio. Seguín, despite his brave service during the revolution, was among those forced to leave. When Santa Anna learned that Seguín had fled to Mexico to escape the San Antonio roughnecks, he had him collared and offered the choice of indefinite imprisonment or service in the invasion. Seguín chose the latter.)

When news of the assault on San Antonio spread, a relief column commanded by Captain Nicholas Mosby Dawson marched west from La Grange to aid the Texas garrison facing Woll. Before reaching San Antonio, however, Dawson's men were surrounded by Woll's. Of fifty-five men in the Texan company, thirty-three, including Dawson, were killed in the fight. The remainder surrendered, most of whom either died as prisoners in Mexico or were, in the Santanista tradition, executed.

Woll held San Antonio for nine days, and when he returned to Mexico he had in tow fifty-three civilian prisoners. On his arrival he had found a trial in progress; surrounding the courthouse, he rousted all out, including judge and jury. They were taken to Mexico City and corked into Perote Castle, along with the remnants of Lamar's Santa Fe Expedition.

Popular opinion demanded that a punitive foray now be mounted, and a force under General Alexander Somervell headed toward the Rio Grande in November. While one purpose of the expedition was to rescue the captured Texans, all that the seven hundred men were after was some high jinks of terror and pillage in the border towns. They managed to take Laredo, after which two hundred returned home, and then seventy miles to the south, they took Guerrero. But with their supply lines stretched to snapping, with legion Mexican reinforcements coming up, and with it obvious that the captives could not be rescued, Somervell on December 19 ordered a return to Gonzales. Fewer than two hundred of his command obeyed; the rest insisted on continuing the fight until they had enough stock and booty to pay for their trouble. The penchant of Texan volunteers to throw over officers and ride off to battle against overwhelming Mexican odds was getting to be a habit. Moreover, most of the rebellious leaders had become anti-Houston politicians, and they could make important political hay of sponsoring a plundering expedition in Mexico.

To lead them the men elected Colonel William S. Fisher (Secretary of War in Houston's first cabinet), and headed downstream on December 20. Forty men under Houston enemy Thomas J. Green floated on four small river craft taken in Guerrero. Ben McCulloch led a small company of Rangers to scout the Mexican side of the river, while Fisher and the main body marched down the Texan side. With a total strength of just over three hundred they arrived opposite Mier, an important Mexican garrison town about one hundred miles upstream from Matamoros, on December 22.

McCulloch's Rangers reported massive Mexican troop movements in the vicinity, and counseled retirement. Fisher scoffed, and the Rangers disgustedly quit the scheme and sought safer territory. Fisher and about 250 men entered Mier on December 23 and demanded supplies and provisions. The town complied, but as no transport could be found to carry the goods to the river (short of the Texans lugging it themselves, which they refused), Fisher retired with a promise of delivery on the morrow, and with Mier's alcalde as hostage. The goods did not arrive, and on Christmas Day Fisher learned the reason: Mexican forces had forbidden it.

Leaving a camp guard of 42, Fisher and 260 Texans reentered Mier to seize the supplies. They were met by General Pedro de Ampudia and some 3,000 regulars. A vicious battle lasted until the afternoon of December 26. Fisher's men, better marksmen with better weapons, inflicted terrible losses on Ampudia's army—perhaps 600 killed and 200 wounded. Fisher lost only 12, but he was trapped, and running out of powder and provisions. When Ampudia sent the Texans a white flag under which to surrender, Fisher accepted.

Only after they were disarmed did the Texans learn that they were not prisoners of war; they had, as the Santanista phrase went, surrendered at discretion. The order for their execution was immediate, but Ampudia managed to win them clemency on December 27. Fisher and the other leaders were spirited off to Mexico City at once. The wounded were left at Mier, where they later bribed their guards and escaped. The others were marched to Matamoros, and soon thereafter, on down the road to the capital.

While in transit Captain Ewen Cameron led an escape from the town of Salado that was almost made good, on February 11, 1843. After disarming their guards and shooting their way out of town, they tried to make their way east. After terrible suffering during a week lost in the desert, however, most—176—were retaken in small groups. Only three were known to turn up in Texas again; about fourteen disappeared.

Santa Anna angrily ordered the execution of all the fugitives. This time they were saved by Francisco Mexía, governor of Coahuila, who resisted the presidential order until foreign diplomats in Mexico City persuaded Santa Anna to soften his order. He

MIER PRISONERS AND GUARDS. Three captive members of the expedition heft their chains in this retouched daguerreotype. Serape-wrapped guards boast a baroque display of arms, including a cavalry lance and broadsword.

did, somewhat: instead of shooting everybody, now one in ten, a total of seventeen, were to be executed. According to survivor Thomas Jefferson Green, "the decimation took place by the drawing of black and white beans from a small earthen mug. The white ones signified *exemption,* and the black *death.* One hundred and fifty-nine white beans were placed in the bottom of the mug, and seventeen black ones placed upon the top of them. The beans were not stirred, and had so slight a shake that it was perfectly clear that they had not mixed them together. Such was their anxiety to execute Captain Cameron that [he] was made to draw a bean from the mug in this condition.

HENRY JOURNEAY, one of the Mier prisoners, occupied his time while in Perote dungeon with the making of this violin, for the construction of which he had only a razor and a piece of glass.

"He said, with his usual coolness, 'Well, boys, we have to draw, so let's be at it;' so saying, he thrust his hand into the mug, and drew out a white bean. . . .

"Some of lighter temper jested over the bloody tragedy. One would say, 'Boys, this beats raffling all to pieces;' another would say that 'this is the tallest gambling scrape I ever was in,' and such like remarks. . . .

"Poor Major Cocke, when he first drew the fatal bean, held it up between his forefinger and thumb, and . . . said, 'Boys, I told you so; I never failed in my life to draw a prize.'

"[L. L.] Cash [of Victoria] said, 'Well, they murdered my brother with Colonel Fannin, and they are about to murder me.'

"Several of the Mexican officers who officiated in this . . . expressed great dissatisfaction thereat, and some wept.

"Captain Cameron, in taking his leave of these brave men . . . wept bitterly, and implored the officers to execute him and spare his men.

"Just previous to the firing they were bound together with cords, and their eyes being bandaged, they were set upon a log near the wall, with their backs to their executioners. They all begged the officer to shoot them in front, and at a short distance. . . . This he refused; and, to make his cruelty as refined as possible, fired at several paces, and continued the firing from ten to fifteen minutes, lacerating and mangling . . . in a manner too horrible for description."

One Henry Whaley, who had said he was satisfied to die, knowing he "had killed twenty-five of the yellow bellies," was wounded fifteen times. His savage taunting of the Mexicans' marksmanship was silenced when a pistol to the head splattered his brains on the wall.

"Such was the effect of this horrible massacre upon their own soldiers, who were stationed as a guard on the wall above, that one of them fainted, and came near to falling over, but was caught by his comrades."

When Santa Anna learned that Cameron had been among the survivors, a special express sped out with his death warrant. He was executed on April 26, near Mexico City. Spurning both the blindfold and the priest who offered to hear his confession, Cameron said, "For the liberty of Texas, Ewen Cameron can look death in the face." He opened his shirt to the firing squad and ordered, "Fire!"

The other Texans were conveyed on to the capital and, after three months' labor as road gangs, were dungeoned in Perote. There they encountered the San Antonio captives whose liberation had been one purpose of Somervell's expedition. Many of the Mier men died in Perote of exposure and starvation. Some had escaped while on the road gangs; a few others tunneled—a small miracle—out of Perote and made their ways home. From time to time the United States, Britain, or France would use their influence to win the release of one or a few. The last of them were paroled under a general amnesty on September 16, 1844.

The Regulators
and the Moderators

HOUSTON'S second term was also disrupted by one of the worst feuds that ever occurred in Texan—or American—history. It began when the trouble that Stephen F. Austin had feared over land fraud broke out, in huge and unorganized Shelby County, along the Louisiana border in that part of the state known as the Redlands. A preexisting boundary dispute between the United States and France resulted in the land along the Sabine becoming a no-man's-land in which neither Texas nor the United States exercised jurisdiction, and thus a haven for the fugitives of both. Wrote a resident from the area at the time: "It is nothing uncommon for us to inquire of a man why he ran away from the States. Few persons feel insulted by such a question. They generally answer for some crime or other which they have committed. If they deny having committed any crime or say they did not run away, they are generally looked upon suspiciously." Noah Smithwick was also familiar with pine-forested Shelby County: "The Redlands had a hard name, and there is no denying the fact that there were many hard characters there, its geographical position making it a convenient retreat for renegades. . . . The settlers [who were] too weak to protect themselves, and having neither civil nor military protection, were completely at the mercy of these outlaws."

It had been in 1837 that the respected Judge Robert M. Williamson was sent to establish the first district court, only to have one of the local bosses inform him that it could not be. Thumping his Bowie knife down on the crude bench, he declared, "This, sir, is the law of Shelby County." Three-Legged Willie, the Tom Paine of the Texas Revolution, instantly drew his pistol. "Well this," he roared, "is the constitution that overrules your law!" Williamson's successors were less inventive of local-color rulings, however, and after his departure the county judiciary degenerated into a farce.

Alfred George was running for sheriff of Shelby County. In 1839 George had sold a slave to a certain Joseph Goodbread, and been paid in fraudulent certificates for forty thousand acres of land. Both men knew the papers were counterfeit; printing fake land scrip was a thriving local business and—curiously—many people traded in them with hardly a discount from the real thing, especially when, like these, they issued from the county commissioners. Such printing operations, however, worked to the detriment of the national government, whose principal resource was its public domain. The Texas Congress created a board with authority to approve legal land scrip and invalidate absolutely the bogus paper. In July of 1840 the board undertook an examination of land certificates relating to Shelby County, and the scrip paid to Alfred George for his slave was declared worthless. George went to Goodbread demanding compensation for his

Negro, and Goodbread refused. Soon after, the slave in question disappeared, and Goodbread learned that George, rather than risk the man being resold, had persuaded him to hide in the thick pine forests, and was sneaking food out to him. Goodbread made the whole transaction public, perhaps hoping to cause George's defeat in the election. George was angered and embarrassed; he knew that Goodbread had shared previous acrimony with a certain Charles W. Jackson, which was long since agreeably settled. George went to Jackson and told him that Goodbread would kill him the next time he saw him. Jackson rode over into town and found Goodbread talking to another man. Warning the bystander aside, Jackson coolly leveled his rifle and shot Goodbread through the heart. He then rode to the justice of the peace's office, and posted a bond of two hundred dollars with the requirement that he appear at the next sitting of the district court. Alfred George won the election.

Sometime later, Jackson learned that he had been indicted for murder, and knew he had to do two things. First he sought a change of venue to Harrison County, to the north. The judge granted the request but ordered the sheriff—Alfred George—to hold him in close confinement, without bond. George demurred that the jail was too dilapidated to hold prisoners. The judge then ordered George to keep Jackson under guard; as soon as the judge left on his circuit, Jackson was set free. The second necessity was more complicated; many people in Shelby County had been friends of the deceased and could testify against the conspirators Jackson and George. Knowing that the "Piney Woods" outside the towns were a paradise sheltering outlaws and fugitives of every describable stripe, Jackson organized local rangers to clean them out, and many well-intended men joined his "Shelby Guards" with that object in mind. Priority of whom to attack lay with Jackson, and once in the saddle, his guards became known as the Regulators, intent on destroying or driving away those who had been friends of Goodbread. Most of the latter lived in the northern part of the county. After horsewhipping a certain Squire Humphries, the Regulators rode through the vicinity of McFadden Creek, looking for three men in particular—brothers William and Bailey McFadden, and James (Tiger Jim) Strickland. None of the targets were at home, and the Regulators had to content themselves with burning their cabins, having refused to let the families save any possessions whatever.

John M. Hansford assembled his court on July 15, 1841, in special term; the trial of Charles Jackson, for murder, was the only case on the docket. The "prisoner" arrived, guarded by twenty or so of his own men, and himself armed. Hansford fined Sheriff George for letting Jackson appear with weapons, whereupon the prisoner surrendered his arms to the judge, quickly followed by his coat and shoes. There were looking on perhaps a hundred amused Regulators, in addition to the guard, when he then dared the judge to try him. Hansford used the entire day to empanel a jury, then adjourned. He left town during the night, leaving the sheriff a note: "Being unwilling to risk my person in the courthouse any longer where I see myself surrounded by bravos and hired assassins, and no longer left free to preside as an impartial judge at this special term of court for the trial of Charles W. Jackson, I order you to adjourn the court tomorrow at eight o'clock by proclamation without delay. From you at the regular term I shall expect the prisoner. You will secure the prisoner and keep him safely until then, by causing him to be securely ironed and keeping a strong guard until delivered by due course of the law." Jackson's lawyer lectured the jury on the rights of accused persons, and after a quick vote the prisoner was acquitted and released. Judge Hansford was later assassinated.

Thinking that his trouble over killing Goodbread was finally at rest, Jackson turned his attention to bounty hunting. Shelby County was a rich field to harvest, and common sense told the fugitives that the surest way to avoid being delivered up to the law in Louisiana was to join Jackson's Shelby Guards; thus his Regulators prospered. What

THREE-LEGGED WILLIE. Born in Georgia sometime around 1805, Robert McAlpin Williamson acquired his nickname after a disease, probably polio, bent back his right leg at the knee when he was fifteen, necessitating the use of a wooden peg. He became a lawyer before arriving in Texas in 1826 to take up a career as a newspaper editor. From this platform he was a fiery advocate of independence; the scouts and Rangers he commanded during the Revolution shepherded citizens through the Runaway Scrape and rounded up stock and supplies for the army. He went to Shelby County as judge of the Third Judicial District, which made him a member of the Supreme Court as well. A senator and four-term congressman of the Republic, Williamson named one of his seven children Annexus, in support of joining the Union. He retired from public life after his defeat in the race for lieutenant governor in 1851, and died in 1859.

Williamson was never slowed by his physical disability. He was a renowned dancer, and held his own in a frontier society where "gliding around" was frowned upon and the success of a dance was measured in the number of splintered floorboards that had to be replaced.

he had not counted on was the fury of those he had beaten and burned out. One day when Jackson was returning from the Louisiana border town of Logansport, he was ambushed and shotgunned into oblivion by Squire Humphries, the McFadden brothers, and a number of other men who had formed a second guard force to oppose the Regulators. They became known as the Moderators, and with the killing of Jackson, the feud was on. Sheriff George went into hiding in Nacogdoches.

The Regulators lost no time in selecting a new leader, a tall, goateed young psychopath and Mississippi forger named Charles W. Moorman. By the time Sam Houston was elected to his second term, the Moderators had been driven to their strongholds in northern Shelby County. "Watt" Moorman held Shelbyville in an almost medieval grasp, leading large mobs of Regulators even into adjoining counties in search of Moderators, rallying and deploying his men with blasts on a hunting horn. Early in October 1841 William and Bailey McFadden were overhauled and taken back to Shelbyville for trial. The jury voted 174 to 0 for hanging, and the sentence was summarily executed, from the same tree. The McFaddens' young brother Rufus, fourteen, also took part in killing Jackson, but was let off with twenty strikes of a blackjack.

The feud claimed its most prominent casualty in the spring of 1842. Colonel Robert Potter had signed the Declaration of Independence and served the Republic of Texas as the first Secretary of the Navy, and had entered his second term in the Senate. A neighbor of Potter's, Captain William P. Rose, had a five-hundred-dollar reward over his head for several murders. Potter was a Moderator, Rose a prominent ringleader of the Regulators who operated in Harrison County. After Congress adjourned, Potter went to his estate on Caddo Lake; his attempt to capture Rose was foiled by the latter's hiding in a brush pile. Several days later Rose and his men surrounded Potter's house. The colonel tried to escape by diving into the lake, but was shot in the head when he surfaced to breathe.

Watt Moorman, meanwhile, continued to run more or less amok in Shelbyville and surrounding towns. One suspected Moderator he shot dead in a Baptist revival meeting in San Augustine. When a new district judge, William B. Ochiltree, tried to bring to justice those responsible for the McFadden lynchings, Moorman and his Regulators wheeled up a cannon and trained it on the courthouse, but the effort was unnecessary. Nearly every man on the grand jury had participated in the killings, so no indictments were returned. Moorman himself clubbed an elderly spectator at the hearing, but defied arrest. For the next two years the Regulators and Moderators passed through truces and reorganizations, but gradually the complexion was assumed of the Regulators as the established authority, and the Moderators trying to end the reign of terror. A number of pitched battles were fought that eventually took perhaps fifty lives and brought commerce and new settlement to a virtual standstill. Goodbread and Jackson were all but forgotten; fighting continued from one act of vengeance to the next, and many honest men were badgered into joining one faction to avoid being murdered as a member or sympathizer of the other. As one observer noted, "the most foolish and extravagant infatuation" had taken hold.

During the summer of 1844 Watt Moorman hatched a political scheme of unknown proportions; whether he intended eventually to act against the central government, or stop after solidifying his empire in Shelby County, cannot be known. But when his riders posted notices for twenty-five leading citizens to leave the area within two weeks or be executed, so many men—Moderators and neutrals—enlisted under the deputy sheriff, who had been a recipient of the Regulators' ultimatum, that Moorman was stretched to calling in all his supporters from the surrounding counties. As the two armies maneuvered and skirmished, the people of San Augustine finally prevailed on the government to act, and President Houston arrived with General Rusk late in August. After the President listened—whittling, as was his habit—to Judge Ochiltree and others recite the horrors of the previous four years, Houston proclaimed an order to end the feud. He also issued a call for militia that brought six hundred volunteers almost instantly to obey his directive to arrest ten leading men of both sides. The Moderators came willingly; Watt Moorman had to be forced.

Judge Ochiltree assembled all the principals in Shelbyville, and Houston mediated their differences; although bitterness continued for years, the feud ended at that meeting. It seems remarkable that a four-year feud in which fifty people lost their lives should have been quelled by what one historian described as a "fatherly talk." But of course, both sides were exhausted, and moreover, the war between the Regulators and the Moderators pointed up a central characteristic of any feud that is often overlooked today—that it was actually "not lawlessness. It was an appeal to a law which was felt to be a reasonable substitute for legal redress which could not be obtained." A feud took justice into its own hands, and when the power of the government was asserted, the reason for its existence ceased to be.

WATT MOORMAN, even after his fiefdom collapsed, continued to make a hard name for himself until he was killed in a Louisiana gunfight.

The Germans in Texas

CARL, PRINCE OF SOLMS-BRAUNFELS had a good heart and noble intentions. However, he missed the ambience of his castle and hounds and groveling peasants, and stayed in Texas only a year before returning to Germany.

JUST as Sam Houston, when President Jackson sent him to treat with Comanche Indians in Texas, had been largely pursuing his own interests, just so was Henry Fisher, when Houston commissioned him to represent Texas to the German states of the Rhine. The Texan Government, like the Mexican before, seized upon the empresario-colony system to populate empty tracts of the frontier, and Fisher had acquired a huge grant north and west of Austin, in country still held, unchallenged for the most part, by Penateka Comanches. Fisher's eye was open for colonists, and he could not have arrived at a better time. Political and economic conditions in the German states were so ripe for emigration that some twenty-five altruistic noblemen had formed the Adels-verein, or Society for the Protection of German Immigrants in Texas, to give the movement some order and allow the Germans, once in Texas, to stay together. Under the leadership of Carl, Prince of Solms-Braunfels, they contributed $80,000 as a fund to purchase a colony and settle their pioneers, who would pay $240 per family for transportation, a 320-acre stake, and food until the first crops were brought in.

Fisher, German-born himself, had little difficulty convincing the good-hearted but gullible Prince Carl to authorize the expenditure of $9,000 for 4 million acres of Comanche territory, on the representation that the colony was accessible, fertile, and wonderfully suited to coastal commerce. The bargain was struck in June of 1844; the first contingent of 439 immigrants would arrive in December, and Prince Carl left in advance to make preparations; only on his arrival did he find he had been taken.

Settling the Fisher grant with so little preparation was impossible, so Prince Carl shopped for a second site where his people could settle and marshal their resources before expanding into the Indian country. For $1,111 he bought two leagues—nearly nine thousand acres—on the Guadalupe River thirty miles northeast of San Antonio. At the foot of the Balcones Escarpment, amid scenery not dissimilar to that of the middle Rhine, he laid out a town named, not surprisingly, New Braunfels. His work done, the Prince of Solms-Braunfels resigned his position with the Adelsverein and left his immigrants in the spring of 1845. In Galveston to board a ship for home, he met his successor, thirty-three-year old Ottfried Hans, Baron of Meusebach. The red-bearded nobleman knew five languages, and was trained in political science, law, economics, forestry, and mining. Where Prince Carl had earned considerable ridicule for his hunting parties with noble friends, clattering through the forests in their Prussian uniforms, Baron von Meusebach renounced his titles and became John O. Meusebach, citizen of Texas, and set to work.

He inherited a hard job. While Prince Carl was off looking for land, he generously left an open credit line for his colonists as they arrived at the coast, and they very nearly ate the Adelsverein into bankruptcy. The immigrants arrived at New Braunfels in April of 1845 but planted no crops; a bargain was a bargain, and they expected to be fed for a year, and they believed, wrongly, that it was too late in the season to plant. Many of the Germans endured terrible hardship making their way inland to the colony; a considerable number of them died. But the Society forwarded more money, more settlers, and the colony took in a big way. In a year the four hundred became four thousand, and two years later, seven thousand. By 1855 Texas was home to some thirty-five thousand Germans who could not have been happier.

East Texas, with its tobacco-chewing, slave-beating, Anglo-American cotton planters, looked on with horror. Not only did the Germans outstrip them economically, they did it without benefit of slaves. Unlike the Southerners, who came seeking fortunes, the Germans came for political freedom, and "did for themselves"; almost unanimously they detested the idea of owning other men. By the mid-1840s, slaves accounted nationwide in Texas for just over a quarter of the population, and in eastern counties heavily dependent on cotton it was not unusual for blacks to outnumber whites. At the same time, in almost exclusively German Gillespie County there were only five slaves in a population of 1,240. The Germans reveled in their political franchise, and in places like San Antonio where American office holders had begun to take unchallenged tenure for granted, they began to be voted out, with predictable reaction from American-controlled newspapers:

"On election day a horde of political lepers crawled to the ballot-box and there nullified the votes of thousands of your countrymen, who had weighed well the principles in controversy. Great God! Shall these things always exist?

"The unanimity with which the German and Mexican vote was cast *against* the American candidates [cannot mean] that the thousands and tens of thousands of these ignorant, vicious, besotted *greasers* who swarm the land, are more capable of self-government than [we are]."

Rumors began to circulate in East Texas that the Germans planned to rise up, separate from the rest of Texas, and establish a new government where slavery would be outlawed. Americans traveling in East Texas were often primed with stories of the Germans' sloth and mean character; some, however, went on west to see for themselves, and had a shocking surprise.

"We stopped one night at the house of a planter, now twenty years settled in Eastern Texas. He was a man of some education and natural intelligence, and had, he told us, an income, from the labor of his slaves, of some $4,000. His residence was one of the largest houses we had seen in Texas. It had a second story, two wings and a long gallery. Its windows had been once glazed, but now, out of eighty panes that originally filled the lower windows, thirty only remained unbroken. Not a door in the house had

A German House, Fredericksburg. While most American Texans seemed satisfied with their drafty lean-tos and dogtrot log cabins, the Germans whom they vilified for laziness and mean character were busily building snug houses. Many of them were *Fachwerk,* a half-timber frame chocked with cut limestone; some even had copper roofs.

Other German improvements included a preference for stoves over inefficient fireplaces, dietary variety from closely tended dairies and vegetable gardens, and a devotion to culture that put Germans—and other Northern and Central Europeans—in the forefront of fine arts development. From German and Czech smokehouses evolved that most quintessentially Texan contribution to the American diet: barbecue.

ever been furnished with a latch or even a string; when they were closed, it was necessary to *claw* or to ask someone inside to push open. (Yet we happened to hear a neighbor expressing serious admiration of the way these doors fitted.) The furniture was of the rudest description.

"Our supper-table was nothing else than the *eternal* pork fry, corn pone and coffee. Butter, of dreadful odor, was here added by exception. Wheat flour they never used. It was 'too much trouble.'

"[A neighbor] told us that the only reason that the people didn't have any comfort here was, that they wouldn't *take any* trouble to get anything. Anything that their negroes would make they would eat; but they would take no pains to instruct them, or to get anything that [they] didn't grow. . . . They owned fifty cows, she supposed, but very rarely had any milk and scarcely ever any butter, simply because his people were too lazy to milk or churn.

"On entering Texas we had been so ignorant as not to know that there were larger settlements of Germans there than in any other Southern State. At Bastrop, at a watch-maker's shop, I had seen, with surprise, a *German newspaper,* the *San Antonio Zeitung* of the week previous, and found that it contained more news of general interest than all the American Texan papers I had come across. . . . However, no one could give us any precise information about the Germans, and we had not the least idea that they were so numerous, and had so important a position in Western Texas, until we reached them. . . .

"I never in my life, except, perhaps, in awakening from a dream, met with such a sudden and complete transfer of associations. In short, we were in Germany.

"There was nothing wanting; there was nothing too much. The landlady enters;

JOHN O. MEUSEBACH, formerly Baron von Meusebach, married Agnes Coreth, formerly Countess Coreth of Tyrol, in New Braunfels in 1852 and served as state senator. He lived out a long retirement tending his farm, rose garden, and orchard, and survived until 1897. One of the first buildings in his town of Fredericks-burg was the Lutheran VEREINSKIRCHE *(right),* lo-cally known for obvious reasons as the Coffee-mill Church. The structure shown here was later destroyed, but was replaced by one iden-tical to it.

CASTROVILLE, named for its founder and patron, Texan diplomat HENRI CASTRO, never became a great city, a fact that allowed it to maintain its Alsatian charm.

she does not readily understand us, but we shall have dinner immediately. In two minutes' time, by which we have got off our coats and warmed our hands at the stove, we are asked to sit down. An excellent soup is set before us, and in succession there follow two courses of meat, neither of them pork and neither of them fried, two dishes of vegetables, salad, a compote of peaches, coffee with milk, wheat bread from the loaf, and beautiful, sweet butter. . . .

" 'How can you make such butter?' we asked in astonishment. 'Oh, ho! it is only the American ladies are too lazy; they not work enough their butter. They give us fifty cent a pound for our butter in San Antone! yes, fifty cent! but we want to eat good butter, too.

"We went out to look at our horses; a man in a cap and jacket was rubbing their legs—the first time they had received such attention in Texas. They were pushing their noses into racks filled with fine mesquit hay. They seemed to look at us imploringly. We ought to spend the night. But there is evidently no sleeping room for us in the little inn. They must be full. We concluded to ask if they could accommodate us; yes, with pleasure—would we be pleased to look at the room they could afford us? Doubtless in the cock-loft, as usual. No, it was in another little cottage in the rear. A little room it proved, with blue walls, and oak furniture. Two beds, one of them would be for each of us, the first time we had been offered the luxury of sleeping alone in Texas."

After Meusebach had restored the Adelsverein to a workable if not sound footing in New Braunfels, he moved to take possession of the original grant that Henry Fisher had stuck them with. The town of Fredericksburg was founded about a hundred miles west of Austin, and elsewhere in the Hill Country were founded Sisterdale, Castell, Leiningen, and numerous others. The Germans in Texas have also been given credit for one other accomplishment that eluded American Texans—they made peace with the Comanches. However, by the time Meusebach met Hard Penis' Penatekas in council, at the crumbling San Sabá Presidio ruins in 1847, the Comanches had been so thoroughly whipped by Anglo Rangers that the sight of friendly white faces was not unwelcome. The Germans paid them one thousand dollars for permission to survey the Fisher grant;

whites on the Penateka range were not to be molested, Indians were welcome to visit the German towns, and all infractions were to be mutually reported and dealt with.

While ground for the Meusebach-Comanche Treaty had been prepared by warfare in which the Germans did not take part, it was still the closest thing to a successful agreement ever undertaken with a tribe of Comanches. It held good until the Penatekas removed to a distant reservation in the mid-1850s.

While the Germans came to outrank the Mexicans as the second most numerous ethnic group in Texas, they were far from the only nationality to arrive from Europe. Swedes, Norwegians, Danes, Belgians, Dutch, French, and Slavs also immigrated and started communities that retained their distinctive atmospheres. The most successful of the minor empresarios was Henri Castro, the Texan consul general in Paris. A highly literate descendant of Portuguese aristocracy, his several hundred Alsatian colonists began a thriving community on the Medina River west of San Antonio in September of 1844. Where German success was guaranteed by massive numbers and hard work, Castro's advantage was money. Starting and organizing the colony and providing for his settlers cost some two hundred thousand dollars of his own fortune.

The Pig War

THE seat of government was moved to Austin in 1839, just in time for French recognition. The finest house in town, with imported chef and wine cellar, was built by the thirty-year-old chargé d'affaires, Jean Peter Isidore Alphonse Dubois, Comte de Saligny. He admired President Lamar, but was otherwise abysmally ill suited to life in the wilds. The product of a turreted château in Brittany, touchy and pretentious, he proved a godsend to frontier ruffians in need of a butt for their jokes. When the elegantly sashed and bemedaled young noble called on former President Houston to pay his respects, the old warrior called his bluff, dropping his Indian blanket from his scarred shoulders, growling, "A humble republican soldier, who wears his decorations here, salutes you." The count was mortified and the town guffawed for days. The prank was less than fair, for de Saligny was himself wounded in the street fighting that put his king, Louis Philippe, on the throne. Houston made amends; it was he and not Lamar who supported the count's Franco-Texienne bill.

De Saligny met his downfall over what became known as the Pig War. On February 19, 1841, Secretary of State J. S. Mayfield was startled to receive a hot communiqué from the French chargé that one of his servants, Eugène Pluyette, suffered an unprovoked attack by a stick-wielding local named Bullock. "These acts, Sir," he wrote, "constitute one of the most scandalous and outrageous violations of the Laws of Nations," and demanded an apology and punishment of the culprit.

More facts surfaced the next day, when Bullock, keeper of Bullock's Hotel, wrote the President of the Republic himself on the matter:

"Your memorialist would most respectfully represent to your Excellency . . . that the Charge d'affaires of France, M. Saligny, has become his debtor, to the amount of two hundred seventy dollars and seventy-five cents par money.

"Your memorialist further states, that soon after his debtor refused payment (for the first time) that he has suffered further detriment in the loss of hogs, which have been most maliciously and wantonly killed with pitchforks and pistols used by his debtor and a Frenchman in his employ called Eugene. . . ."

Bullock went on to complain that he couldn't prosecute for the debt because of de Saligny's immunity. On February 21 de Saligny wrote Secretary Mayfield that Bullock had again threatened Pluyette, and Mayfield arranged a judicial hearing on the whole matter for February 22. The count refused to appear before any such lowly tribunal; the dignity of France was deeply involved, and Bullock must be punished in accord with "the Laws of Nations." Mayfield apologized that international law did not provide for punishment of petty crimes, and the hearing was held. De Saligny forbade Pluyette to appear, but even without him the judge found sufficient evidence to bind Bullock over for trial. This might have satisfied the count, until Bullock's bail was provided by a friend of his, John Chalmers, who happened to be the Secretary of the Treasury. De

Saligny was furious at this apparent official involvement, but did manage to compose his version of the dispute.

He had offered time and again to pay Bullock the amount owed, not the padded bill of $270, "which everyone has termed scandalous . . . but according to that fixed by arbitration, conforming to (his) known prices," which was $123.75.

"As for the complaint of the said Bullock concerning his pigs, here is the truth of it. For a long time I have been tormented, and still am tormented every day, like everybody, from the numerous pigs that infest the city. Every morning one of my servants spends two hours repairing the boards of my fence that these animals break in order to eat my horse's corn; 140 pounds of nails have been used in this way! One day three pigs came even into my bedroom; ate the linen there and destroyed my papers. Another time a dozen of these animals, in order to eat the corn, rushed my stable and trampled one of my servants who was rescued half dead. It was then that following all my neighbors' example, I ordered my people to kill all the pigs that should come into my yard. Did they belong to Mr. Bullock or someone else? I do not know." All that his forbearance brought him was that Bullock "was permitted to vomit, every day, against me, the Representative of France, the grossest insults, the most insulting calumnies."

Before Mayfield could reply, Bullock struck again, laying hands on the count himself. "You will understand, Monsieur," he wrote the Secretary, "that I would not be

ALPHONSE DUBOIS, COMTE DE SALIGNY came to Austin with a chef in his entourage, whose resourcefulness was undoubtedly taxed by the frontier produce. The count's carefully numbered diplomatic dispatches are missing about five reports—presumably the ones eaten by pigs.

THE FRENCH LEGATION, AUSTIN, was at the time of its completion the finest residence
in the capital, but was not proof against stray pigs who explored the bedchambers
and wine cellar.

able to remain any longer with a government [unable] even to protect my life from the
assaults of a scoundrel." He demanded to know what was being done, and Mayfield
replied that the trial was docketed and the law would take its course.

When de Saligny declared that insufficient reparation for France's dignity, Mayfield wrote on April 5, "I have the honor to state that you can obtain your passports
when you choose to demand them."

The Count of Saligny—or as Texans took to calling him, the No-Count of Saligny
—sniffed over his shoulder and left town.

De Saligny presented the French Foreign Ministry with a problem, as he was a
notorious hothead who had been in trouble before. But in this case they sustained him,
reluctantly, and diplomatic relations with Texas were broken off for a time. As the
Foreign Minister later explained to the Texan chargé in Paris, "France can afford to be
wrong on occasion, but she cannot afford to be ridiculous."

In this instance it was de Saligny who had the last laugh. Texas had been vigorously promoting a $5 million bond sale in France, which bankers there refused to touch
unless the French Government guaranteed them. This they agreed to do, until the
Comte de Saligny spoke to the Finance Minister, who was his brother-in-law, and the
bond issue failed.

Annexation

THE most important political question in Texas during the early 1840s was whether to apply for annexation to the United States. It would eventually guarantee security from Mexico and would hasten Texas' internal development as well. Individual Texans treasured nothing more than the great measure of independence they enjoyed, but family ties and cultural heritage were a strong pull toward union. There were hard economic reasons as well, not least of which was that the United States could be expected to assume Texas' national debt, which, thanks to President Lamar's military policies, had ballooned to a hopelessly unmanageable $8 million. American currency in Texas was already more acceptable than their own.

At the time Sam Houston was elected to his first term in September of 1836, a national referendum on the question passed by a lopsided majority. The Revolution had left Texas prostrate as well as victorious at the time Houston wrote his idol Andrew Jackson about annexation. "It is policy to hold out the idea . . . that we are able to sustain ourselves against any power . . . yet I am free to say *to you* that we cannot do it.

"I look to you as the friend and patron of my youth and the benefactor of mankind to interpose on our behalf and save us."

President Jackson, however, had problems of his own. His term was nearly up, and his support was committed to his Vice President, Martin Van Buren of New York, to succeed him. Northerners and abolitionists were hostile toward Texas annexation and Jackson dared not provoke them. Van Buren was not a strong candidate, and supporting Texas could lose the election. Not until Van Buren was safely the winner did he act; as Jackson's last official act, in March of 1837, he recognized the Republic of Texas.

Most Texans were bitter at Jackson's evasion, but bided their time. Their minister at Washington broached the subject again the following summer, but the Van Buren administration refused to touch them. Mexico had vowed war on America if Texas were swallowed up, and moreover, Texas' entry as a slave state would wreck the hard-won balance of slave and free states in the Senate. A resolution of annexation was introduced in that body, but John Quincy Adams killed it in a twenty-two-day filibuster. Jilted, Houston withdrew the offer of annexation in 1838, and the imperial-minded Lamar scarcely mentioned the subject during the three years of his presidency.

The United States, however, had underestimated Texas' hand. The heroism of the Alamo had gained a wide following in Europe, and immigration to the new country was massive. France and Great Britain needed a dependable, heavy supplier of high-grade cotton, and a moneyed customer for their manufactured goods, which a healthy Texas could buy. But more than for trade advantage France and Britain groomed Texas' nationhood as a thorn to stick in the side of the United States. Texas cotton would free them to drive a harder bargain with American traders, thus subverting American tariffs.

Britain, particularly, could use a sphere of influence driven like a wedge into North America midway between British Oregon and the British West Indies, thus thwarting further American expansion. European motives allowed Texas to play the United States and Europe against each other, and Texans loved it.

Jackson's recognition of Texas was his way of passing the annexation problem on to Van Buren, but it left the door open for Europe to follow suit without incurring American displeasure. French recognition came late in 1839. The treaty with Britain, subscribed with a legibly feminine "Victoria R." arrived a year later. (At least one additional British interest in Texas lay in the swelling tide of German immigration. The president of the Adelsverein, the Prince of Leiningen, was Queen Victoria's half brother, and the Prince of Solms-Braunfels was an intimate of her husband, Prince Albert of Saxe-Coburg-Gotha. The Duke of Coburg-Gotha was also a member). Recognition from Belgium, Holland, and various German states then followed in a line.

At the beginning of his second term Houston warmed again to the United States, but was not encouraged. His devotion to the annexation cause never wavered, but as the direct approach had failed, the Talleyrand of the Brazos went, crablike, back to work. He promoted the Franco-Texienne scheme, by which a gigantic French colony would be promoted deep in Texas' interior. He made certain that British and not American diplomats handled the redemption of the Mier prisoners. Then to demonstrate that if Texas had to be a nation she meant to rule every acre of territory she claimed, Houston blessed a filibustering expedition north to the Santa Fe Trail, similar in many respects to the one Lamar organized. Led by former Acting Secretary of War Jacob Snively, the group fought and defeated a Mexican column near the Arkansas River crossing, and hovered about the trail, looking for caravans on which to levy duties. When a force of United States Army dragoons compelled them to surrender and escorted them, considerably disarmed, back where they came from, Houston elevated the dispute to an international incident.

Advocates of American expansion viewed the situation with little less than horror, and Houston's many American admirers were vocal in their denunciation of him. Only later did he explain his strategy:

"Supposing a charming lady has two suitors. One of them she is inclined to believe would make the better husband, but is a little slow to make interesting propositions. Do you think if she was a skillful practitioner in Cupid's court she would pretend that she loved the other 'feller' the best and be sure that her favorite would know it?

"If ladies are justified in making use of coquetry in securing their annexation to good and agreeable husbands, you must excuse me for making use of the same means to annex Texas to Uncle Sam."

Houston's team, his Secretary of State, physician Anson Jones, the chargé d'affaires in Washington, Isaac Van Zandt, and his roving minister in Europe, also a doctor, Ashbel Smith, all played their parts deftly, keeping a calculated distance from American diplomats, encouraging the French and the British.

The ruse, if anything, worked, as Jones summarized that "the attitude of the United States government, toward the Texas question, from 1836 to 1843, was one of weak and blind indifference . . . and from 1844 to 1846, one of ludicrous alarm and haste." Even Andrew Jackson was fooled. Although retired to the Hermitage and in failing health, he was still powerful, and he roused himself long enough to write his connections in Washington that Texas must be acquired, "peaceably if we can, forcibly if we must." Houston sent Jackson a confidential letter explaining that all was well, for which Jackson was at once grateful and lost in admiration for the strategist he had created.

Back in Washington, Van Buren was out and John Tyler, a Virginia slave owner who favored annexation, was in. After some rough negotiating, a treaty of annexation was signed, providing for the United States to assume Texas' debt and take control of her public domain. She would become a territory, and be carved up into smaller states as they qualified for admission. Houston was displeased with most of it, but he endorsed it, warning Jackson: "My venerated friend, you will perceive that Texas is presented . . . as a bride adorned for her espousal. . . . She has been sought by the United States, and this is the third time she has consented. Were she now to be spurned, it would forever terminate expectation on her part, and . . . she would seek some other friend."

The American Senate rejected the treaty in June of 1844, and further diplomatic steps were suspended to give the subject a full airing in the 1844 election. Texas' humiliation was slight, however; the Texas Congress also rejected the treaty, and gave ear to ever more interesting overtures from France and England. They still held the upper hand, and indeed the Houston faction had to take care that Texans not enjoy independence so much that annexation was jeopardized. Anson Jones ran, and won, the presidency in 1844 on a platform so ambiguous it was hard to tell what he favored.

Van Buren tried for renomination, but lost his place on the 1844 ticket to a go-

ED BURLESON, who ousted General Cós from San Antonio, also played a leading part in President Lamar's Indian policy. He was Vice President when he ran against Anson Jones in 1844, but his chief claim to the presidency was that he "had killed more Mexicans and Indians than any other Texan." He lost.

ahead expansionist, James Knox Polk of Tennessee. His election that autumn was a clear sign of the national will, and lame duck President Tyler produced a novel suggestion: Texas could be annexed by a joint resolution of the Congress. It was faster than a treaty, and needed to pass by only a simple majority instead of two thirds. Texas would enter directly as a state, not a territory; she could keep her debt and her public domain —the only state ever given such a concession—and would enter the Union in her present monolithic size, although she might divide later if she chose. The American Congress passed the joint resolution on February 28, 1845, and sent a representative packing to Texas to lay out the welcome mat; the offer was good until the end of the year. Except for the debt question, it was everything Texans wanted.

At this juncture Britain and France played what they believed was their trump card. If there was one thing Mexico hated worse than Texas independent, it was the thought of Texas as an American state. On European advice Mexico agreed to recognize Texas, provided annexation be forever refused. "Houston," wrote Special Minister J. Pinckney Henderson, "has played it off well." Texans could be anything they chose.

President Jones himself wavered at this last offer: peace with Mexico, trade with Europe, eventual repair of relations with America, and above all, independence. But Mexico was historically faithless, trade with Europe could mean domination, and the people were clamoring for statehood. Jones called a session of the Texas Congress for June 16, and a convention for July 4. Congress decided for annexation, and the convention completed a state constitution that was adopted in October.

The documents were hurried to Washington. At the instant they were accepted, December 29, 1845, the Lone Star became the twenty-eighth in the American galaxy.

Governmental authority was transferred on February 16, 1846. At the hewn-log capitol in Austin three days later, President Jones told a gathering that "the final act in this great drama is now performed. The Republic of Texas is no more." He reached out to the flagpole and lowered the Lone Star; Sam Houston stepped forward and took it.

J. P. Henderson was elected Texas' first governor, and Houston and Thomas Jefferson Rusk went to Washington as senators.

The question of annexing Texas was intimately connected with the status of slaves like those in Texas. Admission of Texas as a slave state would upset the balance of free and slave states in the federal Congress. And slavery in Texas had a different complexion than it did in other Southern states. Most owners were not the lords of great plantations, but rather had emigrated from the plantation country of the Deep South because they were the have-nots. Most owned one or a very few slaves, and were themselves often hard-pressed to get by. Moreover, the rough-and-tumble conditions on the frontier and the amount of work attendant to taming a wilderness meant that their slaves had, if possible, an even more arduous existence than those on the large plantations. These factors, and the presence along the western fringe of a slave-owning country of thousands of prosperous German farmers who found slavery repulsive, combined to produce a vague awareness among modest slave owners that the institution was inherently evil. As one astute traveler noted: "We were several times struck, in Eastern Texas, with a peculiarity in the tone of the relation between master and slave. Elsewhere at the South, slavery had seemed to be accepted generally, as a natural, hereditary, established state of things. . . . But in Texas . . . there seemed to be the

TEXAS SLAVES.

consciousness of a wrong relation and a determination to face conscience down, and continue it; to work up the 'damned niggers,' with a sole eye to selfish profit, cash down, in this world. As to 'treasures in Heaven,' their life is a constant sneer at the belief in them."

The slave who as a teenager was Sam Houston's personal attendant, Jeff Hamilton, later said he believed that about one master in four was a really cruel "driver." Such slaveholders were not widely respected; indeed, Houston had bought Hamilton out from under just such a man to show his contempt for him, and tried to reunite the split family by purchasing the boy's mother, but was unable to do so.

Another slave asserted that the harshest masters of all were the free blacks who had been citizens in Spanish Texas. As he said bitterly, "One nigger's no business to sarve another. It's bad enough to have to sarve a white man without being paid for it, without having to sarve a black man. There ain't no nations so bad masters to niggers as them free niggers." At the time of the first federal census in Texas in 1850, there were only 397 free blacks in Texas, which had a total of 7,747 slave owners—not a high percentage to have gained such a wicked reputation.

The Lone Star State

TEXANS had achieved their hearts' desire, but still had a ways to go in their quest for civilization. After a visit to Austin early in 1854, noted traveler and landscape architect Frederick Law Olmsted commented on what he considered one of the more remarkable social eccentricities of the region. At one house, "where everything was extremely neat, and where we had silver cups for drinking, there was no other water-closet than the back of a bush or the broad prairie—an indication of a queerly Texan incompleteness in cultivation of manners.

"From something a German gentleman afterwards told us, it would appear that water-closets are of recent introduction in Texas. He had lived some time in . . . quite a large settlement, before he had time to erect one of those little social necessaries. Though the first to do so, he had no idea that it was a matter of interest to any other person than himself; but no sooner did it appear, than he was assailed for *indecency,* and before he well knew on what account, his edifice was torn down and dragged away by a nocturnal mob. He shortly rebuilt it. It again disappeared on the sly. Nothing daunted, he caused a third to be put up, and as the thing was founded on a real want in human nature, it *took,* and two or three others appeared."

Outhouses were, of course, not the only social improvements on the scene. Dramatical societies and organizations for intellectual improvement began to augment, if not displace, horse races and cockfights. There were even a few bands and orchestras, and every German town had its *Singverein.* Most importantly, religion began to take hold.

During colonial days, when Catholicism was a condition of settlement, Austin's colonies were served by a single, circuit-riding priest, Michael Muldoon. That he was a merry Irishman who partied and winked at bond marriages until he could perform a ceremony, did much to offset the intrinsically odious fact that he was Catholic. The fact was, however, that most Texans practiced no religion but the right to do as they pleased.

Probably the first Protestant sermon in Texas was preached by a Methodist, William Stevenson, in 1817, but it was not until 1834 that a regular minister was appointed to Texas. Three more followed in 1837. Although of a different denomination than Padre Muldoon, they adopted his practical circuit-riding habits. So did Robert Emmett Bledsoe Baylor, who helped organize the Texas Baptist Union Association in 1840 and the Texas Baptist Education Society in 1841, from which sprang Baylor University in 1845. Baylor's circuit riding happily coincided with his duties as judge of the Third Judicial District. The Baptist denomination came more or less to dominate in the contest for converts, and a milestone was reached on November 19, 1854. During one of his leaves from the Senate, Sam Houston shocked the state with his immersion in the "Baptizing Hole" in Rocky Creek, near Independence. Ever since their marriage Margaret had been waging a quiet campaign for his soul; Houston's behavior had undergone astonishing improvement, but piety still escaped him. When a friend later teased him about his sins being washed away, Houston, recalling his drinking and swearing and days with the Cherokees, replied, "I hope so, but if they were *all* washed away, the Lord help the fish down below."

Most Texans shared Houston's pragmatic optimism, about religion, and about their future; Texas was booming. During ten years as a Republic the population quadrupled,

ABNER COOK, who designed many of the prominent structures in Austin, was probably the finest architect in antebellum Texas. His great talent, exemplified in this residence completed about 1855, lay in his ability to adapt the prevalent Greek Revival style to conditions on the frontier. Deep verandas and floor-length windows, usually on the east side, kept homes cool in summer, and substitution of limestone for brick held costs down. Visiting landscape architect Frederick Law Olmsted marveled how in Austin building-quality limestone could be picked off the ground in much of the city and worked "as easily as wood."

The buildings that line Congress Avenue demonstrate the abundance of native limestone. The fine new capitol was built of it also. The columned building on the street
corner at left is Bullock's Hotel, whose owner cost the Republic French recognition
when he "phlabotomized" the nose of the chargé d'affaires in a billing dispute. In
this view, board siding covers the hewn logs that formed the exterior at the time of
the Pig War.

and by the time of the first federal census in 1850 had increased to 212,000. Ten years
later, at the next census, there were over 600,000. Nearly all of them were rural, but the
cities did well during the decade. Austin, which had only 600 residents in 1850, ballooned to 3,500 ten years later. In 1850 the largest city was Galveston, with 4,100
people; in 1860 its 7,300 were eclipsed by San Antonio's 8,200. Houston held 4,800,
double the 1850 figure. The southern port of Brownsville had nearly 3,000, and Dallas,
a northern plains village in 1850, now had 2,000. Marshall, the largest of many northeast Texas commercial centers, had 4,000; mostly German New Braunfels had 3,500. In
each place shops, mills, and forges could hardly keep pace with the growth. In New
Braunfels alone there were twenty carpenters, seven wagonmakers, eight blacksmiths,
and a smattering of butchers, bakers, tailors, cobblers, and even a button maker.

Some towns, of course, suffered for want of forecast. Civic leaders in the former
national capitol of Washington-on-the-Brazos spurned interests who sought rail connections for the city, favoring instead two new river steamers, the *Washington* and the
Brazos. They guessed wrong, and the town withered. Railroads were the coming thing.
General Sidney Sherman, hero of the Revolution, turned entrepreneur and in 1851
began laying tracks for the Buffalo Bayou, Brazos and Colorado Railroad, the first in
Texas. By 1860, several companies operated more than four hundred miles of line, all of
it linking cotton centers of the Gulf Plains to shipping ports.

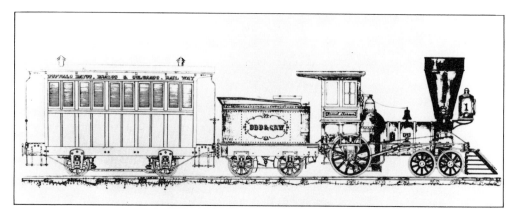

The first working railroad in Texas was pulled by this locomotive,
named for its owner the GENERAL SHERMAN.

HENRY KINNEY. Not all the business ventures in antebellum Texas were success stories. Indeed, some development occurred as the serendipitous fallout of visionaries whose reach forever exceeded their grasp.

Henry Kinney of Pennsylvania was twenty-four when he came to Texas in 1838. Settling in Brownsville, he began ranching and then wheeling and dealing in land ventures on a grand scale—with other men's capital, mostly, and realizing little profit. Kinney served as a senator in the last Congress of the Republic and the first four sessions of the legislature; after the Mexican War he sought a new fortune in seagoing trade.

In 1852 he lavished resources on a fair and exposition to promote the town of Corpus Christi he had founded—his only permanent legacy.

Two years later he went filibustering to Nicaragua, envisioning himself as the beneficent ruler of an experimental state on the Mosquito Coast. Failure there was dismal; his New York financiers either died or withdrew, and his followers deserted him for a rival filibuster. He returned to Texas and won a seat in the Eighth Legislature, from which this photograph dates. Unwilling to stomach secession, he resigned in March of 1861 and retired to obscurity and a violent end in Matamoros.

King Cotton

THE fuel that fired Texas' economy was, first and always, cotton. The first export, 300 pounds in small bales, was forded on muleback across the Rio Grande. Edwin Waller was shipping it to Matamoros on his schooner by 1831, and in 1833 Stephen Austin reported thirty gins in operation in two areas alone. The total crop that year was 7,500 of the standardized 500-pound bales.

Texas cotton was of a finer grade than that grown elsewhere in the South, and commanded higher prices in Liverpool and other European exchanges. After independence Britain and France encouraged the industry; in 1844, the year before annexation, the value of cotton exported through customs houses was some $580,000, by far the most valuable commodity of the cash-poor Republic.

COTTON GIN.

Business was bigger and grew even faster during statehood. The 1848 crop of nearly 40,000 bales grew to 62,000 bales four years later. Of the 1854 crop of 110,000 bales, 84,000 were shipped overseas from Galveston alone. In 1860 Texas produced over 420,000 quarter-ton bales of cotton.

Even of that monstrous sum, most of it was produced by small landowners who held only four or five slaves; great plantations were an exception. Average income for a modest planter was perhaps $3,000 a year, earned at 9¢ a pound on cotton that would have cost 5¢ a pound to grow. By far his largest investment was his slaves; a prime field hand might cost between $800 and $1,000, which, said one owner, "was a great deal of money to be laid out in a thing that might lie right down the next day and die." He would also buy three or four women ("half-hands") and hope for an increase.

An investment almost as risky was selecting the land: "It is difficult to fix an

COTTON YARD. This gin and cotton yard near Austin give only a small idea of the vastness of the Texas cotton industry, but the brunt of the labor still fell on black field hands like those shown in the stereograph on page 137.

average price. . . . Where land can yet be bought at $2.50 per acre, it is probable that the freight and charges on cotton hauled to the coast would destroy all profit. To be within profitable reach of market, the planter must pay $5 to $10 per acre for a suitable tract of 1,000 acres." Ten thousand dollars was usually enough to get a small plantation going, and with the bottomlands producing as much as 2,000 pounds per acre, total failures were uncommon.

Some landowners in the plantation country also experimented with such exotic crops as silk and indigo, but only rice and, more importantly, sugar, caught on. Most of the sugar crop went into production of molasses, of which more than 400,000 gallons were barreled in 1850, along with 3,500 tons of sugar. This industry centered in Brazoria County, where General Sherman's Buffalo Bayou, Brazos and Colorado became known as the Sugar Railroad.

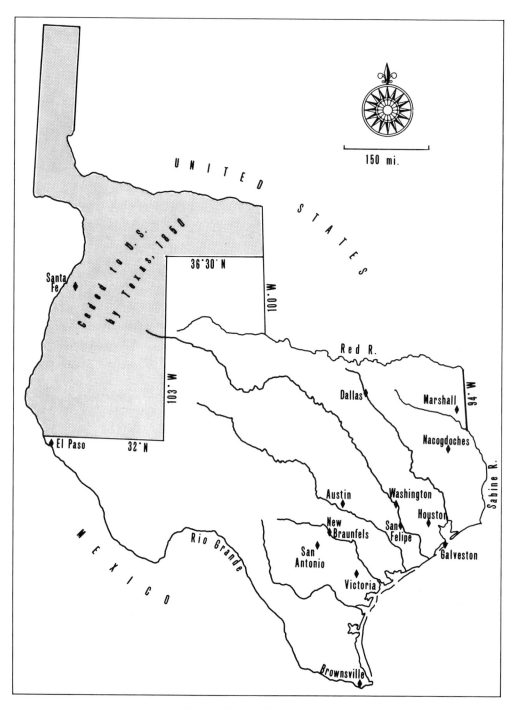

UNITED STATES

Ceded to U.S. by Texas, 1850

Santa Fe

36°30' N

100° W.

Red R.

103° W

Dallas

Marshall

94° W

Nacogdoches

Sabine R.

El Paso

32° N

MEXICO

Rio Grande

Austin

Washington

Houston

New Braunfels

San Felipe

San Antonio

Galveston

Victoria

Brownsville

150 mi.

TEXAS STATE BOUNDARY
FIXED BY COMPROMISE OF 1850

Sectionalism

ONE thing the cotton economy depended upon was slaves, an issue that daily reminded Texans, in spite of the good economic times, that as a mere state they could no longer do as they pleased in matters of international policy. The United States had outlawed further importation of slaves into the country, which led in Texas to a chronic labor shortage, illegal landing of slave traders at remote points on the coast, and even a few cases of kidnapping black West Indian seamen from aboard British vessels in Galveston. (This last problem led to a considerable diplomatic row, but not so loud that Britain would endanger her cotton supply.) Texas' admission also threw an unworkable wrench into the Missouri Compromise. It happened this way.

At annexation, as northerners feared but Texans could hardly wait, Mexico tried to reassert sovereignty over at least that part of Texas south of the Nueces River, which had been for a time a Mexican state boundary. It was not much of a claim—as much could be said of most rivers in Mexico—and it was intended as a first step in the reconquest of Texas. But when Mexican troops crossed the Rio Grande in May of 1846 and, as President Polk put it, "shed American blood upon American soil," the Mexican War was on. Some eight thousand of the sixty-nine thousand American troops were Texans, including Rangers who did invaluable scouting for Zachary Taylor's army. They fought splendidly, but their treatment of captured towns and people was often needlessly harsh. The result of the war was a humiliating defeat for Mexico. Santa Anna was returned from banishment to lead the fight, but he was beaten everywhere and as at San Jacinto, fled the field of the last battle, for Mexico City itself. Mexico lost over a third of her territory by the Treaty of Guadalupe Hidalgo—California and New Mexico. Texas was admitted in 1845, however, with no mention of relinquishing her claims to New Mexico east of the Rio Grande.

The working mode of the American slave-or-free question extended back to the Missouri Compromise of 1820, when, to preserve the balance of slave and free states in the Senate, Missouri was admitted slave, Maine free, and a boundary drawn indefinitely westward along the 36°30' parallel. New states admitted above it were to be free, new states below it, slave. Texas spilled far above that line. General Taylor, now President, tried to have New Mexico organized as a free territory. Texan commissioners did manage to organize El Paso as a Texas county, but were thrown out by the American Army when they ventured north of there. Texans were livid.

A solution seemed at hand in the omnibus Compromise of 1850, which provided in part that Texas could keep El Paso but give up her claim to eastern New Mexico in exchange for $10 million. The northern boundary was marked at 36°30', the old Missouri Compromise line, and Texans were satisfied to have their public debt retired, with enough left over to invest $2 million in a permanent school fund.

The rest of the South, however, was not satisfied with the rest of the 1850 Compromise. Their hand strengthened by the election of a weak President, Franklin Pierce, and the placement of Jefferson Davis of Mississippi in his Cabinet, Southerners openly threatened to pull out of the Union if the right to slavery were not extended. They won it, in the Kansas-Nebraska Bill of 1854, by which the Missouri Compromise was repealed and new territories given the right to decide on slavery for themselves. The South was confident that they could flood border areas with slave owners, win slavery referendums, and gain a Senate majority.

Sam Houston was virtually alone among Southern senators in seeing the measure as shortsighted, vicious, and incendiary. He was right, of course, but when he voted against it the entire South vilified him as a traitor and blackguard; his popularity in Texas plummeted to nearly nothing.

SAM HOUSTON AS UNITED STATES SENATOR. The lifelike realism of this painting derives from its being a copy of a photograph taken in New York in 1856. This picture in turn served as the model for the famous portrait that hangs in the Texas House of Representatives.

The Cattle Empire

WEST of the soggy rice and cane fields and the endless rows of cotton, conditions were too dry for profitable agriculture. The brush country was ideal, however, for stock raising, and here developed Texas' second great empire.

After independence many Mexican landowners, fearing to share in the retribution of San Jacinto, either joined march with General Filisola on his way out of the country or followed soon after. Most abandoned their herds of "range cattle" as the price of losing the war, and thought ahead to starting a new life beyond the Rio Grande. The cattle were raw-boned, leggy, foul-tempered descendents of the stock that accompanied the earliest Spanish explorers. (Oñate alone had brought seven thousand in 1598.) They turned feral, and by the time Texas entered the Union, about a third of a million wild longhorns roamed loose on the range, considered as a resource belonging to whomever claimed them. As one observer wrote: "Texas is, perhaps, one of the finest portions of the world for raising cattle. . . . Provided for in the rich pastures of nature, [they] grow enormously large; and thousands of them are raised almost entirely without expense. And yet, so well are they situated for commerce, that their market is fine, and beef brings a good price. Hence, some are making fortunes in this way, who could do, perhaps but little in any other. A man who is weak handed, can, nevertheless, raise stock."

A few ranchers drove some herds east to market in New Orleans, but most were content to capitalize just on the tallow and hides. Most table beef was consumed locally, in the growing cities, where prices were high enough to make stock raising profitable, but where it was still one of the cheapest staples on the menu. In town, beef brought 3¢ to 4¢ per pound, about half the price of pork and far below cured bacon or ham at 20¢ per pound. (Eggs, by contrast, were 25¢ a dozen, "inferior" apples 75¢ a dozen, and sugar 19¢ a pound. Milled flour was still expensive, $15 a barrel, and bread from a good German bakery 8¢ a pound. Only corn and sweet potatoes, at 50¢ a bushel, were cheaper than beef.)

Most stockmen in this era were small operators, but the great ranching dynasties also had their beginnings here. One of the greatest was born in Florida, at the chance meeting of two yankee steamer captains en route to the Mexican War. Mifflin Kenedy was twenty-eight, from Chester County, Pennsylvania; he had gone to sea at sixteen and been as far as Calcutta. New Yorker Richard King was twenty-two, a cabin boy from the age of ten, with most of his experience as a river pilot in Alabama. They did good service on the Rio Grande and stayed in Texas after the war, forming a riverboating partnership in 1850. Kenedy was also engaged in trading with the Mexican interior and ranching sheep and cattle. In 1852 King bought the sprawling, seventy-five-thousand-acre Santa Gertrudis, an old Spanish land grant, and later sold half to Kenedy. At its height the legendary King Ranch covered some 1.25 million acres. Kenedy later organized his part into what became the Texas Land and Cattle Company, a concern almost as magnificent. King and Kenedy remained partners in various business ventures until 1875.

RICHARD KING.

The Cortinas Wars

JUAN NEPOMUCENO CORTINAS.

IT was impossible for Mexican-Texans pushed across the Rio Grande not to view the prosperity of Anglo ranchers like King and Kenedy with resentment. Especially after the humiliation of the Mexican-American War, cattle-rustling raids from south of the border became more numerous and better organized. Juan Nepomuceno Cortinas was the most celebrated operator.

The uneducated son of a ranchero, at the time he began his career "Cheno" Cortinas' only claim to substance were the estates of his mother, the heiress of sprawling Spanish land grants around Brownsville, on the Texas side of the river. At the outbreak of the war Cortinas fought under Mariano Arista at Palo Alto, but his popular reputation stemmed more directly from an incident in 1847. Then, the story had it, Cortinas murdered the owner of a string of mules who had hired him as a driver, and sold the animals to the United States Army. Such double-dealing machismo appealed to the downtrodden rancheros of the valley, and gained him a large camp of hangers-on whom he sheltered at his mother's Santa Rita estate a few miles north of Brownsville. With the American Army having abandoned Fort Brown after the war, Cortinas established a kind of local barony over the next ten years, stealing stock from Anglo ranchers and selling them across the river.

Cortinas was indicted for his operation, but he never went to trial and was not in awe of the law. In mid-July of 1859 the marshal in Brownsville took into arrest for drunkenness, and mistreated, a former Cortinas employee, and Cortinas, after being insulted by the officer, shot him in the shoulder and claimed his man.

Perhaps startled by his own audacity, Cortinas and his following scattered from Santa Rita and reassembled safely in Matamoros. They stayed there two and a half months, nursing their grievances; then on September 28 Cortinas and about sixty followers stormed into Brownsville, shot the jailer and three other men, emptied the jail and set up a headquarters at Fort Brown. The Cortinas Wars were on.

Cooler heads in Matamoros prevailed on him to withdraw from the city back up to Santa Rita, where he issued a proclamation declaring himself protector of Mexicans in Texas and vowing destruction to Anglos who opposed him. He and his army then returned to Mexico. Anglos in Brownsville were ashamed for their city of two thousand having been caught off guard and held in terror, and for having to apply to the Mexican Government for aid. The citizens organized into posses, and early in October they caught and jailed one of Cortinas' lieutenants, Tomás Cabrera. Cortinas demanded his release on pain of burning Brownsville to the ground; when the town defied him, Cortinas reoccupied Santa Rita and made plans. Before he could attack, he was himself assaulted on October 22 by the Matamoros militia and about forty Mexican Texans who united with twenty Anglos who organized themselves as the "Brownsville Tigers." The attack was not vigorously prosecuted, and Cortinas' men easily chased them back into Brownsville on October 24, capturing two small cannons in the process.

Defeat of the Brownsville Tigers left Cortinas master of the countryside. He intercepted and read all mail into and out of Brownsville, shanghaied recruits for his growing army, and sent out squads to rake in "contributions" from those he was protecting. On November 10 a company of Texas Rangers arrived to restore order. Cortinas' reply was a second declaration, naming himself leader of a movement for social justice. Tomás Cabrera was lynched and the Rangers attacked Santa Rita on November 24; after Cortinas defeated them, the Mexican tricolor was hoisted over Santa Rita, and arms and sympathizers began to show up from the interior.

By now, however, the American Government had had enough. Fort Brown was reoccupied, and on December 14 a force of 285 men under Major S. P. Heintzelman—120 of them Rangers under Captain John Salmon (Rip) Ford—moved against Santa Rita. Cortinas and his 350 retreated continually, not engaging until two days after Christmas, at Rio Grande City. In the fight Cortinas was badly whipped, losing sixty men to Heintzelman's none.

Cortinas vanished for a few weeks, but materialized at La Bolsa on February 4, 1860, intending to capture King and Kenedy's river steamer *Ranchero*. As the boat hove into view, Rip Ford's Rangers splashed across the stream and scattered them again. Soon after this one of the American Army's most capable officers arrived in Texas to settle things once and for all. Colonel Robert E. Lee had orders to demand that Mexico collar Cortinas, and if they failed, to enter Mexico and take him. Threatened with reinvasion, Mexico complied and the Cortinas Wars passed, but their heart was not in it. Later the Mexican Government made Brigadier General Cortinas governor of Tamaulipas, an excellent position from which he pestered Texas ranchers for years.

Cheno Cortinas still excites controversy in the discussion of whether he was an outlaw bully or a champion of social justice. Before and after Cortinas, Mexicans in the Rio Grande Valley were subjected to humiliating and often violent discrimination. At best, however, Cortinas illustrated how much plunder a clever man can accumulate by playing his causes right: of the 245 men who were killed in the war, only 15 were Anglos; 80 were anti-Cortinas Mexicans who did not care for his brand of protection.

Two Ways to Control Indians

THE pressure of westering settlement, which brought closer contact between white pioneers and "Brazos" Indians—a generic term that included a number of small central Texas tribes—prompted the legislature to consider establishing a reservation for them. The moving force was Texas' Indian superintendent, Major Robert S. Neighbors, who selected a four-league (18,576-acre) site on the upper Brazos River, twelve miles south of Fort Belknap, and practically on the boundary between settled ranch land and untamed Comanche domain to the northwest. The area was soon doubled to include bands of Penateka Comanches—the same tribe that made its peace with Meusebach's Germans in 1847—who wished to come in.

By the end of 1854 the Brazos Reserve was a going concern with some two thousand Indian inhabitants. The Comanches were difficult to control, owing largely to the proximity of uncontrolled territory, the influence of wilder Comanche bands, and the ease with which young Penateka warriors could resume the old life. The Brazos Indians, however, regularly rationed and supplied by the federal government at a cost of eighty thousand dollars a year, made, for the most part, model citizens. They planted about six hundred acres in grain and vegetables; Brazos Indian warriors were eager to enlist as scouts against their traditional enemies, the Comanches (except, of course, the next-door Penatekas). The quiet respect that the Indians earned from neighboring ranchers was not enough to offset the storm of racist outrage that issued from frontier towns and newspapers.

Those who hated the idea of subsisting Indians with government money blamed virtually every unsolved crime on the reservation Indians, and whipped up such a storm of insistence on their extermination or removal that even Sam Houston joined the governor in petitioning the federal government to transport them, for their own protection, to the Indian Territory.

The day after Christmas, 1858, Brazos Indians on a pass to go hunting in Palo Pinto County were ambushed by a group of whites; eight were killed as they slept before the rest escaped. Governor Runnels ordered a hundred Rangers to the area under his best officer, Rip Ford, and issued a warning to citizens to leave the Indians alone. The identities of the bushwhackers were learned, but a grand jury refused to indict them.

Principal among the Texas Indian haters was John Robert Baylor, who had fought Comanches at eighteen in 1840 as a ranger and been elected to the state legislature at thirty-one. When Neighbors became superintendent, he had hired Baylor as agent to the Comanches, but soon fired him for his harshness and insensitive bullying of his charges.

In late May, 1859, Baylor materialized at the Brazos Reservation, followed by a ragtag gaggle of frontier ruffians. He demanded the persons of certain Indians he accused of depredations, and declared that if the federal troops at the agency fired on him he would shoot back. When the Army called his bluff and prepared to fight, the Baylor mob hustled off to a safe distance, scalping an old Indian man as they left the reservation and killing a woman as she tended her garden. Warriors from the Brazos tribes swarmed like hornets in pursuit and overhauled the Baylor party at a nearby ranch where they had stopped to eat. The troops, too, clattered out, but as they had no authority outside the reserve—a special agreement with Texas, the only state that owned its public lands—they merely observed the Indian attack. One Indian chief and two of Baylor's men were killed, and others wounded, before the battle subsided.

Seeing no peaceful future for the Brazos Indians in Texas, Neighbors hastily rounded up them and the reservation Penatekas for a long march north to the Wichita Agency in the central Indian Territory. Neighbors, as was his custom, traveled with them, his escort protecting them en route from other mobs like Baylor's. He delivered them safely to the Wichita Agency on September 1.

Back at Fort Belknap only two weeks later, Superintendent Neighbors was gunned down by a local settler incensed by his Indian policy. The Comanches against whom the Brazos Indians had scouted soon found the refugees huddled at the Wichita Agency, and swooped down in vengeance. The few surviving Texas Indians became more or less assimilated with the Wichitas who took them in.

The Neighbors assassination and the persecution of the Brazos Valley Indians rival the Cherokee removal as the moral nadir of Texas-Indian history.

MAJOR AND MRS. R. S. NEIGHBORS. Robert Simpson Neighbors was twenty when he came to Texas in 1836. During the years of the Republic he served as acting quartermaster of the army before joining Captain Jack Hays' Ranger company. At the second Mexican invasion of 1842, Neighbors was one of the Anglos captured in San Antonio and marched off to a dungeon in Mexico, not released until spring of 1844. His career as an Indian agent began early in 1845, as the country's representative to the Tonkawa and Lipan Apache tribes. After annexation his duties were expanded to include Comanches as well. The federal government confirmed his position with an appointment as U. S. Indian agent in spring of 1847, but the job was one of political patronage which he lost with the election of a Whig President in 1848. Neighbors was then elected to the state legislature, where he sponsored a law enabling the creation of Texas Indian reservations. He was recommissioned superintendent of Texas agents after the election of Franklin Pierce in 1852.

Neighbors' success in dealing with native inhabitants lay in his willingness to spend much time traveling among them in their own domain. It was a gesture of trust and respect to which the Indians responded with a loyalty unprecedented in Texan-Indian relations.

CYNTHIA ANN PARKER. The wilder Comanches of bands other than the Penatekas, bands such as the Nokonis (Wanderers) and Quahadis (Antelope Eaters) provided a more justified target for Texan wrath. Neither Army nor Rangers nor citizen posses were able to stop their forays into the ranch country for plunder and "coups"—war glory that elevated a warrior's social standing. Occasionally, however, a significant victory was won. RANGER CAPTAIN SUL ROSS attacked a large Comanche village at the head of the Pease River in 1860. It was a rout in which many Indians were killed and a female white captive retaken. She proved to be Cynthia Ann Parker, captured at the age of nine in the bloody Parker's Fort raid of 1836. She had been taken to wife by the chief of the Nokoni band, Pe-ta Nokoni and had borne him three children. Shortly after her "rescue" —watchful relatives prevented her escape back to the Comanches—her portrait was taken by a daguerreotypist in Fort Worth. Her hair is cut short in the belief that Pe-ta had been killed, she is shown here nursing her daughter, Prairie Flower.

Cynthia Ann Parker is remembered mostly for her second child, a boy named Quanah ("Fragrance"). He later switched his affiliation from the Nokoni to the Quahadi band and became the last of the great Comanche chiefs. Prairie Flower died within a couple of years, followed by her unhappy mother, who had never reconciled herself to becoming white again.

Secession

THE SEVEN WHO VOTED AGAINST SECESSION *(Top row, left to right)* A. P. Shuford, James W. Throckmorton, Lemuel H. Williams, Joshua Johnson. *(Bottom row, left to right)* William H. Johnson, George W. Wright, and Thomas P. Hughes.

CORTINAS' cattle rustling during the 1850s fueled a scheme on which Senator Houston expended much time and energy—the forcing of an American (principally Texan) protectorate over Mexico. Enumerating twenty-five coups, revolutions, and uprisings there in the previous twenty-eight years, Houston argued to the Senate that the southern border would never be peaceful until order was imposed by a more enlightened people. The Congress, however, ignored him. Indeed, Houston's influence in the Senate had been declining ever since his Kansas-Nebraska vote. He felt it was time for a change himself, and without resigning his seat he returned home and ran for governor in 1857.

The state Democratic organization had disowned him, so he ran as an independent, but in unspoken affiliation with the Know-Nothings, a short-lived political animal of antiforeign and anti-Catholic leanings. Traveling by buggy during the heat of summer, which not coincidentally gave him a chance to appear bare-chested and expose his old war wounds to public view, Houston delivered two- and three-hour harangues in forty-three towns in two months. But it was an ill-starred campaign. States' righters finally had a chance to scald him for his Kansas-Nebraska treason, and the Know-Nothing affiliation alienated Mexican Catholics and German immigrants; Houston was, as he admitted, "skinned" by a majority of four thousand. It was the only election he ever lost, and the state Democratic Party punished his heresies by naming a replacement for his Senate seat, which became vacant in March of 1859.

With nothing now to lose, Houston announced for governor again in that year, but waged a completely dissimilar campaign. He made only one speech, at Nacogdoches on July 9. Again he explained his stand on the Kansas-Nebraska Bill, concluding, "If I was wrong, I own it . . . if you were wrong, I forgive you." Against the charge that he had deserted the Democratic Party, Houston insisted that he had stuck to his principles, that it was the party that had moved. He spoke against blind political affiliation and especially party platforms, which he said clever politicians "contrived to gull the people, secure party success," and cloud the real issues. Later in the speech part of the staging behind him gave way and collapsed. As dignitaries picked themselves out of the crashed lumber Houston wagged triumphantly, "There! Did I not tell you platforms were dangerous?"

The coalition of enemies that toppled him from the Senate, led by former presidents Burnet, Lamar, and Jones, scorched against the "bloated mass of iniquity," but this time Houston carried the day, trouncing the same man who had beaten him two years before, by more than double the margin.

As governor, Houston spent ever less time on his protectorate over Mexico and more time trying to head off the breakup of the Union. His stand on the Kansas-Nebraska issue had made him something of a hero in the North, and formidable political forces began promoting him as a presidential candidate in 1860. Sectional sentiment had gone too far, however, and the Democratic Party preferred to split in two rather than compromise on a moderate candidate. On the first ballot of the Constitutional Union Party's convention, Houston was only one half vote behind John Bell, who was short of a majority. Had Houston made a fight of it, he could have won, but old whispers about his morals and his drinking caused him to remove himself from contention. There was considerable justification for the widespread feeling that, had Houston gotten a nomination, he and not Abraham Lincoln would have been elected. He therefore confined his pro-Union speaking to Texas, addressing a Unionist rally in Austin on September 22: "—I come not here to speak on behalf of a united South against Lincoln, I appeal to the nation. . . . The Union is worth more than Mr. Lincoln, and if the battle is to be fought for the Constitution, let us fight it in the Union and for the sake of the Union."

In Huntsville a few weeks later he clarified his stand on the usurpation of state rights, with a reference to his own career:

"I need not assure you that whenever the time shall come, when we must choose between a loss of our Constitutional rights and revolution, I shall choose the latter.

"[But] if the Union be dissolved now, will we have additional security for slavery? . . . Our Treasury is nearly empty. We have near half a million dollars in the Treasury of the United States. A million of our school fund is invested in U. S. Bonds. . . . Are we justified in sacrificing these when they are yet protected and secured?"

The battle, however, was a losing one. Lincoln was elected without even appearing on Southern ballots, and when Texas secessionists brought pressure to bear on the governor to call a special session of the legislature to declare Texas out of the Union, Houston fended them off with the excuse that there was not enough money to pay the per diems. He asked the state supreme court to obviate the issue by declaring secession unconstitutional. The court refused, and the chief justice, Oran M. Roberts, made his own feelings known with an unofficial call for a secession convention to meet, whether Houston wanted it or not. The idea took, and delegates were chosen in local elections, to meet in Austin on January 28.

Still maneuvering, Houston relented and called the special session of the legislature for January 21, but that body when it met bestowed legal status on the upcoming convention, thus blessing Texas' withdrawal from the United States, only fifteen years after she entered.

Sam Houston: A Last Look

SAM HOUSTON IN 1863. One of the last, possibly the last, photograph taken of him, an engraving made from it was used to promote town lots in the city of Houston.

AFTER passing the secession ordinance on February 1, the convention announced a popular referendum for February 23. Their authorized work was completed, but before adjourning on the fifth the members bounded far beyond their power, electing delegates to the Confederate Government that was organizing in Montgomery, Alabama. They also created the Committee of Public Safety that was not only given broad powers to defend the state, but authorized to keep its business secret.

Houston utilized the three weeks before the referendum to campaign against splitting the Union, arguing with the passion of a proud old man about to see his life's work undone. But he was too experienced a politician to mistake the popular sentiment; audiences were so hostile to his message that at times his entourage would beg him not to risk his life by appearing. From the balcony of a Galveston mansion, less than a week before the voting, Houston surveyed the angriest crowd of all, and only after several minutes did he glare them into enough quiet to make himself heard. Then he intoned prophetically: "Some of you laugh to scorn the idea of bloodshed as the result of secession. But let me tell you what is coming. Your fathers and husbands, your sons and brothers, will be herded at the point of the bayonet. You may, after the sacrifice of countless millions of treasure and hundreds of thousands of lives, as a bare possibility, win Southern independence . . . but I doubt it. I tell you that, while I believe with you in the doctrine of state rights, the North is determined to preserve this Union. They are not a fiery, impulsive people as you are, for they live in colder climates. But when they begin to move in a given direction, they move with the steady momentum and perseverance of a mighty avalanche. . . . They will overwhelm the South."

Just like the mutinous volunteer army in 1836 that grumbled against Houston while bragging that one Texan could whip ten Mexicans, the 44,317 people who voted to secede were as naïve as they were cocky. Only 13,020 voted with Houston. The convention reassembled on March 2 to canvass the vote, and on the fourth, as Abraham Lincoln delivered his inaugural address, Houston published the declaration of secession. The next day the convention extended its power again by voting to join the Confederate States, one act that Houston finally declared illegal. Texas, he felt, would do better to fend for herself again as an independent nation, but in any event, such a step was the prerogative of the regular legislature, due to convene on the eighteenth, not for an ad hoc rump packed with secessionists. The convention responded by passing a requirement aimed directly at the governor, that all state officers take an oath of

THE GOVERNOR'S MANSION as it appeared in the 1860s. Like the house on page 134, it was the work of architect Abner Cook.

allegiance to the Confederacy. Two days were set aside to hear the public confessions of devotion, after which any remaining Unionists would be removed from office. Houston failed to appear on March 15, and that evening a delegate called on him, conveying a directive to appear before the convention at twelve o'clock noon the next day to take the oath.

That night Houston retired upstairs early, leaving strict orders not to be disturbed by anyone for anything. All night he paced the second-floor hall of the Governor's Mansion in his stockinged feet, stopping only to pray, or write a thought; in the morning he came down and told his wife, "Margaret, I will never do it."

Later in the morning he crossed over to the capitol with his speech and his whittling knife. W. M. Baker, a Presbyterian minister, witnessed what followed, that as "the old governor [sat] in his chair in the basement of the capitol . . . the gathering upstairs summoned the old man . . . to come forward and take the oath of the Confederacy. I remember as yesterday the call thrice repeated—'Sam Houston! Sam Houston! Sam Houston!' but the man sat silent, immovable . . . whittling steadily on."

After the issue was decided, Houston walked up the stairs and addressed the convention. He had just turned sixty-eight years old; he was nearly bald on top of his head, but still had a generous shock of white around the sides. His face, now clean shaven, revealed a mouth that had wrinkled and turned distinctly down at the corners. But he was still six feet four inches tall.

"My worst anticipations as to the assumption of power by this Convention have been realized.

"It has elected delegates to the Provisional Council of the Confederate States . . . annexed Texas to the Confederate States and Constituted themselves members of Congress.

"It has appointed military officers and agents under its assumed authority. It has declared by ordinance, that the people . . . ratify the Constitution . . . of the Confederate States. . . . It has changed the State Constitution and established a 'test oath' of allegiance to the Confederate States.

"Fellow-Citizens, in the name of your rights and liberties, which I believe have been trampled upon, I refuse to take this oath.—

"[But] I love Texas too well to bring civil strife and bloodshed upon her. To avert this calamity, I shall make no endeavor to maintain my authority as Chief Executive of this State, except by the peaceful exercise of my functions. When I can no longer do this, I shall calmly withdraw from the scene, leaving the Government in the hands of those who have usurped its authority; but still claiming that I am its Chief Executive.—

"It is perhaps but meet that my career should close thus. I have seen the patriots and statesmen of my youth, one by one, gathered to their fathers, and the Government which they had created, rent in twain. . . . I stand the last almost of a race. . . . I am stricken down now, because I will not yield those principles, which I have fought for. . . . The severest pang is that the blow comes in the name of the State of Texas."

The regular legislature convened on the eighteenth and declared the office of governor vacant. The Houstons were ordered out of the Governor's Mansion, but before leaving, the governor received a visit from Noah Smithwick. "I went to see General Houston and had a long talk. 'General,' said I, 'if you will again unfurl the Lone Star from the capitol, I will bring you 100 men to help maintain it there.'

BEN MCCULLOCH, a Tennesseean, planned to come to Texas in Davy Crockett's entourage, but did not settle his affairs in time to join him at the Alamo. McCulloch did open the Battle of San Jacinto as gunner of one of the Twin Sisters, the beginning of a long career as Republic congressman, state legislator, Ranger, and Indian fighter. He enjoyed a close relation- ship with Sam Houston until they split over the secession issue. After seizing the federal arsenal in San Antonio, McCulloch was commissioned a Confederate brigadier, assigned to defend Texas' northern frontier and the Indian Territory. He won the Battle of Oak Hills before losing his life in the Battle of Elk Horn on March 7, 1862.

" 'My friend,' said he, 'I have seen Texas pass through one long, bloody war. I do not wish to involve her in civil strife. I have done all I could to keep her from seceding, and now if she won't go with me I'll have to turn and go with her.' "

Smithwick's appeal to Houston was his last hope to stay in Texas. Like many ardent Unionists, he was driven from his locality by secessionist neighbors, forced to abandon without compensation the sawmill he had come to own. When Houston declined to resist, Smithwick sold him his remaining property—a slave—for about half his value, and moved to California. (After the war he eventually settled, to his undoubted irritation, in the town of Santa Anna, California, where he lived until October of 1899.) The move was wise, though. During the course of the war several dozen suspected Union sympathizers were lynched by local committees of "Public Safety." At least forty were strung up at the "Great Hanging" in Gainesville.

Houston received a similar, though more substantial, offer of aid, from President Lincoln: enough troops to sustain Houston in office if he would keep Texas in the Union. Houston was tempted, even though his friend-turned-antagonist Ben McCulloch had already seized the American military headquarters in San Antonio. For one of the few times in his career Houston consulted friends on what to do; only one believed that Houston should accept Lincoln's offer, and Houston reluctantly destroyed the message. If he were ten years younger, he said, he would make a fight of it.

The ousted governor took his family, which now included eight children, into a retirement that was not lavish. To settle his debts he sold most of the parcels of property he owned, including Woodland, the home in Huntsville that he had designed himself and loved dearly. They moved to the summer place at Cedar Point, on the north shore of Galveston Bay, and made ends meet by shipping firewood down to Galveston. He occupied himself with visits to friends, and growling complaints about zealous provost marshals who kept an eye on him for some hint of Unionist activity. They found none. "The time has come," he said in one of his increasingly rare speeches, "when a man's section is his country. I stand by mine . . . and await the issue." He also continued to scheme in the last great preoccupation of his life, the plan to extend a Texan protectorate over ever-anarchic Mexico.

Practicality brought him back to his senses, however. In the autumn of 1862 Galveston fell to a Union task force and the Houstons, with their income shut off, returned to Huntsville. He tried but failed to repurchase Woodland, and so rented the unorthodox "Steamboat House" of Dr. Rufus Bailey, president of Austin College. Houston was frequently ill and his unhealed war wounds gave him much pain. In June of 1863 he journeyed to Sour Lake, north of Beaumont, to soak in the mineral muds. It was clear when he returned that the end was near; he took a cold that turned into pneumonia. The night of July 25 he slept fitfully; his teenage slave, Jeff, fanned the flies away all night, hearing the old man murmur repeatedly, "Oh, my country!" He died at six o'clock the next evening.

Most people in the North did not learn of his death until after the war.

WOODLAND. Sam Houston kept no secret of the fact that he considered his Huntsville residence "a bang-up place." On summer afternoons he would nap on the second-story breezeway, a cooling feature of his own design. First occupied in 1848, Houston reveled in "my woodland residence, with my wife and brats . . . farming in a small way and busy as a 'bee in a tar barrel.' [Here] I feel no disposition to return to scenes of official conflict."

Texas in the Civil War

GENERAL DAVID E. TWIGGS.

SOUTH Carolina had seceded from the Union on December 20, 1860. Hostilities did not commence until the following April 12, but the war momentum in Texas was unstoppable. The Secession Convention's Committee of Public Safety, a full week before the referendum to approve withdrawal from the Union, rode under arms to San Antonio, headquarters of the U.S. Army in Texas. At their head was ex-Ranger Ben McCulloch, confronting Major General David E. Twiggs, a distinguished but seventy-one-year-old holdover from the Mexican War, who had run the Texas Department since 1857.

Governor Houston had earlier inquired of Twiggs what he meant to do if Texas seceded, and had been answered that Twiggs had received no instructions on that point. Still no orders were forthcoming, and by February 18 Twiggs capitulated, surrendering his entire department. Two months before the war began, McCulloch gained for the Confederacy more than $3 million in military equipment, and neutralized twenty-seven hundred federal troops, more than ten per cent of the prewar standing army.

Twiggs, a Georgia native, was discharged from the Union army, but late in May the Confederate army restored his rank of major general. He was given command of the New Orleans defenses but soon retired from poor health. He died in July of 1862.

Once the war began, ardent Texans flocked to the cause; before the struggle was over some sixty-seven thousand of them took up arms. Some of the Texas regiments became legendary for their courage and skill. Foremost among them was the 8th Texas Cavalry, organized by Benjamin Franklin Terry, a forty-year-old Kentucky native who owned a sugar plantation in Fort Bend County. Like McCulloch a delegate to the Secession Convention, he had then gone to Virginia, where he participated in the Rebel victory at the First Battle of Manassas, or Bull Run. Back in Houston he organized ten 100-man companies, composed largely of former Rangers. They traveled by makeshift conveyances to New Orleans, where they received an invitation to join another Texan, Albert Sidney Johnston, then forming an army in Kentucky.

Terry himself was killed only a couple of months later, leading a charge near Woodsonville, Kentucky, but "Terry's Texas Rangers" fought gallantly in a number of savage engagements, including Shiloh—where General Johnston was killed—Murfrees-boro, and Chickamauga.

John Robert Baylor, the implacable Indian hater who had wrecked the Brazos Reservation in 1859, also figured prominently in early battles, in a different theater. He had been ranching near the town of Weatherford, close to the scene of his Indian triumph, when he was elected to the Secession Convention. Now as lieutenant colonel

COLONEL BENJAMIN FRANKLIN TERRY, 8th Texas Cavalry.

of the 2nd Texas Mounted Rifles he was stationed in El Paso, from where he struck north to drive federal troops out of New Mexico. By the end of the summer he had occupied Fort Fillmore and won victories in the Organ Mountains and at Valverde. After his drive stalled at Glorieta, he retired to establish a capital at Mesilla, where, in his typical fashion, he created a "Territory of Arizona" and named himself governor.

His title was confirmed by the Confederate Congress, and Baylor settled in to govern his little empire. His principal headache was Mescalero Apache Indians, who since the federal evacuation had been running amok through local ranches. In March of 1862 he issued orders to one of his officers which would have surprised no one who knew him: "I learn . . . that the Indians have been in to your post for the purpose of making a treaty. The Congress of the Confederate States has passed a law declaring extermination of all hostile Indians. You will therefore use all means to persuade the Apaches or any tribe to come in for the purpose of making peace, and when you get them together kill all the grown Indians and take the children prisoners and sell them to defray the expense of killing. . . . Leave nothing undone . . . and allow no Indian to escape."

In due time a copy of the orders crossed the desk of Jefferson Davis, President of the Confederacy. Davis, as the American Secretary of War in 1853, had relieved a New Mexico general for browbeating these same Indians. He likewise stripped Baylor of his command and ordered him out of New Mexico. The change mattered little, for the Confederate jig in the Southwest was about up, anyway. Union volunteers from Colorado and California retook it during the summer.

Baylor was not finished yet, however. He turned up as a representative in the Confederate Congress in 1863, and served until the collapse of the government.

JOHN ROBERT BAYLOR.

Hood's Texas Brigade

John Bell Hood.

Four Soldiers of Hood's Brigade.

WHEN the war started, John Bell Hood was a twenty-nine-year-old infantry officer on duty station in Texas. He was a Kentucky native, and he resigned his Union commission on April 16 to assume command of the 4th Texas Infantry. They became one of the South's crack combat units, fighting under the sobriquet of Hood's Texas Brigade. An officer who preferred to fight alongside his men rather than plan strategy from the rear, Hood was wounded in the arm at Gettysburg and was considered a hero for his performance at Chickamauga, where he lost his right leg. Immensely capable, he was promoted to brigadier general in March of 1862 and gained a second star after Antietam, commanding the largest division in James Longstreet's Corps. He became lieutenant general on February 1, 1864, and succeeded Albert Sidney Johnston as commander of the army of Tennessee in July. That force was virtually annihilated by George H. Thomas at Nashville on December 15–16; Hood was relieved of command shortly afterward and resigned his commission.

During the final stage of the crushing defeat at Nashville, Union General John Schofield praised Hood's leadership of his men. "I doubt if any soldiers in the world," he said, "ever needed so much cumulative evidence to convince them they were beaten."

In the photograph above, four Texans of Hood's Brigade pause to mug while doing camp chores. When a British observer commented on their makeshift uniforms, Robert E. Lee reassured him, "Never mind the raggedness. The enemy never sees the backs of my Texans."

Triumph at Second Manassas

WAUD'S VIEW OF SECOND MANASSAS.

AT the Second Battle of Manassas in 1862, J. E. B. Stuart ransacked a federal headquarters and drew Union General John Pope and his sixty thousand men into the
waiting twenty-five thousand of Stonewall Jackson. After a firefight on August 29,
Pope felt sure of overwhelming Jackson's thin lines, and attacked with all his might the
next day. He had ignored intelligence of danger to his left, however, and only after
committing his reserves to the attack against Jackson did he discover he had been
flanked by thirty thousand more Confederates of Longstreet's Corps. The latter's front
line was composed of Hood's Texas Brigade. After a furious cannonading the Texans
led the charge, shrieking "like demons emerging from the earth." Two Union regiments
crumbled beneath them, one of which, manned by romantically pantalooned New York
"Zouaves," suffered the highest federal fatality rate of the entire war. Of a regimental
strength of nearly five hundred, one in four died.

The sketch above by Alfred Waud depicts the assault, a mounted officer trying to
rally his men as a battery fires into the charging rebels.

Disaster at Antietam

CONFEDERATE DEAD, ANTIETAM.

AFTER the sweeping victory at Second Manassas, Robert E. Lee headed his army northward, probably intending to neutralize the Union railroad center at Harrisburg, Pennsylvania. A copy of his orders, however, fell into Union hands, and the drive north only reached Sharpsburg, Maryland, on Antietam Creek just above the Potomac River, before stalling under the weight of stiff Union pressure. Lee took up a defensive position in Sharpsburg, his left (north) flank consisting of two patches of woods separated by a forty-acre cornfield, up the left side of which ran the road north to Hagerstown. It was anchored in the West Woods by Hood's Texans, with other units spread across the cornfield and into the East Woods. At daybreak on September 17 Union Major General "Fighting Joe" Hooker raced his I Corps down the Hagerstown Pike and assaulted Lee's units in the cornfield, pushing them back and creating a dangerous bulge in the defensive line. Hood's Texans, furious at the interruption of their first hot meal in days, crashed into the unsuspecting Hooker's right side and pushed them back across the cornfield.

Hooker had placed his artillery in the barnyard that adjoined the cornfield. The Union troops fell back apace and the Texans came dashing on. When the bluecoats regained the barnyard with Hood's Brigade only twenty yards behind, the six-gun battery primed with double-shotted canister roared to life. The Texas Brigade was mowed down like grain. Hooker's advance was stalemated, but Hood was left to mourn, when asked the status of his division, that it lay "dead on the field."

This and other body-littered fronts at Antietam did little more than point up the terrible extravagance of the Civil War. At San Jacinto twenty-three hundred men altered the flow of Western civilization. At Antietam twenty-three thousand fell, to the apparent advantage of no one.

This photograph by Alexander Gardner shows Confederate casualties outside the cornfield fence.

Galveston Falls . . . and Rises

WHILE Texas contributed to the Glorious Cause regiments renowned for their bravery, the state was far removed from the devastation of the major battlefronts. It became an economic bulwark of the faltering Confederacy, from the powder secretly manufactured in a deep cavern west of Austin to the hard cash gained in trade with Mexico. Richard King and Mifflin Kenedy, the steamer captains turned ranching magnates, returned to sea and raked in a fortune running cotton to buyers in Europe. This was the principal reason that an increasing number of federal officers felt it imperative to make some move to strike at Texas herself.

On October 4, 1862, Union naval forces captured Galveston without much of a fight, steaming into the harbor under flags of truce and demanding that the city capitulate. The Confederate commander refused, but asked for and got four days to evacuate civilians to the mainland. Not until Christmas Day did federals occupy any of the city, when about three hundred troops made a small fortification on Kuhn's Wharf.

The commander of the District of Texas, General John Magruder, began rounding up troops almost at once to counterattack. During the night of December 31 his forces silently surrounded the wharf, and before dawn on New Year's Day, Magruder himself opened the artillery barrage against the Union positions. The attack began badly. The federals were covered by heavy ordnance on the gunboats *Owasco* and *Harriet Lane,* which quickly silenced Magruder's artillery. With most of his troops deployed to isolate the wharf, Magruder's second force attacked along the waterfront, but the move failed when their scaling ladders proved too short to reach from the beach up to the wharf.

Unable to rout the entrenched federals, Magruder played his tactical ace. He had assembled a small squadron of two "cotton-clad" coastal defense vessels and two tenders, which sortied into the Union ships. The first, the *Neptune,* rammed the *Harriet Lane* but damaged herself more than her victim, and pulled away to nearby shallows to sink. The second cotton-clad, the *Bayou City,* likewise rammed the *Harriet Lane,* and General Tom Green's marines succeeded in capturing the vessel.

It was a mortal blow to the Yankees on the wharf, for with the loss of the *Harriet Lane* they lost their main fire support and their only means of retreat. Trapped, they surrendered, and with the land force captured, the remaining Union ships hoisted white flags and got up steam. The flagship, the gunboat *Westfield,* grounded on Pelican Spit, however, and was blown up to prevent her capture. The others, the *Clifton,* the *Owasco,* and the *Mary Boardman,* departed.

The Texans had killed 50 Union soldiers and taken over 600 prisoners, while losing 26 dead and 117 wounded. Galveston was freed, and the victory was sweetened further by acquiring the 600-ton *Harriet Lane,* a fast ex-Revenue Service steam cutter that became a successful blockade runner.

One of the units of Magruder's force was a company of artillery gunners comprised entirely of Irish Catholic immigrants from around Houston, led by a twenty-five-year-old redheaded saloonkeeper, Lieutenant Richard W. Dowling. Three weeks after the liberation of Galveston, Dowling's company and a smattering of other available men, all commanded by Dowling's wife's uncle, dealt another hard blow to the Union's West Gulf Blockade Squadron. Mounting two guns on each of two other cotton-clads, the *Josiah A. Bell* and the tiny *Uncle Ben,* the Southerners sortied from their hiding place in Sabine Pass, east of Galveston. They pounced on and outdueled two federal vessels, the 1,000-ton sailing ship *Morning Light,* mounting nine guns, and the blockade schooner *Fairy.* The larger ship was burned when she proved too heavy to get over the shallow bar into Sabine Pass, but the *Fairy,* like the *Harriet Lane,* was refitted for Confederate service.

JOHN BANKHEAD MAGRUDER, West Point class of 1830, was an artillery specialist three times promoted for gallantry during the Mexican War.

A Virginia gentleman fond of the good life, he was an elegant host to other officers, who nicknamed him Prince John. After resigning his federal commission and joining the Confederacy, he was primarily responsible for delaying McClellan's Richmond campaign, but was exiled to the Texas command in October of 1862 after fumbling the close of the Seven Days' Battles.

Magruder refused to accept Union victory in 1865, offering his services instead to Maximilian in Mexico. He returned to the United States after the collapse of the imperial caper, and died in Houston in February of 1871.

MAJOR LEON SMITH.

USS WESTFIELD
a rare action view of the Union's heavy
gunboat lost in the battle for Galveston.

USS HARRIET LANE.

BATTLE OF GALVESTON.

In this view, the twin-stacked Confederate cotton-clads *Neptune* and *Bayou City* have already rammed and captured the *Harriet Lane,* and the *Neptune* limps off to sink in shallow water. In the foreground the *Westfield,* hopelessly aground, is blown up to prevent her capture. Major Leon Smith commanded the rebel squadron that saved the day for General Magruder.

Loss of the sleek new *Harriet Lane* was a mean blow to Union morale. Named for the niece and White House hostess of bachelor President Buchanan and launched in 1857, she was the first of the vessels that would become known as Coast Guard cutters. Before the war she had seen such varied duty as gunboat di-

plomacy up the Paraná River to Paraguay, transported the Prince of Wales on his visit to America, and steamed up the Platte River to punish hostile Indians. The *Harriet Lane* was the first ship ordered to sea when the Civil War broke, and was instrumental in the capture of New Orleans, where, according to Admiral Farragut, she "supported us most noble." On the Mississippi she was David Dixon Porter's flagship in the runs past Vicksburg. At Galveston both her captain and executive officer were killed during the capture. Rechristened the *Lavinia,* she ran the federal blockade until being interned in Cuba in May of 1864. Under still another name, the *Elliott Richie,* she was wrecked off the coast of Brazil in 1884.

Texas' Moment of Glory:
The Union Invasion Defeated

AFTER the capture of the two Union blockade vessels, Dowling's artillery company resumed their station at Fort Griffin on Sabine Pass, improving their gunnery with firing practice when there was enough ammunition. They also staked range markers down both the east and west channels every three hundred yards, and reworked their sighting tables to withering accuracy.

The recapture of Galveston by the South had not diminished rumors that Texas was to be invaded, but the prospect of its actual occurrence increased when the fall of Vicksburg in July 1863 left the entire length of the Mississippi River in Union hands, severing Texas and western Louisiana from the rest of the Confederacy. Texas had long concerned the federal high command; it was the strongest remaining section of the South. What cotton could not be run through the blockade found a market in Mexico, and the French emperor, Napoleon III, constantly worried Lincoln with what his intentions south of the border might be. Texas in Union hands or even in trouble could be counted on to tamp down his ambitions there. The Union commander of the Department of the Gulf, Major General Nathaniel P. Banks, thought it mo important to strike at Mobile, but when he was overruled in favor of a Texas invasi   e was given the consolation prize of deciding where to land.

Strategically, his best bet was Sabine Pass. His forces there would have the shortest and safest supply lines. It was the outlet for the cotton-rich valleys of the Sabine and Neches rivers, and Union intelligence believed there were forty thousand bales stockpiled in Sabine City. It lay within thirty miles of the important towns of Beaumont and Orange, and was in a good position to disrupt Texas railroad traffic, virtually all of which was concentrated in the southeast corner of the state. Best of all, it was lightly defended, by one small, hastily erected fort.

September 6 found Captain Frederick Odlum (Dowling's uncle by marriage) in temporary command of the headquarters at Sabine City. There word reached him from General Magruder that a federal invasion fleet was out, believed headed for Brownsville, or Galveston, or Sabine Pass, or possibly up the Red River to northeast Texas. Odlum relayed the message to Dowling, left in temporary command at Fort Griffin, who posted mounted sentries on the beach on both sides of the pass.

Beginning that afternoon, Dowling and his coast watchers saw through their spyglasses a strange sequence of movements. First a large federal gunboat appeared and anchored off the bar; a short time later the vessel suddenly made all steam back to the east. Late in the moonless night and wee hours of September 7, signal lights blinked constantly across the water, and dawn revealed well over a dozen federal gunboats and transports riding at anchor off the bar. When there was full light, about seven of the

DICK AND ANNIE DOWLING. Dick Dowling was eight when his family fled the potato famine in County Galway, Ireland, for the United States. He was fifteen when his parents died in the 1853 yellow fever epidemic in New Orleans. There was a thriving Irish community in Houston, and at nineteen he opened a saloon and liquor-importing concern, probably financed by the prominent Odlum family. His means were soon comfortable enough to marry one of the eligible Odlum girls.

Annie Odlum Dowling's family was no stranger to service to Texas: her father had served in Fannin's Georgia Battalion and escaped the massacre at Goliad as one of the nurses that General Urrea had managed to save. Her uncle was a captain in the same unit in which Dowling was a lieutenant.

After the Battle of Sabine Pass, Dowling became such a celebrity that he was assigned detached duty to aid in recruitment drives. He remained a popular figure until his untimely death in 1867.

ships crossed the bar into the channels, then reversed themselves and resumed their positions. All day they stayed there. A great many more signal lights were seen that night, and when daybreak revealed a fleet of twenty-two warships off the bar it was clear that the brunt of the invasion would fall on Dowling.

The Union invasion commander was General William B. Franklin, who had commanded the Left Grand Division at Fredericksburg the year before. On the morning of the eighth, Franklin sent his best ship across the bar to reconnoiter and probe the

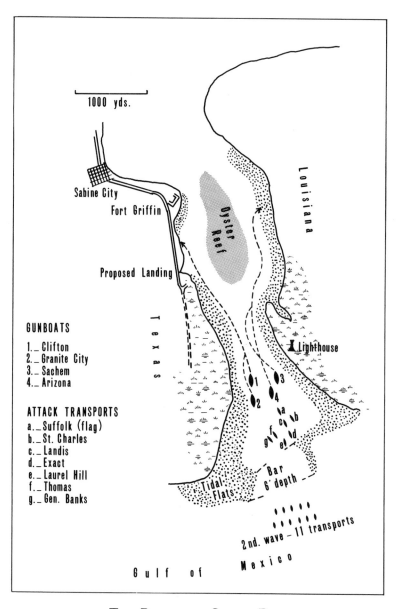

1000 yds.

Sabine City
Fort Griffin

Louisiana

Oyster Reef

Proposed Landing

Texas

Lighthouse

GUNBOATS

1._ Clifton
2._ Granite City
3._ Sachem
4._ Arizona

ATTACK TRANSPORTS
a._ Suffolk (flag)
b._ St. Charles
c._ Landis
d._ Exact
e._ Laurel Hill
f._ Thomas
g._ Gen. Banks

Bar
6' depth

Tidal Flats

2nd. wave – 11 transports

Gulf   of   Mexico

THE BATTLE OF SABINE PASS
SEPTEMBER 8, 1863

strength of the fort. She was the side-wheeled USS *Clifton,* 892 tons, 210 feet long and 40 feet in the beam. A ferry before the war, the navy purchased the vessel in December of 1861 and fitted her with diagonal iron strapping. She mounted eight heavy guns: two formidable 9-inch Dahlgren smoothbores, two 30-pounder Parrott rifles and four long-range 32-pounders.

Under command of the man who bore overall responsibility for the gunboat squadron, Acting Lieutenant Frederick Crocker, the *Clifton* proceeded to within three quarters of a mile of the fort and opened with the forward Parrott rifle. Crocker lobbed two dozen balls about the fort, two of which scored hits on the mudbanked walls but caused no damage. The result perplexed him. He estimated eight guns in the fort, but he drew no fire. Indeed, he saw few men inside the structure, but he was sure Fort Griffin would not be a pushover, because it was impossible to bombard from an effective range. The Texas channel passed barely five hundred yards from the walls, from which his light ships would be blown out of the water. The Louisiana channel was nearly a mile away, too far for accurate shooting. Extending for a mile and a half down the middle of Sabine Pass was an oyster bed half a mile wide, covered by only two feet of water. Fort Griffin, designed by a former Austrian military engineer on Magruder's staff, Valery Sulakowski, was a small post, but placed for maximum effect.

The only way to take the fort was to flank it, and for a final conference Crocker signaled the assault force to join him inside the bar: the transports *Suffolk* (the flagship, carrying Generals Franklin and Godfrey Weitzel), *St. Charles, Landis, Exact, Laurel Hill, Thomas,* and *General Banks,* and Crocker's other three gunboats, the *Sachem,* the *Granite City* and the *Arizona.*

Aboard the *Suffolk,* Crocker persuaded General Franklin that a landing of troops was imperative if the fort was to be taken, although they knew that almost the entire length of the Texas shore of Sabine Pass consisted of mud flats. To ascertain the feasibility of a landing, a few small boats were lowered and rowed over; their bottoms grounded in the mud well over a hundred feet from shore, and the sailors who jumped out sank up to their calves in the sucking ooze. At this point a cotton-clad that Crocker had seen anchored behind the fort in Sabine Lake—it was the *Uncle Ben*—steamed out to investigate. Three heavy balls from the *Sachem,* however, flew high over the little vessel and sent her back under cover.

Because the element of surprise was lost—the parade of coming and going that Dowling had observed was the result of communications foul-ups—and because therefore rebel reinforcements were feared at any hour, a landing on the sandy coast of the Gulf was not considered. The only choice was to land at the one stretch of firm ground on the Texas channel, a low bluff that was the site of an abandoned fort, only half a mile from the guns at Fort Griffin.

The plan finally adopted called for two gunboats, the *Sachem,* a shallow-draft screw steamer of 197 tons, 121 feet long, mounting four long 32s and a Parrott 20-pounder; and the lumbering *Arizona,* nearly 1,000 tons, 200 feet long with a mixed battery of six guns, would steam up the Louisiana channel to draw fire from the fort. As soon as the rebel guns were trained on them, Crocker would bring on his *Clifton* at all speed up the Texas channel for close bombardment. In his wake the assault transports would land the first wave of the invasion, twelve hundred men of the XIX Corps' 1st Division (New York), with artillery support. The landing would be covered by the 450-ton

THE BATTLE OF SABINE PASS. In this contemporary engraving the United States gunboats *Clifton (left)* and *Sachem* begin their runs up the Sabine Pass channels.

Granite City, mounting a respectable battery of one 12-pounder rifle and six 24-pounder howitzers. After the troops were ashore, the *Granite City* would follow the *Clifton* up the channel. At least one of the gunboats would have flanked the fort by reaching Sabine Lake, and with the infantry assaulting their rear, the Confederates could not hold out. After that the other eleven ships still off the bar could land their thirty-eight hundred more troops, including four companies of Union Texas cavalry. Some ten thousand more soldiers were projected to follow once a hold was secure.

Against this staggering firepower, Lieutenant Dowling mustered barely enough men to field a good choir. Of the sixty-four men in his Company F, 3rd Texas Heavy Artillery, seventeen were on detached service or leave. Only forty-seven were available to service the six guns. Of his ordnance, the two 24-pounder smoothbores faced north, and could not be brought into action at all until he had been flanked and the battle, probably, lost. The other four guns, two 32-pounder smoothbores and two 32-pounder howitzers, were not in good repair. Only one was rated as safe for sustained fire.

The ships began moving at three-thirty in the afternoon. The *Sachem* surged up the Louisiana channel, opening fire with her forward Parrott 20-pounder, followed by the *Arizona.* The *Clifton* started forward, slowly, up the Texas channel, waiting for all of Dowling's guns to train on *Sachem* before making his move, opening at extreme range with the forward 9-inch Dahlgren.

Information concerning the strength of the federal fleet had reached headquarters, and Dowling received a message letting him off the hook: it was within his discretion whether to fight, or spike his guns and retire. Much apocryphal Texana has grown out of the decision to stick and fight. Some accounts have Dowling haranguing his four dozen men from atop a parapet, saber in hand. Others have him marking a line in the dirt, like Travis at the Alamo, or adopting as their own Travis' Victory or Death motto. To a historian the simple decision to oppose so much with so little was sufficient heroism.

After deciding to fight, however, there were no options about how to do it. The *Sachem* had to be engaged, at once. As her guns came to bear, the bang of her Parrott gun was dwarfed by booming salvos from the long 32s. As the 24-pounders couldn't yet bear, Dowling lined her up in his own 32-pounder howitzer, christened "Annie" after his wife. His engineer, Lieutenant N. H. Smith, directed fire from the 32-pounder smoothbores. The first salvo from the fort was high, and Dowling narrowly escaped decapitation as, seconds after backing away from the Annie to fire her, a 9-inch ball from the *Clifton* carried away the top of the sighting screw. The second salvo was also high.

The *Sachem* now entered the area staked with range finders, and the gunboat shuddered as Dowling's third salvo carried away her stack, lifeboats, and part of the cabin. But there was little cause to celebrate: one of Dowling's howitzers had backed off its carriage and lay useless, the *Arizona* had freed herself from a mudbank and was opening fire, and Lieutenant Crocker, seeing the fort's battery trained across the pass, suddenly brought on the *Clifton* as fast as he could.

For the moment, though, Dowling had to ignore him; it was imperative to stop the *Sachem* before she reached Sabine Lake. Further hits holed her deck and superstructure; two and then three of her guns were silenced. Suddenly, the *Sachem* veered crazily to starboard and stuck fast in the mud on the Louisiana shore. She was so close to Sabine Lake that Dowling's 24-pounders could now work on her, and one of the first shots from them holed her amidships and ripped open her steam drum before exiting the starboard side.

Up to this point Dowling had been lucky. None of his men had been injured, and the undermanned crews set their sights now on the *Clifton*. The remaining guns fired at a rate of one shot every two minutes—very fast for heavy cannon. Singes and powder burns resulted from muzzle blasts; barrels heated beyond safety blistered the hands that worked them.

Back aboard the *Sachem,* her master, Acting Lieutenant Frederick Johnson, signaled the *Arizona* for aid. His engine power was gone, and many of his men were torn by shrapnel or scalded by live steam. The *Arizona*'s skipper, however, Acting Master Howard Tibbets, refused to tow the *Sachem* free, even though Fort Griffin's guns were turning on the *Clifton*, nor did he stop to take off the wounded. Had he continued his run up the channel, he could have flanked the fort, opposed only by the two 24-pounders and perhaps some harassment from the *Uncle Ben*, and possibly saved the day for the Union. But he didn't; he backed down the channel and removed himself from the action. Perhaps he was concerned about the size and draft of his ship; he had already grounded once and had to power himself free. If he grounded again in Sabine Lake he would be a sitting duck. Whatever his considerations, his lack of initiative earned him savage criticism from fellow officers.

On the opposite side of Sabine Pass, Lieutenant Crocker showed considerable skill as he brought his *Clifton* into the fight, preceding the *Granite City* and the troopships. He managed to bring all his guns into action except the aft Dahlgren, while zigzagging up the channel, denying Dowling a steady target. His fire, unanswered at first as Fort Griffin concentrated on the *Sachem,* repeatedly gouged into the mudbanked walls but failed—except for shooting off Annie's sighting screw—to find a target inside.

Once the *Sachem* was finished, though, and with the *Clifton* now coming within the grid of range markers, the Texan gunners found Crocker's ship before any landing could be effected. A lucky ball disengaged the *Clifton*'s steering ropes; the churning, 900-ton vessel heeled uncontrollably to port and ploughed fast into the mud on the Texas shore, immobile, only three hundred yards from Dowling's guns.

The furious cannonading was clearly audible in Sabine City, and Captain Odlum arrived in the middle of the action. To the delight of the gunners, he declined to assume command of the action; Dowling had started the fight, and he should finish it. The gun crews gave him three cheers and pounded the *Clifton* to pieces. Iron balls holed the deck and superstructure; one penetrated the steam drum, cutting pressure to the engine and halting the effort to back out of the mud. One ball banged its way down the deck, causing several casualties and killing Crocker's executive officer. Still Crocker fought back, his sharpshooters trying desperately to pick off Dowling's crewmen. With his starboard guns being silenced one by one, Crocker directed the crew of the port Parrott gun in shooting a hole through the cabin to bring it to bear.

Dowling responded to the whiz of sharpshooters' bullets by changing his solid shot for grape and canister, which sent them scurrying below. When the *Clifton*'s boiler exploded, the ship's surgeon deserted the wounded in the dispensary and crouched, sheltered, on the rudder. As Crocker went forward to direct fire from the 9-inch Dahlgren, he ordered his new executive officer to form a detail to extinguish a fire. He ran up a white flag instead.

Back aboard the steam-wreathed wreck of the *Sachem,* acting Lieutenant Johnson also lowered the stars and stripes and ran up a white flag, as most of his surviving crew slopped their way across the marsh into Louisiana. By the time the *Uncle Ben* steamed out to take his surrender, Johnson had flooded his magazines and destroyed his signal books, and spiked his only remaining gun, the forward Parrott that had opened the action. Soon after, Dowling himself took Crocker's surrender aboard the *Clifton.*

The fight was over well before sundown, a complete Confederate victory. Aboard the assault transports that were to have landed the troops, rumors flew that massive Rebel reinforcements were at hand. The vessels disgorged stores and even livestock to lighten ship and retreat back into the Gulf. The only trouble taken was to hobble the mules before they went over the side, to insure that they drowned and did not swim ashore, and the fleet quickly disappeared.

As a result of the Battle of Sabine Pass, Texas remained uncowed by the military might of the Union, and federal bonds sank to their lowest premium of the war. Dowling and his company were cited for gallantry by President Davis himself, and special medals were struck. The captured vessels were refitted for service in the Confederate navy, except for the walking beam of the *Clifton,* which was triumphantly installed as an amusement in a Beaumont playground.

The Union Tries Again

GENERAL NATHANIEL BANKS, the Union's commander of the Department of the Gulf, opposed the invasion of Texas. In the field neither he nor his officers were prepared for the walleyed resistance that drove them back.

A second invasion attempt from General Banks' department managed to take Brownsville on the Mexican border—the local garrison evacuated without a fight—two months after Sabine Pass. Few were surprised that the 6,000 federals found little happening there and withdrew during the summer.

In some quarters of Washington, however, the idea of intimidating French ambition in Mexico by dominating Texas had become a fixation. Instead of capitalizing fully on the fall of Vicksburg, some 27,000 troops were diverted for Banks to lead across Louisiana, capture Shreveport, and invade Texas from the northeast. General Magruder rushed as many men northward as he could to oppose them. At Mansfield, forty miles south of Shreveport, on April 8, 1864, 8,800 rebels under Generals Richard Taylor and E. Kirby Smith attacked Banks' advance unit of 8,000. The Confederates captured 150 loaded supply wagons, 22 cannon and took 2,500 prisoners before retiring in the face of Union reinforcements. Banks fell back to Pleasant Hill, thirty miles west of Natchitoches, to regroup. The next afternoon, all 12,000 Southern soldiers fought savagely to cut off the Union escape route, but were driven off with a loss of 1,500. Although Banks lost not quite so many, his campaign was wrecked and he quit the Texas scheme for good.

SITTING DUCKS. After the Mansfield and Pleasant Hill defeats, General Banks withdrew so rapidly that he left behind on the Red River his screen of more than a dozen heavy gunboats, plus transports and river steamers. The flotilla, which was commanded by one of the Union's most capable officers, Rear Admiral David Dixon Porter, was then stranded in Alexandria by a fall in water level to nearly four feet below the minimum needed to negotiate downstream rapids. "No amount of lightening [of the ships]," grieved Porter, "will accomplish the object. In the meantime, the enemy are splitting up into parties of 2,000 and bringing in the artillery . . . to blockade points below here."

Threatened with annihilation, Porter had stone crib dams *(above)* built across the river and waited nervously for the water to back up. When a hole was finally opened in the dam, Porter's gunboats careened down the crest to safety. But it was not a clean getaway. The *Eastport* was sunk on April 15, the *Champion No. 3* was captured and the *Champion No. 5* was sunk on April 26, and the transport *Warner* and gunboats *Covington* and *Signal* were all lost on May 5. Nearly all the surviving ships were holed and battered by what Porter called "the heaviest fire I ever witnessed."

The spectacular retreat ended Northern attempts to punish Texas before the end of the war.

Rear Admiral David Dixon Porter.

Final Victory of a Lost Cause

COLONEL THEODORE BARRETT *(left)* could not have known what a tough old bird he was up against in COLONEL JOHN SALMON (RIP) FORD *(right)*. The famous Texas Ranger-turned-Confederate officer had acquired his nickname during the Mexican War, when he wrote so many condolence letters to families of Ranger casualties that he began abbreviating "Rest in Peace" to "R.I.P."

ROBERT E. Lee surrendered at Appomattox on April 9, 1865, and General Joseph Johnston capitulated to Sherman eight days later in North Carolina. The war over, Union commanders throughout the South were ordered to take control of the governmental apparatus.

Among them was Colonel Theodore H. Barrett, commanding a federal encampment on Brazos Island off the extreme southern coast of Texas. On May 11 he dispatched Lieutenant Colonel David Branson and some three hundred men, mostly black infantry, to claim Brownsville, about twenty-five miles inland.

Twelve miles from the town, at Palmito Ranch, the troops overran a force of 150 Confederate cavalry under Captain W. N. Robinson. When the latter regrouped and opened a skirmish, Branson assumed they had been reinforced and fell back about four miles to a defensive position. In fact, Southern reinforcements did not arrive until afternoon on the thirteenth: seventy men and six 12-pounders under Colonel John S. (Rip) Ford. Almost at once Ford directed a cannonading and a shrieking Rebel charge. The Union force broke ranks and fled back to their post, losing some thirty casualties. Ford lost five wounded and three captured; the Texans took 113 federal prisoners, from whom they learned that the war had ended a month before.

Palmito Ranch is considered notable as the last land engagement of the Civil War.

Reconstruction

GENERAL GORDON GRANGER.

PRESIDENT Lincoln signed the Emancipation Proclamation on January 1, 1863, but the instrument had little effect in the South outside those areas occupied by Union troops. This was especially the case in Texas, where the slaves were not effectually freed until liberation was reiterated by General Gordon Granger. When he disembarked at Galveston on June 19, 1865, to assume command of the forces of occupation, his message included the declaration that ". . . in accordance with a proclamation by the executive of the United States all Negroes are free." Blacks in Texas, the descendants of freed slaves like those shown below, have traditionally celebrated "Juneteenth" as the anniversary of their real emancipation.

FREED SLAVES.

A Clutch of Governors

O<small>N</small> June 11, 1865, with Union occupation imminent, about forty ruffians took advantage of the chaos and robbed the state treasury of some seventeen thousand dollars of its one hundred thousand dollars in specie before a citizen mob drove them off. The incident seems to be unconnected with the fact that the next day Governor Pendleton Murrah vacated for Mexico. Executive power was left with his lieutenant governor, Fletcher Stockdale who served only a few weeks before President Johnson appointed A. J. Hamilton, a Unionist Texan and Republican who had served in the Northern army, to be governor instead.

Scalawags and carpetbaggers held a convention in February of 1866, which adopted a new constitution. In the election the following July, in which white Democrats were disenfranchised by what was called the Iron-clad Oath, J. W. Throckmorton, who as a legislator had dared to vote against the secession ordinance, was elected governor. The Congress in Washington, however, decided to humiliate the South a little

P<small>ENDLETON</small> M<small>URRAH</small>.

F<small>LETCHER</small> S<small>TOCKDALE</small>.

A. J. HAMILTON.

EDMUND J. DAVIS.

J. W. THROCKMORTON.

ELISHA PEASE.

more, and army rule was reinstated. The military governor, Lieutenant General Philip Sheridan, replaced Throckmorton in August of 1867 with the still more tractable former governor Elisha Pease, whom Throckmorton had just trounced better than four to one in the election.

Sheridan could not get along with Pease, either. That governor resigned in disgust on September 30, 1869, and Texas was ruled by military decree until the installation of Edmund J. Davis, a carpetbag Republican from Florida, in January of 1870. Not all Texas Republicans were radicals, however. Hamilton came to head a conservative wing of the party, and even with former secessionists barred from voting, Davis had beaten him by only 800 votes out of 80,000 cast.

Texas was finally readmitted to the Union in March, after completing still another constitution, this one finished under military supervision to go farther than did the 1866 document in the protection of freedmen.

The Warren Wagon Train Massacre

ALONG the northwestern frontier of the settled portion of Texas, the Comanche and Kiowa Indians who roamed the plains with undiminished freedom were quick to notice the change in status quo that came with the Civil War. They had never forgiven the *Tehannas* for the Council House Fight, and when the federal troops who had been maintaining some presence on the frontier marched east to fight each other, the Plains Indians raided among the thinly settled whites with unparalleled savagery. By 1865 they had heaved the line of settlement a full 150 miles back to the southeast.

The precise extent of Comanche-Kiowa responsibility for all the violence on the frontier, however, was impossible to determine, because white outlaws murdered and pillaged just as freely, often disguising themselves as Indians and scalping their victims to hide their own guilt.

As early as 1855 an article in the Goliad *True American,* under the heading "Indians. May-be-so," reported of one such raid that "a party of Indians (so supposed) visited the farmhouses of several of our citizens living on the San Antonio River, some ten or fifteen miles above this place, and drove off from eighty to one hundred head of horses. . . .

"This report may be true, but we don't believe the *Indian* story. We feel satisfied that this stampede was made by the *whites*—or, as Jim Burk, an old ranger, would say, if they were not white then, they could be made so by taking them to a water-hole, and use a little soap on them."

The Army was familiar enough with the ploy that when troops returned to frontier duty, many officers tended to pooh-pooh as extravagant the settlers' tales of Indian horror. The government concluded the Little Arkansas Treaty with the Comanches and Kiowas in 1865, and in further councils two years later at Medicine Lodge, Kansas, the Army, while admitting that incidents had occurred and that the tribes were turbulent and dangerous, agreed with the Indian Bureau that the "testimony satisfies us that since October 1865 the Kiowas [and] Comanches have substantially complied with their treaty stipulation entered into at that time at the mouth of the Little Arkansas. . . . We are aware that various other charges were made against the Kiowas and Comanches, but the evidence will pretty clearly demonstrate that these charges were almost wholly without foundation."

Enough violence occurred in 1868 for the Army to authorize a full-scale war in the Indian Territory, but the brunt of it was borne by the Cheyenne tribe, whose principal raiding grounds were Kansas and Colorado. By 1869 most bands of Comanches and Kiowas had still never suffered a significant defeat from the American military. In that year the government undertook the "Peace Policy," a radical reform in Indian management which replaced military agents with missionaries authorized to promise liberal rations to tribes who came in to learn the "white road." When the Comanche-Kiowa feeding station was established at Fort Sill, in the southern Indian Territory, settlers in Texas complained bitterly that it was nothing more than a city of refuge, a place where the Indians could rest and load up supplies for more raids south of the Red River. By spring of 1871 citizen abuse of the Army for its alleged inaction led William Tecumseh Sherman, who had succeeded U. S. Grant as General of the Army, to undertake an inspection tour of the Texas forts and ascertain the facts for himself.

May 18 found Sherman traveling from Fort Griffin northeast to Fort Richardson. In the company of Inspector General Randolph Marcy, two staff colonels, and a cavalry escort of only fifteen, they used a road that, Sherman was told, had been abandoned as too dangerous. He kept a constant lookout for Indian sign, but saw nothing. The party arrived that evening at Richardson, and after dinner Sherman listened skeptically to a group of local citizens hold forth on the horror of the Indian menace.

During the wee hours of May 19 a wounded man named Brazeal was admitted to the post hospital; General Sherman was soon at his bedside, listening to the particulars of a terrible massacre the previous afternoon on the Salt Prairie. A wagon train, the property of army supplier Henry Warren of Weatherford, had been en route to Fort Griffin when pounced on by at least a hundred Indians. Seven of Brazeal's companions had been killed, the stock stolen, and their cargo, a contracted load of corn for the Army, destroyed. Sherman had doubts; he had come over that road only a few hours before Brazeal's train, and seen no hint of hostiles. The regiment on duty at Richardson was the 4th Cavalry under Ranald Mackenzie; deciding quickly, Sherman ordered Mac-

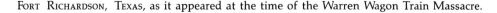

FORT RICHARDSON, TEXAS, as it appeared at the time of the Warren Wagon Train Massacre.

kenzie out to the site, and if he found there had been an incident, he was to track and punish the Indians responsible, or else pursue them to their alleged "refuge" at Fort Sill. There Sherman would await Mackenzie and his report.

Mackenzie followed his orders, and Sherman left for Fort Sill, soon having in hand the brief post mortem prepared by Assistant Surgeon Patzki: "Sir: I have the honor to report that in compliance with your instructions I examined on May 19, 1871, the bodies of five citizens killed near Salt Creek by Indians on the previous day. All the bodies were riddled with bullets, covered with gashes, and the skulls crushed, evidently with an axe found bloody on the place; some of the bodies exhibited also signs of having been stabbed with arrows. One of the bodies was even more mutilated than the others, it having been found fastened with a chain to the pole of a wagon lying over a fire with the face to the ground, the tongue being cut out. Owing to the charred condition of the soft parts it was impossible to determine whether the man was burned before or after his death. The scalps of all but one were taken."

Within hours Mackenzie's men found the other two bodies, lying where they had fallen in an attempt to flee the massacre. The Indians' trail was washed out by rainstorms, so Mackenzie proceeded on to Fort Sill. Sherman was already there, sobered to discover how close the General of the Army had come to losing his own graying red hair. He quickly determined that if Sill was indeed a City of Refuge, it was not so with the complicity of either the post's commanding officer, Colonel Benjamin Grierson, or the agent at the close-by Kiowa-Comanche Agency, Lawrie Tatum. The latter, although an emissary of the Quaker Church, had become increasingly stern with his Indians, and had already queried his superiors on the touchy question of closer cooperation with the Army in punishing raiders. When Sherman staggered him with news of the Warren Wagon Train Massacre, Tatum assured him he would investigate on the next issue day, when all the prominent Indians would be in for their rations.

Issue day was Saturday, May 27, but the chiefs found the commissary locked, and a clerk told them that Tatum was waiting in the meeting room for a council. Once the Kiowas were seated, Tatum inquired whether they knew anything about the destruction of a wagon train near Fort Richardson. After a silence the man who rose to reply was Satanta (White Bear), who of all the Kiowa leaders was the best known to the whites. As a consequence of his strutting and boasting at the Medicine Lodge treaty councils in 1867, news correspondents had smirked and given him the sobriquet "Orator of the Plains." But he was an important leader and feared raider, and his reply was not at all what Tatum expected. Satanta looked straight at him and thumped his chest.

"Yes, I led that raid. I have heard that you have stolen a large portion of our annuity goods and given them to the Texans; I have repeatedly asked you for arms and ammunition, which you have not furnished, and made many other requests which have not been granted. You do not listen to my talk. The white people are preparing to build a R.R. through our country, which will not be permitted. . . . When Gen. Custer was here two or three years ago, he arrested me & kept me in confinement several days. But arresting Indians is plaid out now & is never to be repeated. On account of these grievances, I took, a short time ago, about 100 of my warriors, with the chiefs Satank, Eagle Heart, Big Tree, Big Bow, & Fast Bear. We went to Texas, where we captured a train not far from Fort Richardson, killed 7 of the men, & drove off about 41 mules. Three of my men were killed, but we are willing to call it even. We don't expect to do any raiding around here this summer, but we expect to raid in Texas. If any other

Indian comes here and claims the honor of leading the party he will be lieing to you for I did it myself!"

Satanta interpreted the gasps of astonishment as admiration for his boldness and repeated his demand for arms. Tatum explained that he was not allowed to issue guns, but told Satanta of Sherman's visit. If he wanted to ask guns of Sherman, a meeting would be arranged. Tatum then ordered the Kiowa rations issued, and penciled a note to Grierson and Sherman:

"Satanta, in the presence of Satank, Eagle Heart, Big Tree, and Woman's Heart, has, in a defiant manner, informed me that he led a party of about 100 Indians into Texas and killed 7 men and captured a train of mules. He further states that the chiefs, Satank, Eagle Heart, and Big Bow were associated with him in the raid. Please arrest all three of them."

Sherman prepared to interview Satanta and the others on the porch of Colonel Grierson's house, hiding troops inside ready to crash open the shutters and secreting mounted cavalry in a nearby warehouse. After a tense and momentarily brawling confrontation, three of the chiefs—Satank, Satanta, and Big Tree—were loaded onto a wagon and with a cavalry escort started for Texas, to stand trial in Jacksboro for the wagon train killings. The procession had scarcely cleared the fort compound when the oldest, Satank, sang his death song, slipped his shackles, and attacked his guard until he was shot dead.

SATANK (SITTING BEAR) at the time of the Warren Wagon Train Massacre was considered by his people to be "highest in the tribe." In this photo the leather strap draped over his left shoulder identifies him as a member of the Kaitsenko, the most exclusive of the Kiowas' six warrior societies. The last joint of the little finger is missing, an act of self-mutilation occasioned by grief at the death of a relative.

GENERAL WILLIAM TECUMSEH SHERMAN *(right)* was only the third man in American history to wear four stars on his epaulets. He doubted Texans' relentless tales of Indian pillage, and at Fort Richardson was embarrassed by one woman who fell on her knees and begged his mercy in corralling the Indians and recovering her captive children. LAWRIE TATUM *(left)* tried his best to administer a fumbling and contradictory Indian policy. He ran afoul of his pacifist superiors when he recognized that force was sometimes needed to control turbulent, primitive tribes. This photo of SATANTA *(below right)* AND BIG TREE *(left)* probably dates from their trial or prison term. After being paroled once, Satanta was returned to prison in 1874, where he committed suicide four years after. Big Tree later became a Christian and taught Sunday school.

At the trial Satanta denied any part in the Warren massacre, and offered to kill with his own hands the chiefs he claimed were responsible. The jury at Jacksboro didn't buy it, and on July 6 Satanta and Big Tree were sentenced to hang. By now the case had gained wide attention. Eastern Indian reformers urged clemency, and Tatum argued that it would be easier to control the rest of the tribe with the two chiefs alive in prison than dead. To the fury of Texans living along the fringe of settlement, Governor Davis commuted their sentences to life imprisonment, and in autumn of 1873 paroled them back to their tribe.

A lenient Indian policy was not the only issue that made E. J. Davis unpopular.

Although Texans had contributed thousands of lives to the war, the state had suffered only negligible material damage. The economic disaster of occupation and Reconstruction, however, was one she shared in fully. While Texas emerged from the war with more manufacturing capability than before, the population, swelled to more than eight hundred thousand by refugees from the Armageddon of the Old South, was more than nine-tenths rural. Governor Davis was honest and personally genial, but as the minion of a despised system, he caught the blame for a host of ills: in eastern counties, farms had lost two thirds of their value. The worth of farm machinery had fallen by a like amount, and the estimated value of farm animals had fallen from more than $42 million before the war to less than $30 million. At a time when some farmers recognized the need to switch from subsistence farming to producing for markets, a financial crash in 1873 halted railroad construction and made credit virtually unobtainable.

Davis was responsible for some good laws, in such fields as education, but other of his policies sparked widespread hatred. He disbanded the Texas Rangers and replaced them with the State Police Force, composed largely of freed slaves, who enforced the preferred position of white Unionist radicals. During the war, secessionists had openly abused and humiliated suspected Union sympathizers. Now it was their turn to live under the lash, and the frequency with which Davis invoked martial law, giving his State Police absolute rule over local trouble spots, made him seem as vindictive as the freedmen who exulted in their new power.

Abuses and indignities by the State Police sparked an insistence on revenge among white Democrats. Denied the right to vote, they joined organizations like the Ku Klux Klan for expression. In widespread violence perhaps a thousand Texans, half of them freedmen, were murdered in the first three years of Reconstruction.

A MASSACRE VICTIM. It was in the nature of Indian attacks, carried out usually against small parties in remote places, that they were difficult or impossible to photograph. Probably no image survives of a killing by Kiowas.

Sergeant Frederick Wyllyams of the 7th Cavalry was killed near Fort Wallace by warriors led by a Satanta ally, Roman Nose. To today's society now sensitive to injustices suffered by Native Americans, this gruesome image is a somber reminder that the revulsion felt by frontier whites to Indian methods was not without foundation.

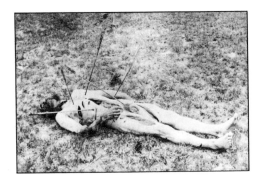

Reconstruction Ends

Hastily called militia prowl the capitol grounds during the paramilitary coup d'état that put Richard Coke into the governor's chair.

E. J. Davis stood for reelection in 1873, but the Iron-clad Oath had been lifted, and he was blistered by a barrel-chested Democrat, Richard Coke, 85,549 to 42,633. Davis challenged the result in court, won his case, and refused to vacate his office. By now, however, most Texans were fed up with anything to do with Reconstruction. The new legislature convened and ratified Coke's election. As the city of Austin armed and militia converged on the capitol, Davis and a guard of police barricaded themselves in a few rooms, while the legislature held most of the building. Davis telegraphed Washington for aid, but when President Grant refused to involve himself, Davis struck camp and left office.

Long regarded as little more than a colorful arabesque of Texas political history, the coup d'état that swept Richard Coke into power illustrates something fundamental in the Texan character: their fearlessly literal interpretation of democracy. It is usual for a government founded by revolution, after justifying its own violent birth, to armor itself with treason laws and codify other punishable offenses, to prevent what it did from happening to itself.

Texans never succumbed to this hypocrisy. To them government reflects the will of the majority; when it does not, it is thrown off. In revolution, in secession, and in Coke's coup, the willingness to act on their contempt for a government that puts on airs of its own sanctity is a peculiarly Texan heritage.

Buffalo Days: A Portfolio

THE following pictures are believed to be the only series of photographs ever taken on a buffalo hunt in Texas, as well as the earliest buffalo hunt pictures taken anywhere. The man responsible for them was W. J. Oliphant of Austin, the proprietor of a second-story studio on Pecan Street (now Sixth Street). After the Civil War he had studied photography in Washington with the famous Alexander Gardner, in whose studio he struck a friendship with another apprentice, George Robertson. When Oliphant returned to Texas, he made good income by selling series of slides for the stereoscopic viewers that were then becoming fashionable. Robertson moved to Austin to join him in the enterprise, and the most popular series they produced was entitled "Life in the West." Robertson went into the field at least twice to take photographs for this series, once on a geological survey, and once—in January of 1874—on a buffalo hunt. His self-portrait *(page 190)* was proudly labeled, "Our Special Artist."

"Robertson was just the man for the job," recalled Oliphant, "mechanical, something of a tinkerer by disposition. He worked hard and carefully to manufacture the equipment that he had to have. He made a darkroom out of an old trunk with a screen window of yellow glass in the top. He made openings in the trunk, one for each arm, and fitted over these holes sleeves of dark cloth through which he could put his hands in order to manipulate the plates and chemicals inside this 'darkroom.' He constructed another box in which to carry his cameras, tripods, and other needed equipment."

The expedition itself had its inception in another venture to the same country the previous autumn. Rumors had been current that vast copper deposits surfaced in the region. Shares were sold to outfit teams to recover the ore. Although copper deposits do occur in north central Texas, no such easy lode was found, and the wagon train returned, broke, to Austin. The expedition members were impressed, however, with the vast numbers of buffalo in the area, and the hunt was organized to pay off the debts of the first trip.

The photographs that Robertson took dropped out of sight until discovered in an Austin residence in 1926. Investigating their story became the project of the great historian Walter Prescott Webb, who located and interviewed Oliphant and the last survivor of the expedition, Emil Oberwetter of Houston, who died less than a year after the information was gathered. According to Oberwetter, "We struck camp [at Buffalo Gap] and remained for two months, moving but one time. All these pictures were made around those two camps. The weather was cold, as you can see by the snow in one of the pictures, and the cold, especially a norther, would bring the buffalo through by the thousands.

The frigid blasts caused little discomfort among the hunters, however. As one old buff runner recalled, "The camp bed of a frontiersman was a thing of art. A tarp was spread upon the grass, the blankets spread upon it and the tarp was drawn back over the top and carefully folded in at the sides. The sleeper then crawled in at the head of his bed and drew the tarp entirely over his head, shutting out the cold and prowling animals and snakes." The night of a norther, one hunter "crept in with his trousers on, but soon found the bed so snug and warm, in spite of the . . . chill, that he had to

George Robertson poses by his tentful of paraphernalia while making
a photographic record of a buffalo hunt.

shed them. Two inches of snow fell during the night, and when the tarp was thrown back the next morning we looked out on a white world."

For the daily hunts, most of the men were armed with Sharps .44 caliber rifles, with which they shot buffalo at 150 yards or so. Some owned the heavier "Big Fifty," a more effective weapon for "taking a stand," the technique of working downwind from a herd, shooting the leader, and then dropping the others one by one as they milled in confusion. An expert hunter might kill a hundred buffalo before the herd finally bolted or wandered out of range. Frank Collinson of Kansas once got 121.

"We aimed to hit the buffalo just behind the shoulder," recalled Oberwetter, "so that the bullet would pass through the lungs and the bottom of the heart. When fatally wounded in this way, the buffalo would stop, switch his tail and walk off by himself. If he lowered his head and began to cough up blood we knew it was useless to bother with him any more. He would go down on one forefoot, then on the other, then would drop on his hind feet and roll over on his side to die." Professional hunters came to prefer their own custom-made bullets, some repacking the bottlenecked, three-inch Big Fifty cartridges with an extra twenty grains of powder. Old hands got to where they could identify other hunters sight unseen just by the peculiar reports of their buffalo rifles. "In those days," said Oberwetter, "I have heard the guns booming like an artillery battle."

Not all the buffalo were gunned down on the open plains. Many were shot
in dense brush along trails to waterholes.

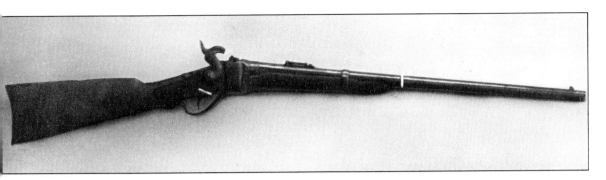

THE BIG FIFTY. The favorite gun on the hunting range was Sharps' massive .50-caliber buffalo rifle, one model of which weighed sixteen pounds and was usually fired from crossed rest sticks. The "Big Fifty" developed 2,000 foot-pounds of muzzle velocity, and its average operating range was 300–500 yards. Many hunters preferred to dismantle the 3-inch cartridges and augment the 90-grain powder charge; buffalo then sighted down the $10\times$ and $20\times$ telescopes could be dropped at three quarters of a mile.

With a day's hunt completed, teams of skinners would go out. According to one old hider, killing more than could be skinned in a day "would waste buff, which wasn't important; it would also waste ammunition, which was."

"There was an art in skinning a buffalo," said Oberwetter.

"First, you cut the hide around the neck, rip up the belly, and down each leg to the hoofs. Then pull the hide from the neck until a rope could be tied on it. Then the animal was snubbed to a tree or peg, the rope hitched to the wagon and the hide stripped off by driving up the team. Men stood ready with knives to keep the flesh cut away from the hide in case it began to tear. The cow hides were more valuable in the market than the bull hides, and as a result we killed as many cows as possible."

As well as hides, the teams would also collect meat. Bulls were too tough to use anything but the tongues, but from the cows they would also take backstrip, hump, tenderloin, and hindquarters. Back in camp the meat was salted and placed in a hide-lined pit for five or six days before being taken out and hung up on a wooden scaffold. Then, said Oberwetter,

"The next thing was to build a slow smoke fire under the scaffold. This fire had to be kept up day and night for two weeks. We made it of green mesquite, or willow with enough brush and dried wood or buffalo chips to keep it going. In time a crust would form on the outside of the chunks of meat, and the longer the meat smoked the thicker the crust would get. The right method was to stop as soon as a good crust formed, leaving the meat inside fresh and sweet. After being treated in this fashion, the meat could be handled like stove wood.

"The green hide of a buffalo might weigh anywhere from seventy-five to 150 pounds. The bull hides—especially the old ones—were likely to be thick and scabby, and of less value than the cow hides which were darker, glossier and easier to handle. They made beautiful robes, then becoming popular as winter lap robes for buggies and carriages and northern sleighs. The hides were brought into camp and pegged down to dry as shown in the picture. When the sun hit them they would contract, pull the

SKINNING A BUFFALO. While the Robertson group divided chores pretty evenly, a more professional hunter might hire two or three different teams of skinners to handle what he brought down. According to one old hunter, to kill more in a day than could be skinned "would waste buff, which wasn't important. It would also waste ammunition, which was."

DRYING HIDES AND TONGUES. By 1874 about the only remaining paying market for buffalo meat was for tongues, shown here racked up to smoke, and hindquarters.

LOADED WAGONS. The Buffalo Gap, seen here in the background, is located a few miles from where the town of Abilene was later founded.

stakes, and curl up. Then it was a job for two or three men to get them down again. When dry, they were tied together and were ready for market."

When Oberwetter's expedition finally broke up camp, they packed the cured meat into the wagon beds, stacked the hides atop them, and set out southeast to the nearest settlement, some two hundred miles away. They had stacked the hides with the tails hanging outside, and when they regained civilization, a number of city folks asked for buffalo tails to send as souvenirs to relatives back East.

Members of this outfit profited about a hundred dollars apiece for their trip. The hides brought $1.55 apiece, considerably less than what was being paid in Kansas, and the meat they sold for 13 cents per pound. Buffalo tongues were in heavy demand for the hotel and restaurant trade, and these brought $9.00 a dozen.

This hunt, having been made in dead of winter, led to no clash with hostile Indians, who seldom strayed from their snug, sheltered strongholds until spring. Standard issue for a buffalo hunter, however, was his "bite," a Big Fifty cartridge emptied of powder and filled with cyanide. Then, if he found himself surrounded by Indians and out of ammunition, he could at least commit suicide and spare himself the maniacal tortures of the Comanches. A couple of months after Oberwetter's group left the area, two other buffalo hunters, Dave Dudley and Tommy Wallace, were found scalped, staked, gutted, castrated, and their genitals stuffed into their mouths. How much was done before they died couldn't be determined, but their heads had been propped up so they could watch.

Almost every hunter on the plains could tell of someone who had "bit the bite."

The Red River War—1874

The Mooar Brothers, Josiah Wright *(left)* and John Wesley, always in the vanguard of the buffalo hunters' movements, were among the first to hunt on the Staked Plains of the Texas Panhandle.

THE party that Robertson accompanied out of Austin was far from being the only one preying on the migrating buffalo herds. In fact, far greater inroads were being made by hunting outfits based in Dodge City, Kansas. Their activity was damaging not only to the stock of game, but also to relations with the South Plains Indians who were, increasingly, hemmed in to the southwestern part of the Indian Territory: the Comanches, Kiowas, Southern Cheyennes, and Southern Arapahos.

In 1870 it had been one of the Kansas hunters, Josiah Wright Mooar, who had started the business of hunting buffalo for their hides. Prior to that time they were shot only for lap robes, meat—primarily tongues and hindquarter hams—or sport; no tanning process had been formulated to render the tough hides into workable leather. Mooar was a tall, blond Vermont Yankee, not yet twenty, when he went West to seek his fortune. He took a job as wood contractor to an army post and made friends with the meat contractor, who stocked the commissary primarily with buffalo meat. When a British firm contacted the meat contractor to supply them with a few hundred buffalo hides to experiment on, he hired Mooar to help fill the order. Mooar shot over his quota and sent the skins to his brother in New York, who sold them to a tannery in Pennsylvania. They developed a workable process, and when they offered the Mooars a contract for two thousand skins at $3.50 apiece, the chase was on. The money was easy, and the business exploded; soon it seemed like every undirected youth and impoverished drifter in Kansas had become a buffalo hunter. The toll taken on the huge herds was suddenly staggering; in the following years the rail lines serving Dodge City alone carried away nearly 4.5 million skins to eastern tanneries.

The Plains tribes in the Indian Territory, whose subsistence, except for spotty and inconsistent government rations, depended entirely on the herds, were aware of the slaughter, but took nothing like united action to stop it, because the hidemen stayed north of the "Dead Line," the Arkansas River. The Medicine Lodge Treaty of 1867 had guaranteed these Indians the right to hunt in the large section of Kansas that lay south of that stream, and of the few hunting outfits that dared cross the Dead Line, enough were picked off and massacred by the Cheyennes that the rest confined their hunting to northern Kansas. One of the most successful of them was a fellow in his early twenties, Billy Dixon of West Virginia: "During the fall and winter of 1872 and 1873 there were more hunters in the country than ever before or afterwards. Thus came the high tide of buffalo hunting. More were killed that season than in all subsequent seasons combined. I feel safe in saying that 75,000 buffaloes were killed within sixty or seventy-five miles of Dodge. . . . We had to make hay while the sun shone."

By this time the northern Kansas buffalo were gone. The hunters, who had taken to wintering in Dodge City, decided to cross the Dead Line in such force that the Indians would be driven south of the state line, into their reservation. This took place, with some losses to Cheyenne scalping knives, but the white hunters, incredible as it seems, obliterated the south Kansas herds in only one season. To find buffalo they now had to enter the Cheyenne-Arapaho Reservation itself. The federal Indian Office, in response to frantic warnings and appeals from those tribes' agent, gave them a new

HUNTERS AND SCOUTS, 1876. After the war started and the plains were too dangerous to run buffalo, many of the hunters found employment as army scouts. This gathering was photographed at Fort Elliot, built just after the war at the site where Colonel Nelson Miles spent the winter of 1874–75. Billy Dixon is seated at lower left.

HE BEAR'S CAMP.

reservation southwest of the one of which they were being dispossessed. The new tract cramped them down on the border of the Comanche-Kiowa Reservation, while the Kansas hidemen, again in only one season, cleaned the herds out of the old reservation.

All four tribes were becoming more and more belligerent at the loss of their buffalo (especially as their government-promised rations consistently fell short or failed to arrive at all, though the agents were not at fault). Ever since the parole of Satanta and Big Tree the peace faction of the Kiowas had been in a shaky kind of control, and now its leading chief, Striking Eagle, sought out his agent and tried to explain the importance of the buffalo: "The buffalo is our money . . . the robes we can prepare and trade. We love them just as the white man does his money. Just as it makes a white man feel to have his money carried away, so it makes us feel to see others killing and stealing our buffaloes, which are our cattle given to us by the Great Father above to provide us meat to eat . . . and things to wear."

The hunters who were spending the winter of 1873–74 in Dodge City knew that any deeper penetration into the Indian Territory would be suicidal. The answer, they decided, was Texas. Rumors had been actively traded all year that the Texas Panhandle was roamed by one, last, massive herd of buffalo. Billy Dixon, among others, scouted the Texas Panhandle enough during the winter to confirm the stories, and a large caravan moved southwest out of Dodge City in the spring of 1874. They set up a ramshackle village near the site of an abandoned trading post, Adobe Walls, and waited for the herds to migrate through.

Until the buffalo hunters arrived from Dodge City, the Staked Plains of the Texas Panhandle were the domain of the man pictured at left. He Bear (Parra-o-coom), shown here with two of his wives, was First Chief of the Quahadi band of Comanches, who were so fierce and isolated that even the other bands, when they visited the Quahadis, were careful not to overstay their welcome.

The history of this photograph begins with Satanta's Warren Massacre on Salt Creek in 1871. In response to that event, General Sheridan sent out Colonel Ranald Mackenzie and his 4th Cavalry to the Panhandle. He Bear's Quahadis had had nothing to do with the affair, but American soldiers had never challenged the Quahadis and allied Kotsotekas in their home territory. Mackenzie was soundly beaten, but went back the next year and managed to capture the village of the Kotsoteka chief Mow-way *(below)*. With more than a hundred women and children captive at Fort Sill, Indian Territory, (the site of the Comanche Agency), Mackenzie was able to force the Panhandle Comanches in. It was the first and only time He Bear was peaceably around white people, and itinerant photographer William Soule made sure to add the chief's image to his collection.

Mow-way, whose name was long mistranslated "Shaking Hand," really means "Push Aside." The claw fixed in his hair is that of a grizzly bear that he killed with a knife as the animal was mauling one of his warriors.

OLD MAN WHITE WOLF.

Once at the agency, they discovered a life in which food rations constantly fell short and sometimes gave out entirely, horse thieves based in Texas stole their ponies without fear of interference from the law, and contraband was circulated freely. The Panhandle Comanches did not stay long. As Mow-way told a council in 1872, "I was promised lots of things, but I don't see them. . . . When the Indians in here are better treated than we are outside, it will be time enough to come in."

Another important impetus for putting the Comanches on the warpath came from the Tonkawa Indians of north central Texas. It will be recalled that after the Battle of Plum Creek in 1840, Tonkawa allies of the Texan army roasted some of the Comanche casualties in a celebratory barbecue. They were cannibals, a practice that the Comanches—if not the Texans—found revolting. During the ensuing thirty-four years of war, the "Tonks," as some Texans called them, continued in the alliance with their more powerful white neighbors. They were ancestral enemies of the Comanches, anyway, so whenever Tonkawas killed Comanches, either while scouting for Texan militia or out on their own, the ritual meal was indulged in. This was still the practice in the 1870s.

It was the custom, when a Comanche was killed in war, for a friend or relative to walk weeping from camp to camp, getting up a revenge party. In the case of one of the Tonkawas' victims, the job fell to Quanah, the half-bred son of Chief Pe-ta Nokoni and white captive Cynthia Ann Parker, long since reclaimed by her own race. With a combination of broken English and hand sign, Quanah gave an account many years

QUANAH PARKER's intractability during the Red River War belies his later adjustment to white civilization. After making his peace in 1875 Quanah became recognized as leader of all the bands of the Comanche tribe, a successful rancher, and a judge of the Indian Court.

later to Captain Hugh Scott, who preserved it in his manuscript monograph on the Plains Indian sign language. According to Quanah Parker: "A long time ago I had a friend who was killed by the Tonkaway at Double Mountain Fork Brazos in Texas. That made me feel bad—we grew up together, went to war together. We very sorry that man. Tonkaway kill him, make my heart hot. I want to make it even.

"That time I was pretty big man, pretty young man and know how to fight pretty good. I work one month: I go to Naconie Comanche, call in everybody. I tell them my friend kill him Texas. I fill pipe—I tell that man, 'You want smoke?' He take pipe, smoke it. I give pipe to other man, he say I not want smoke; if he smoke he goes to war —[but] he not refuse—God kill him he afraid. I go see Kiowa on Elk Creek."

After the Kiowas, Quanah took the pipe to his adopted band, the fierce Quahadis of the Panhandle, and then to the Cheyennes, many of whom were camped close by. There were in the Cheyenne village a number of visiting Comanches, including two powerful and respected old chiefs of the Yapparika band, brothers-in-law named Isa-Rosa (White Wolf) and Tabananica (Sound of the Sun). All the leaders knew that Quanah was seeking aid against the Tonkawas. When they called him in for a conference, they offered to back him, but gave his plan a striking modification: "I hear some-body call, 'Quanah, old men want to see you over here!' I see Old Man Otter Belt and White Wolf, lots old men; they say, 'You pretty good fighter Quanah but you not know everything. We think you take pipe first against white buffalo killers. You kill white buffalo hunters, make your heart good—after that you come back, take all the young men, go to war, Texas.' I say, 'Otter Belt and He Bear—you take pipe yourself after I take young men & go to war Texas.' They say 'All right.' "

The Indians knew that the buffalo hunters were at Adobe Walls, and that was where they headed, picking up strength from other bands along the way until they became what was perhaps the most impressive array of South Plains Indians ever to ride together. Accounts vary, but probably they numbered at least five hundred—Comanches, Kiowas, Cheyennes, and even a few Arapahos. As Quanah remembered, "Pretty soon we move Fort Elliott, got no for there that time.

"Pick out seven men (scouts) go look for white men's houses on Canadian (Adobe Walls)—Old Man White Wolf go with them. Gone all night. Next day a watcher on a little hill call out 'Here they come!' We all [illegible] see scouts circle four times right and we know they find houses. Women, children, everybody make long line in front of the village, Old Man Black Beard in the middle—then seven scouts come single file in front of Old Man Black Beard. He say, 'Tell the truth, what did you see?' 1st Scout say, 'I tell you true, I see four log houses, I see horses moving about.' All scouts say same thing. Black Beard say, 'All right pretty soon kill some white men.' Everybody saddle up, take warbonnets and shields. We start sun there (11 am), stop sun there (4 pm). Put saddles & blankets in trees, hobble extra horses, make medicine, paint faces, put on warbonnets, then move in fours across Canadian at sundown. Keep along river pretty

A WHITE BUFFALO. The Mooar brothers, who were the first to hunt buffalo for hides, were not at Adobe Walls during the battle, but their hunting outfit successfully fought off Indian attacks elsewhere. Wright Mooar returned to Texas and settled on a ranch near Snyder. In October of 1876 he shot a white buffalo—a phenomenal rarity —near Deep Creek. The skin here is displayed by the Mooar brothers in their old age; it is still in the family's possession.

Tonkawa Charley. The Tonkawa Indian chief Chiahook became quite a character around Austin between 1860 and 1867. He was said to be "very fond of whiskey and was seldom sober." For liquor money he took to charging a fee to say whether or not Comanche Indians were good to eat. "He was very drunk one day and came up Congress Avenue," and on being paid answered quickly, "Very good, very good."

near Red Hill near a little Creek (Adobe Creek) where houses were. Everybody walk— [enemy] hear trot a long way off.

"At dark, somebody want to go to sleep. He Bear say, 'Dismount, hold lariats in your hand, I call you mount again.' Some sleep, some smoke & talk. He Bear & Tabananica call them—all mount again, travel until a little light—pretty soon we make a line—all chiefs try to hold back young men—go too fast—no good go too fast—pretty soon they call out, 'All right go ahead!' We charge on horses pretty fast—dust thrown up high. [Prairie dog holes]. I see men & horses roll over & over.

"That pretty big fight—sunrise till twelve oclock—then we go back. . . . I had [illegible] I got shot in side. My first wifes father got leg broken by bullet.

"Two white men killed in wagon, Six Comanche, few Cheyenne, some Arapaho. White men had big guns killed a mile. . . ."

The morning of the attack was Saturday, June 27. In or about the four sod buildings—a saloon, a blacksmith shop, and two stores, one with a restaurant—were twenty-six men and one woman, the wife of the restaurateur. Legend had it for years that the settlement was saved by the providential cracking of the saloon ridgepole, which awakened the men and prevented their being killed in their blankets. It now seems more likely, however, that the barkeeper, Jim Hanrahan, who along with the Mooar brothers had been warned of an impending attack, fired a pistol shot and then shouted to the groggy hiders that the roof was collapsing.

The Army responded to the South Plains Indian threat with the largest movement of troops that had ever been thrown against Indians up to that time. Lieutenant General Philip H. Sheridan, commanding the Military Division of the Missouri from headquarters in Chicago, conceived the strategy. He knew that when South Plains Indians were hard pressed, they sought refuge in the canyons at the edge of the Staked Plains. After his troop columns stirred them up, the soldiers would converge on that refuge from five different directions and give them no peace. Constantly on the run and with their tipis and supplies destroyed, the onset of winter and loss of grazing for their pony herds would force the hostiles back in.

The war zone spread over two departments of Sheridan's Division, both commanded by able brigadiers. In the Department of the Missouri, General John Pope would send out two expeditions. Colonel Nelson Miles left Fort Dodge for Camp Supply, Indian Territory, from where he struck southwest on August 20 with eight troops of 6th Cavalry and five companies of his own regiment, the 5th Infantry, plus artillery, Delaware Indian trackers, and white scouts who were mostly ex-buffalo hunters. From Fort Bascom, New Mexico, four companies of 8th Cavalry marched east to support Miles.

In the Department of Texas, General Christopher C. Augur, from San Antonio and then Fort Griffin, organized three expeditions. From Fort Sill, the center of the disturbance, Colonel John W. (Black Jack) Davidson headed west with five troops of his all-Negro 10th Cavalry, plus infantry, artillery, and scouts. At the same time, Lieutenant Colonel George P. Buell departed Fort Griffin with six cavalry troops and two companies of infantry. Eight companies of the Army's crack Indian-fighting unit, the 4th Cavalry of Colonel Ranald Mackenzie began moving from their positions along the Rio Grande as early as August 10, but because of the distances involved were not in place in Mackenzie's old 1872 base camp until September 19.

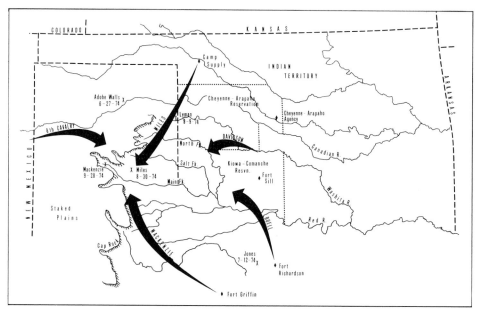

THE RED RIVER WAR
1874

LIEUTENANT GENERAL
PHILIP H. SHERIDAN.

COLONEL NELSON MILES.

GENERAL JOHN POPE.

COLONEL JOHN W. DAVIDSON.

GENERAL CHRISTOPHER C. AUGER.

COLONEL RANALD MACKENZIE.

LIEUTENANT COLONEL
GEORGE P. BUELL.

The custom of the revenge raid was practiced by Kiowas as well as by Comanches, and the second significant fight of the Red River War was the result of a long-nursed grievance. During 1873, cavalry patrols had administered three sound beatings to Ki-owa-Comanche war parties in Texas, in the first of which two popular young members of the Kiowas' aristocratic caste were killed: Tau-ankia (Sitting in the Saddle), the son of Principal Chief Lone Wolf, and Gui-tain (Heart of a Young Wolf), the son of Lone Wolf's brother Red Otter. After inflicting on himself the practice of self-mutilation, Lone Wolf went to Texas to bury them. He gathered up their bones, but was forced to abandon them in the face of yet another attack.

Lone Wolf used the occasion of the Kiowas' annual Sun Dance, held the first week in July, to recruit warriors to share in his vengeance. Most of the Kiowas returned to the reservation, however, led by Lone Wolf's more peaceable rival, Striking Eagle. About fifty men painted themselves for war and followed Lone Wolf to Texas. While visiting the site of Satanta's Salt Creek Massacre, some likely candidates appeared in the form of a couple of dozen of the Texas Rangers' newly outfitted Frontier Battalion, under Major John B. Jones of Corsicana.

A few of the Indians let themselves be seen by the Rangers, and then retreated hastily into the rough valley of Lost Creek where Lone Wolf and the others were waiting. The Rangers thundered obligingly into the ambush. One of the Kiowas, a young man named Hunting Horse who was out to prove himself as a warrior, recalled that the Rangers first crossed the dry streambed and galloped up the valley slope, but when the Indians attacked, Jones pulled his men back to the ravine: "We could see the leader of the whites motioning his men to fall back. One of them was slow. Tsen-au-sain shot him down. 'I got one,' he shouted. But nobody was able to touch the fallen enemy to make coup. . . . We could see the man lying there in plain sight. The heads of the other Rangers could be seen sticking up from a dry streambed. Nobody dared go close enough to make coup.

"Red Otter got desperate. He called for volunteers. Not a warrior spoke up. . . . It was my chance. I said I would go with Red Otter. Red Otter ran forward and took a position behind a large tree. He signaled for me to join him. . . . The bullets were throwing bark in our faces. Then we ran to another tree. But the bullets came thicker. Red Otter said it was too dangerous."

The wounded Ranger, William Glass, regained consciousness and screamed for aid when he saw the two Indians coming for him. The others in the gully laid down a withering fire as three of them rescued him. He died soon after, though, and two other Rangers were wounded. After being pinned down most of the day breathing dust and powder smoke in the July heat, without water, two of the Rangers disobeyed Jones' orders and tried to reach a nearby waterhole. The Kiowas were waiting there, and one of the men, David Bailey, was speared from his horse, and Lone Wolf took vengeance with his brass hatchet-pipe. The other Rangers escaped under cover of night to the Loving Ranch and then to Fort Richardson at Jacksboro. The next day they returned to Lost Valley: "We came upon the body of the boy who had been killed. . . . His cloth-ing was all gone and his body was terribly mutilated. He had been lanced and cut with Bowie knives until it was with difficulty one could recognize the remains as being those of a human. Even his head had been taken entirely away."

GUI-PÄH-GO (LONE WOLF).   TAU-ANKIA (SITTING IN THE SADDLE).

GUI-TAIN (HEART OF A YOUNG WOLF).

R. G. Kimbell
Ex Corp. Co "D"
Frontier Battalion
Texas Rangers 1898-1881
Shot on the Potter Scout
1880 on his mount R E LEE

TEXAS RANGERS, D Troop of the Frontier Battalion,
a rare photograph made in the field.

MAJOR JOHN B. JONES, while defeated at Lost
Valley, became one of the most active and capable of the Texas Ranger officers. The men of
his Battalion were, in the tradition of Texas
irregulars, difficult to control. In an engagement later in the war, Jones commended them
for not stopping to scalp fallen Indians until
after the fight was over.

TSEN-TONKEE (HUNTING HORSE).

Nelson Miles, who had a reputation as a good soldier but a bit of a grabber and braggart, had his 5th Infantry and 6th Cavalry in the field first. He noted with particular satisfaction that this gave him the jump on Mackenzie, who was his chief rival for the next open brigadier's billet. Covering as broad a front as possible, Miles overtook a large band of hostile Cheyennes on August 30, and from the report in army records he came off much the better: "Colonel Miles encountered the Indians near the headwaters of the Washita River, and kept up a running fight for several days, the Indians steadily falling back until they reached the hills . . . where they made a bold stand, but were promptly routed, and pursued in a southwesterly direction across Main Red River and out onto the Staked Plains, losing heavily in men, animals, and baggage."

Two less prominent accounts of the fray, one from a Cheyenne chief and one from Miles' chief of scouts, tell curiously parallel stories suggesting that it wasn't all that easy.

Baldwin's Scout

LIEUTENANT FRANK D. BALDWIN, 5th Infantry, had been on duty at Newport Barracks, Kentucky, when Miles handpicked him to head his scout force of ex-buffalo hunters and twenty Delaware Indians from Coffeyville, Kansas. His diary of the Panhandle campaign, after giving some detail of the punishing drought that afflicted the region, contained the passages:

AUG. 31. Water supply very bad and affecting both men and beast. SEPT. 3. In camp all day resting and preparing for short trip onto Staked Plains. Not feeling well on account of bad water which can hardly drink. SEPT. 5. Got atop [bluffs] before daybreak. . . . Spent the day following big trail. SEPT. 6. . . . warriors we had defeated 7 days before . . . returning to give us all the annoyance they could. One soldier killed and scalped not farther than ½ mile from camp.

IN his haste to crush Indian resistance before Mackenzie had a shot, Miles far outran his supply lines and stranded his command in a drought-stricken desert two hundred miles from his base. The men had only three days rations left when Miles called in Lieutenant Frank Baldwin. "Gen. Miles sent for me about 4 PM and explaining conditions and suggested that if he could find a scout or two to go to Ft. Supply he might discover the whereabouts of supply train. Danger of such a trip fully discussed and I asked for a few moments to consider the proposition and select the men.

"When I reported I told him that considering the importance of the duty I had concluded to go myself and had selected Lemuel T. Wilson, Wm. F. Schwalsh (Schmalsle) and Ira G. Wing without consulting them in any way. They were asked to come to Genl's tent and informed as to what they were to do. When we were about to start at 8 PM our friends came to bid us good luck and dear old companion Capt.

McDonald placed a package in my saddle bag, saying: Frank, enjoy this. It is the last drop in camp. We started out on the trail for Camp Supply and before an hour had passed there was positive evidence that Inds. were closely observing our movement. We veered to westward from main road, getting into foothills which border Staked Plains to conceal our whereabouts while crossing a creek we rode thru water up stream several hundred yards coming out on a solid rock thus hoping to throw Inds off track but this, as it happened, availed us nothing, as the Inds were cunning enough to discover the ruse. A little before daybreak we rode up a long canyon halted and unsaddled and had a pot of coffee boiling on a very small fire with a piece of bacon on a stick about to roast, but at this moment the outlook, stationed just above us, called out: 'They are coming.' Immediately the leading Ind. exposed himself he was shot dead and the whole bunch, not 600 yards away seemed to hesitate, but fired a volley at us, killing the pack horse. The three horses were quickly saddled and just as the outlook was called in an Indian riding a mule was shot dead within 50 yards of us, his body rolling down hill to within 20 ft. of our camp fire, too dead to partake of our abandoned breakfast, as we all remarked at the moment. We soon got into saddles and started off. . . .

"It now began to rain and to increase in violence until daybreak next morning. At

MINNINEWAH (WHIRLWIND). At one time a feared raider, Whirlwind had spent the few years previous to the 1874 outbreak peaceably at the Cheyenne Agency. Apparently, it was just for a round of excitement that he slipped out briefly and encountered Baldwin's unit of Miles' command: "Miles no good. Me lead 'em on long trail, round and round. Braves make big trail for him to follow, then slip back be-hind and scalp stragglers and shoot up rear.

"Got 'em down in breaks on gyp water. Soldiers got sick. Braves get on bluffs and throw rocks at 'em. Too sick to move.

"Sundown, Miles shoot 'em big gun—BOOM—tell every Indian for fifty miles where he camp. Every morning shoot 'em big gun—BOOM—tell every Indian fifty miles he still there. Umph. Heap big bull."

times we could keep our bearing with great difficulty. We knew, however, that the rain would cause the Inds. to abandon pursuit. But the trackless plain now became deep with mud and wearisome to our already fatigued horses . . . until 3 AM morning of Sept. 8. Both men and animals were now played out and rest be taken. We sat down back to back with rifles on laps and remained there until break of day.

"Country open and no timber so we had to keep in the draws. We traveled slowly until reached divide. Secreting horses we crawled to summit and by aid of field glasses located a large camp on Washita. As we were expecting to meet supply train at about this point it never entered our minds that it might be an Ind. camp, their tepees being conical like our tents. We were exultant and could have danced with joy.

"We returned to horses and ate more raw meat. We mounted again and kept in draws. Soon a terrific rain and hail storm broke, even worse than yesterday. . . . At length we approached the brow of bluff overlooking the Washita having ridden in full view of the camp, when it took but an instant to discover our mistake and we soon knew it was a camp of Cheyennes who had just left the agency and gone on war path. Rain was falling in sheets and only sign of life in camp was 2 squaws cutting wood. Backing our horses out of sight, we rode a mile at a good trot when came to head of ravine.

"We rode down the ravine, to keep out of sight, thinking it would lead us below the camp but not so. As we emerged into the valley we rode right into the camp and we saw that under the circumstances it would be folly to turn back, so we put on a bold demeanor and rode right thru the camp at a trot, finally emerging from the lower end of it, into the timber that skirted the bank of the river. In the village we saw only 3 or 4 squaws, of whom we took no notice and they, owing to our slouching blankets and dishevled [sic] hair . . . evidently took us for some Inds. This happened at 5 PM and soon the rainfall ceased.

SCOUT WILLIAM SCHMALSLE.

CAPTAIN WYLLYS LYMAN.

"We had crossed the Ft. Supply wagon trail just below Ind. village. An hour out from the river we halted in good grass and unsaddled horses and remained here some time. After starting again we at length reached south bank of Canadian and on opposite side we saw to our delight the camp fires of the supply train and Co. I, 5th Inf. the escort for it.

"Train was preparing for an early start and I informed officer of train guard the importance of rushing supplies to Miles as soon as possible and that he would be attacked at the Washita. I advised them to corral and stand off Inds. if attacked and go on at night, and get to Miles . . . but they were attacked and held to defensive until morning of 4th day."

The officer commanding Miles' supply train was Captain Wyllys Lyman, 5th Infantry. Baldwin left him one of his scouts, William Schmalsle, and continued with his others to Camp Supply. Lyman was attacked as warned, and on finding himself hopelessly trapped, composed an elegantly distracted message for help to the commanding officer of Camp Supply. He entrusted the paper to Schmalsle and hoped for the best. "That night Schmalsle stole thru Inds. surrounding the train and rode to Ft. Supply for reinforcements. The Inds. detected him getting through and fired on him and hotly pursued. He ran into a large herd of buffalo which stampeded and Schmalsle concealed himself from Inds. by keeping in with the running buffalo. In this way the tracks of his horse were obliterated. When leaving the herd he was miles from his starting point and in right direction for his destination which he reached following PM having covered 80 miles. His information started Kingsbury and Co. to relief of besieged train."

The Battle of Palo Duro Canyon

CHARLES A. P. HATFIELD, shown here as a cadet at West Point. Two years later he was a captain in Ranald Mackenzie's 4th Cavalry, the most respected Indian-fighting regiment in the Army.

BY autumn, 1874, it was apparent that Sherman's strategy of forcing the hostile Indians to collect in their hideouts at the edge of the Staked Plains was working, but no main camp had been found where a decisive blow could be struck. Nelson Miles had had a good chance, but his drive stalled because of inadequate logistical planning.

Ranald Mackenzie and his 4th Cavalry were methodically grinding their way northward along the Cap Rock, their progress hampered by booming, drenching thunderstorms. Indian sign increased, however, and on the night of September 26 an estimated 250 Comanches and Kiowas staged a daring night attack on Mackenzie's camp that lasted well into the morning. The colonel guessed he was close to an important village, and when the hostiles retired to the southwest he increased the number of scouts out looking for it. Mackenzie himself followed the Indians, as remembered by one of his company commanders, Captain Charles A. P. Hatfield of E Troop.

"At one o'clock P.M. we left camp with seven troops and the scouts and followed the broad Indian trail leading southwest. We proceeded leisurely, stopping occasionally to graze the horses, for our following the trail was only pretense, since MacKenzie [sic] knew that the Indians were trying to draw us away from their camp. As soon as it was dark everything changed. We left the trail and . . . marched at a good gait directly northwest, at right angles to the trail, for the Palo Duro Canon.

"About four o'clock next morning the 26th [sic.: it was the 28th] we came again on to the broad trail of the Indians, scarcely an hour old. The Indians supposing they had eluded us had returned to their camp. Knowing pretty soon that we were quite near the Palo Duro, we came to a halt to await the dawn. At the first crack of day we mounted and moved on. Presently we saw directly on our left the dark winding course of the canon Blanco, while in front of us, like a dark blotch on the prairie, was the Palo Duro. We very soon arrived at the head of a well worn trail leading down into the gloomy looking Palo Duro, and dismounting, on account of its steepness, we went running down the trail leading our horses. It happened that Troop E was in the lead which enabled me to observe everything.

"After we had gone about one hundred and fifty yards we ran on to an Indian on guard, who instantly discharged his rifle, waved a red blanket and disappeared immediately afterwards in a marvelous manner.

"When we arrived where the Indian had been we could see the effect of his signal. As far as the eye could see in the fast coming light, Indians were mounting their ponies and hurrying up the Canon.

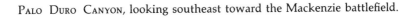

PALO DURO CANYON, looking southeast toward the Mackenzie battlefield.

"The first camp, a cluster of about forty teepees was directly under us. A stone could easily have been pitched into it, but so far below that the teepees appeared the size of a half dollar, and the ponies were mistaken by some for sheep and by others for chickens.

"This first bunch of teepees was at the mouth of the Canon Blanco, and from there the camp extended two miles up the Palo Duro, with intervals between the many small camps scattered along the stream.

"After a half hour of tumbling and slipping down the long trail, the head of the column reached the bottom, when the first two troops mounted and started in rapid pursuit. The Indians, though, had a good start of us and were able to take excellent cover up on the rough sides of the canon. We finally overhauled them, however, and being joined by the other troops a fairly satisfactory fight ensued.

"On account of the alarm given by the Indian sentinel the squaws managed to escape capture, and only four of their men were killed.

INDIAN PRISONERS AT FORT MARION in the spring of 1875. The officer in charge of them there was appalled at the conditions: "The roofs and walls of every casement are dripping with water, and in places covered with a green scum, while all the cells have a musty, sickening odor. . . . A short time in such confinement will destroy [their] general health."

"However, the main point was fully accomplished. The Indians had settled down in a snug winter camp, with ample supplies; if these were destroyed they would be helpless when cold weather came and be compelled to return to the reservation and surrender their arms.

"All of the camps, with the provisions of different kinds, flour and sugar, etc., drawn from the Indian department, and quantities of dried buffalo meat, were destroyed and burned. In addition about seventeen hundred of their horses were rounded up and driven up the long trail and back to the head of Tule Canon where our wagon train with its infantry escort had arrived and established camp.

"On the following morning MacKenzie disposed of the captured horses, ponies and mules. Some . . . were given to the most prominent scouts, and still others were distributed to the troops to replace horses which had succumbed to the hardships of the campaign.

"This left about fourteen hundred and fifty to be disposed of and these were taken out and shot. Of course, this seems creul [sic], but if MacKenzie had tried to keep them, there would have been a stampede on some dark night by the Indians, when he would have lost them and probably some of his own cavalry horses besides. With their horses gone and their teepees and supplies destroyed, the Indians could not face a winter on the plains and shortly began journeying back to the reservation."

There was more to the Indians' return to the reservation than Hatfield mentioned. The rains that broke the drought in early September continued furiously throughout the fall. Constantly kept on the run by the Army, unable to dry out, their horses shot and their tipis burned, hostile Cheyennes, Comanches, and Kiowas for years afterward referred to the closing phase of the Red River War as the "Wrinkled-hand Chase."

After surrendering—some bands held out until spring of 1875—several dozen chiefs and "ringleaders" were sent to Fort Marion, Florida, and imprisoned in the Castillo de San Marcos.

THE GREAT ATLANTIC COAST LINE
Washington, D. C., June 29, 1875
W. J. Walker
Genl. Eastern Passr. Agt.
P. O. Box 582

Hon. Sir:

A Guide to Florida under the auspices of the Atlantic Coast Line is now being prepared for the benefit of those contemplating a trip South next winter.

We are also preparing short sketches of many places of interest in Florida and we desire, if consistent with your official duty, to have photographed some of the prominent Indians now incarcerated at the Old Fort (Marion) at St. Augustine, Florida—all expense necessary thereto to be paid by this line. I therefore respectfully ask your assent, and hope for an early and favorable consideration to my request.

Very respectfully,
(s) *W. J. Walker*
Genl. E. P. Agt.

To the Honorable
Commissioner of Indian Affairs

Texas Comes of Age

CHARLES GOODNIGHT as a ranch manager was strict but fair. He fired foremen who drank and gambled unless they regained his trust, and once forbade another rancher's herd from crossing JA land when he suspected the cattle carried Texas fever. He did, however, send an experienced hand to guide the herd on a shortcut to their destination.

Goodnight had little use for his boss, British moneylender John George Adair. "He was an overbearing old son-of-a-gun," he recalled, "and would have been beaten up several times if it hadn't been for me."

COMANCHE and Kiowa Indians had barely vacated the Staked Plains before ranchers moved in to claim the luxuriant grasslands. The earliest and greatest of them was Charles Goodnight.

Born in Illinois, he was one day old when the Alamo fell; his parents emigrated to Texas in 1846. He was twenty-one when he moved up to Palo Pinto County at the time of the Brazos Reservation troubles. He served as a frontier scout and Ranger during the Civil War, which allowed him to keep an eye on his ranching interests. He wanted to sell some of his cattle, but with Reconstruction the local market was depressed; he could get a better price for them elsewhere, but large-scale cattle drives were not a proven proposition.

Before the Civil War it was unusual for more than fifty thousand head of cattle to

Opening the Panhandle:
Captain Goodnight and the JA Ranch

MOLLY GOODNIGHT. Born Mary Ann Dyer in Tennessee in 1839, she was the cherished only daughter in a houseful of sons. She was fifteen when her father moved the family to Texas; she met Goodnight soon after, but was past thirty when she married him. Molly Goodnight was a woman of delicate sensibilities. She learned much about the west when in Denver soon after her marriage she read of two men being lynched from one telegraph pole. She expressed her outrage at the barbarity to her husband, who replied, nonplussed, that he didn't think the pole would be damaged by it.

be exported beyond Texas borders. A few entrepreneurs had experimented with driving their herds to points as distant as Chicago, but inadequate distribution facilities, and the dangers posed by hostile Indians in getting beef to market, kept traffic to a minimum. In 1865, however, a plainsman and Indian interpreter who spoke fourteen languages, Jesse Chisholm, blazed a wagon trail from Wichita, Kansas, to Yukon, Indian Territory, to establish a trading post for Wichita Indians. Texas ranchers extended this trail southward all the way to the Rio Grande, with alternate routes, cutoffs, and feeder trails, all known collectively as the Chisholm Trail. With safety in numbers en route and a railhead in Wichita, the profitability of large-scale movement was assured, and the age of the great cattle drives began.

It was also in 1865 that Charles Goodnight decided to seek a better price for his

JA Ranch Chuck Wagon. As cattle drives grew in size and labor diversified, the cook rose to rival the trail boss in authority. The JA Ranch's Jerry Shea was reputedly able to cook for and feed forty men in half an hour, and was not afraid to work over Goodnight himself for being slow with a compliment. Goodnight was genuinely grieved to fire him—for drunkenness.

It was probably just such a resourceful range "cookie" who first stewed beef and red peppers into the fiery glory known as chili, although the recipe has antecedents dating back at least to the Revolution. Popularized by San Antonio street vendors in the 1880s, the "bowl of red" was a sensation at the Chicago World's Fair of 1893 and came to rival the Germans' barbecue as the premier Texas dish.

cattle in New Mexico. The next year he and his partner, Oliver Loving, blazed a trail west from Fort Belknap to Fort Sumner; soon other herds began moving along the Goodnight-Loving Trail. After Loving was killed by Comanches, Goodnight continued, driving herds from the ranch of Concho County cattle baron John Chisum to New Mexico market at a dollar-a-head margin. By 1871 the partners were splitting annual profits of seventeen thousand dollars. Goodnight extended his trail north to Colorado before settling down in Palo Duro Canyon at the JA Ranch, named for his partner in this venture, John Adair, who owned the land. Goodnight was hired as manager in exchange for one-third interest.

A number of other large ranches were staked out in the Panhandle, and a new trail, the Dodge City, was cleared, paralleling the Chisholm Trail on the west. This was the heyday of the cattle-driving era. During the next twenty-five years, about 10 million longhorns were herded out of the state to market. The best size for a traveling herd was about twenty-five hundred head, which could be controlled by two "point men" in front, two "press men" at the sides and a few others to round up stragglers. There also came greater organization: the chuck wagon with its centralized cooking made its appearance, followed by the hoodlum wagon for stowing gear. A good remuda held five or six horses for each cowboy; it was each hand's responsibility to see that one of his mounts was saddled at all times to deal with stampedes or Indian attacks.

Another asset that most drovers considered indispensable was the "lead steer," an animal that consistently worked his way to the front of the herd and assumed leader-

JA Ranch Cattle. While Goodnight's early drives were of longhorns and his Palo Duro operation began with Durhams, he began methodical improvement of his herd with the purchase of two hundred registered shorthorn bulls in 1881. In eleven years of breeding experiments with them and Herefords, he achieved a herd that combined the hardiness of the longhorn with the meatier characteristics of the other breeds.

JA Ranch Branding. Cowboy skills, brags, and bets growing out of their daily chores resulted in a unique contribution to American sport. The first professional rodeo in the country was held in Pecos, Texas, in 1885. Of the modern rodeo one old hand grumped, "I never go to such tommy-rot. I used to see better ones every morning.

ship. Goodnight had noticed just such a steer in one of the herds he bought from John Chisum. Fitted with a bell that was muffled at night, Old Blue led Goodnight's drives for eight years. He was somewhat spoiled, sleeping at the horse remuda and demanding handouts from the chuck wagon, but every sunrise found him at the fore of the herd, and once his bell was cleared, he started walking. The hands were in awe of him, and Goodnight treasured him. Old Blue died in 1890 after a dignified retirement; a photograph of his horns appears below.

Old Blue was a longhorn, but Goodnight was an early proponent of herd improvement through breeding. Some earlier Texas ranchers had crossed their stringy range cattle with Eastern types and achieved a meatier longhorn that was still hardy enough to stand the trail well. Goodnight began his operation in the Palo Duro with eighteen hundred Durham cattle, which he decided were not well suited to the climate, then achieved a splendid herd by crossing longhorn cows with Hereford bulls. An active experimenter, he even bred Polled Angus cows to buffalo, resulting in his "cattalo."

Throughout his career Goodnight maintained an interest in buffalo, some of which still roamed wild in the Palo Duro at the time he began ranching. In fact, his first fencing was less to keep track of his cattle than to keep the buffalo off his range. Later, in addition to breeding them with cattle, he also experimented with domesticating them; his hitched buffalo team was a local novelty for many years. He kept a herd of about 250, occasionally donating one to Comanches and Kiowas who rode over from their reservation with a request to kill one for old time's sake.

There was another side to Panhandle ranching that is less examined today than drives and roundups. Goodnight had married Molly Dyer in 1871; after the move to Texas she began keeping house in a mud-chinked cedar pole dugout on the floor of the canyon, two hundred miles from the nearest town. With the men away it was seventy-five miles to the closest neighbor, loneliness so profound that one of her great joys was talking to the three chickens that a ranch hand had brought her in a gunnysack. As she said, "No one can ever know how much company they were to me. They would run to me when I called them and follow me everywhere I went. They knew me and tried to talk to me in their own language."

Her privation was rewarded, however. When Adair died in 1885, having visited the JA only three times, Goodnight, who came to Texas landless, settled with his estate for 140,000 acres and 20,000 cattle. Molly Goodnight died in 1926, her husband in 1929 at age ninety-three.

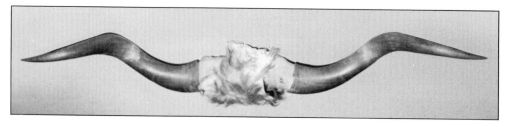

OLD BLUE'S HORNS.

A Ranger's Ranger:
Captain McNelly and the Flores
Affair

LEANDER McNELLY.

As the ranches in the Panhandle began to flourish, the established ranches in South Texas continued to suffer raids from bandits in Mexico. Of course, not all rustling originated there; any number of Anglo outlaws hid out in remote canyons, nabbing unbranded mavericks and even altering existing brands. But since the end of the Civil War at least 150,000 head had been driven across the Rio Grande, and the King Ranch alone lost nearly 35,000 head in four years.

At the time the Texas Rangers were reorganized and John B. Jones placed at the head of the Frontier Battalion, a second group called the Special Force was also organized. It was led by a thirty-year-old captain—tall, thin, and somewhat sickly Leander McNelly. His most celebrated adventure began on the morning of November 19, 1875, when he opened a communiqué and learned that Juan Flores, who had succeeded Cortinas as premier rustler along the border, had filched 250 American cattle and recrossed the Rio Grande into the sanctuary of his Las Cuevas Ranch. McNelly was in the saddle at once, leaving orders for his company of thirty Rangers to follow.

At midday McNelly arrived at the crossing and discovered three companies of U.S. Cavalry in the river-bottom brush thickets, with Flores' snipers firing potshots across the river at every opportunity. The cavalry on the border had standing orders for hot pursuit of rustlers into Mexican territory, but none of the officers seemed willing to assume responsibility, concluding rather to await orders. McNelly's Rangers clattered up at nine that night, tired and dusty but ready for a fight. When McNelly offered to cross the river with his own men, the regulars agreed to cover his retreat if he got into trouble.

The Rangers crossed the Rio Grande at one o'clock in the morning, intending, as McNelly said, to "learn them a Texas lesson they have forgotten since the Mexican War." The river was boggy and treacherous; after struggling to get five horses up the Mexican side, the rest of the men crossed three at a time in a leaking boat, two pulling and one bailing. Setting off on foot the three miles to Las Cuevas, they killed four sentries at an intervening ranch before walking into a terrible surprise—about three hundred Mexican irregulars, a third of them mounted, under Flores' command. McNelly knew that if he fled his men would be cut down like straw; he also knew that most Mexicans preferred to give Texas Rangers—*los tejanos diablos,* as they called them—a wide berth. Committed to a bald bluff, McNelly marched his men forward in the predawn gloom to within one hundred yards of the Mexicans, then retired hastily as though trying to pull them into an ambush. As Flores and his officers smiled at the naïveté of such a primitive ruse, McNelly got his men to cover and made his enemy believe he led a larger force than he had.

The Mexicans opened an attack at daylight, advancing repeatedly but not able to penetrate the Rangers' position. Flores was killed, but other groups arrived during the battle. McNelly, too, sent back for reinforcements; in response thirty cavalrymen crossed and fought with him during the day, but returned that night, calling his position hopeless. As they left, however, McNelly's nerve began to pay off. A Mexican delegation approached under a white flag, and McNelly with ten of his men went out to meet them. When the officers ordered him to quit Mexican soil, he announced the nature of his business, which he would not leave undone. The Mexicans promised to handle the matter officially, but McNelly snorted that the offer was worthless, knowing that it was usually officers who profited most from the rustling.

Clearly uncomfortable, the Mexicans requested a truce for the night. With staggering cheek McNelly demanded the return of a gun and two horses his men had lost in the fight. This they agreed to, and McNelly permitted them to remove the body of one of their officers from the battleground.

By daylight of November 20 the Mexican force had grown to several hundred. The

American consul in Matamoros was trying to negotiate McNelly's surrender and return, and the cavalry across the river had received their orders from Fort Brown: "If McNelly is attacked by Mexican forces on Mexican soil, do not render him any assistance." Flores' men were none the wiser, and the day passed without incident.

Near sundown McNelly again demanded the cattle and thieves, and said he would give the Mexicans an hour's notice before resuming hostilities. Forty minutes later two representatives arrived with their capitulation, and the Rangers reentered American territory that night. The next morning sixty-five stolen cattle were driven north across the river, the Mexicans claiming that the rustler apprehended had been killed, as the saying went, while trying to escape. This was the first time that stolen stock had been redeemed from Mexico, and another Ranger legend was born.

The Salt War

CAPTAIN McNelly was not the only Ranger officer engaged in chasing Mexican outlaws. John B. Jones, who had taken the beating by Kiowa Indians during the Red River War of 1874, was still major of the Frontier Battalion. He, too, was after Mexicans, but in his case the role of villain was less easy to define than with Flores. Large salt deposits spread from the foot of the Guadalupe Mountains, and for as long as anybody could remember, salt had been free for the taking, both to Anglo-Americans from El Paso, just over a hundred miles to the west, and to Mexicans who crossed the Rio Grande in sometimes lengthy cart trains. In 1877 an El Paso politico and newly elected judge, Charles Howard, established a personal claim over the salt beds. When he tried to enforce the claim by charging a fee to those who came for the salt, however, an outraged mob forced him to sign a paper forfeiting any exclusive rights. He was also required to post a twelve-thousand-dollar bond, resign his office, and move from El Paso.

Judge Howard went into exile at Mesilla, New Mexico, but returned on October 12, just long enough to shotgun a political enemy, Luis Cardis, to death. Major Jones arrived to keep the peace, which meant protecting Judge Howard's bondsmen from outraged Mexicans from across the border. The area was so isolated that Jones had to recruit a new company of Rangers and place them under a lieutenant who had no experience. Jones was soon called elsewhere, and Howard returned again—with the Rangers in escort—in December, to attempt to reassert his authority. The Mexican community would have none of it; one of Howard's bondsmen was stabbed to death, scalped, and his body stuffed in a gunnysack and left in the desert. A mob then surrounded Howard and his escort; it was to save the Rangers' lives that Howard gave himself up to his fate. He and two supporters were shot, butchered, dragged behind horses, and finally dumped in an abandoned well.

More Rangers might have been sent to restore order, but as the only real threat to peace had been Howard, the matter was allowed to pass, after an Anglo mob looted the town of San Elizario and sent the Mexican mob leaders packing for Mexico. Thereafter, salt was purchased without violence.

JUDGE CHARLES HOWARD   LUIS CARDIS

A MEXICAN BULL CART, of the type used to haul salt from the Guadalupe pans.

Sam Bass

ONE of the projects that called Major Jones back east from El Paso was quashing the career of a twenty-six-year-old phenomenon of a train robber named Sam Bass.

Originally from Indiana, Bass had worked as a teamster around the town of Denton, northwest of Dallas. He came to own a splendid quarterhorse and supplemented his income by racing, before going north on a cattle drive. In South Dakota he fell in with some bandits, and after lightening a Union Pacific train of sixty thousand dollars in gold, he returned to northern Texas. At his hilltop hideout just south of Denton he formed his own gang, which held up in appalling succession two stages and four trains. A special company of Rangers was formed to trap him, and an insider, Jim Murphy, informed Major Jones of an intended bank robbery in Round Rock, a small town just north of Austin. When the Bass gang rode in on July 19, 1878, Major Jones was waiting. A local resident named Jefferson Dillingham was present. "I saw it all. About 11 a.m., Sebe Barnes, Frank Jackson and Bass went into a grocery across the street from the livery stable in front of which, on a bench, sat officers. The latter noticed the strange men carried bulges beneath their shirts. They went over to inquire about their authority for carrying weapons.

"The Bass gang broke for their horses tethered to a fence in the rear of a hotel operated by a woman. In the melee Barnes fell dead of a gunshot wound as he turned into the avenue. Bass and Jackson mounted their horses, came out of the alley with bullets flying after them and sped westward."

Bass had been hit, once in the arm and once in the chest just beneath his heart. In a thicket near Brushy Creek, Jackson hid Bass in some undergrowth and made his escape. The next morning a black wood gatherer came into town and told authorities of moans he had heard coming from the thicket, and Dillingham's brother-in-law took out his hack and returned with Bass in the back. Bass lingered in agony through that day and night before expiring on his twenty-seventh birthday.

SAM BASS *(center)* poses with two members of his outlaw band—or so he thought. JIM MURPHY *(right)* infiltrated Bass' gang in the service of the Texas Rangers, tipped off the Rangers about the intended holdup in Round Rock, and disappeared before the gunfight.

COLONIAL CAPITOL AFIRE. Plans for a new capitol had been afoot for six years when the old one burned on November 9, 1881. Austin builders were allowed to cannibalize the hulk for its limestone, which found its way into several nearby buildings, and groundbreaking for the new capitol took place less than three months after the fire.

CAPITOL QUARRY. The source of stone used in the new capitol was Granite Mountain, a monolith of high-grade pink granite in Burnet County.

The Biggest Capitol

TEXAS' legislature and state departments had long since outgrown the so-called Colonial Capitol built in the early 1850s, and plans for a new one began with the Constitutional Convention of 1875, which voted a reserve of 3 million acres of the public domain to pay for it. The old capitol was gutted by a fire on November 9, 1881, which rendered a new seat of government imperative. The land payment, with an addition of fifty thousand acres to cover the cost of surveying the rest, was made on New Year's Day of 1882.

Contractor Abner Taylor began construction a month later, on the same site as the old building. He began using limestone quarried by prison labor at nearby Convict Hill, but before the basement was completed the stone proved to be cosmetically defective. Ferrous crystals imbedded in the limestone left streaks of discoloration. After contractual shenanigans by both Taylor and the state, the design was changed to produce a

CONVICT WORKERS. The Stonecutters' Union was infuriated by the use of prison labor to quarry and haul the stone, and by the importation of stonemasons from Scotland to piece the building together. They sued the contractor, who paid a five-hundred-dollar fine for violating the Alien Contract Labor Law.

THE GODDESS OF LIBERTY, fourteen feet high and holding aloft the Lone Star, was cast in zinc, in three pieces, by J. C. McFarland of Austin. She was raised to her home on the dome on February 26, 1888.

building of glittering pink granite from Burnet County, about fifty miles northwest into the Hill Country from Austin. A special narrow-gauge railway was built to haul the 15,700 carloads of stone, cut and transported by a thousand more convicts. With the switch to granite the roof was also redesigned, from slate to fourteen-ounce copper.

The building itself, the design of Elijah Myers of Chicago, was calculated to dazzle, built in the shape of a Greek cross 200 yards long and 100 yards across. For the construction Taylor imported five dozen stonecutters from Scotland, to which the local Stonecutters' Union took vigorous exception, including a boycott and lawsuit. The dome, conceived as brick but built in cast iron, towers 309 feet high, just a shade taller than the Capitol in Washington. Actually, it is two domes, the outer one painted pink to match the granite, the inner one ornately boxed and coved, surmounted by a Lone Star cap suspended by cables from the top of the outer dome.

Inside, no expense was spared. Cast-iron banisters and newels were imported from Belgium. Eight acres of floor space included a rotunda floored in colored glass. Decorative door hinges were specially cast in brass, as were the door knobs, lock sets, and window pulleys. Interior doors and transoms were fitted with intricately acid-etched glass panels, 114 cases of them, from Britain. Chambers and corridors were lined with seven miles of lavishly carved wainscoting in ash, cedar, cherry, mahogany, oak, pine, and walnut, at a cost of $115,600. The twenty-two-foot ceilings were corniced and decorated with $65,000 of plaster work. Only as the Romanesque behemoth neared completion did the builders throttle back, dropping porticoes planned for the ends of the east and west wings. Soon after completion, however, the twenty-six-acre grounds were enclosed in a wrought iron fence crafted in Ohio, painted black and studded with Lone Stars in gold leaf.

When the light switch was thrown on April 20, 1888, the bulbs in each of the

Senate Chamber's five-pointed chandeliers spelled out TEXAS, one letter in each point of the stars. The public was admitted the next day, and gasped.

The 3,050,000-acre land payment was conveyed to Charles and John Farwell of Chicago, two principals of Taylor, Babcock and Company, or the "Capitol Syndicate." It was A. C. Babcock who determined that the land should be ranched until it could be subdivided for farming, and thus in 1885 was born the XIT ("X" for ten members of the syndicate, "in Texas") Ranch, the largest ever, sprawling across nine Panhandle counties. Capital was raised by forming a corporation in Great Britain, the Capitol Freehold Land and Investment Company. The first cattle were driven up from the Fort Concho area by Ab Blocker of Austin, who devised the famous XIT brand, which was said to be rustler-proof. By November of 1886 the herd numbered more than 110,000 head. Some 15,000 of them were driven north to markets that year, and the herd stabilized at about 150,000.

The XIT was not unusual in being owned by a foreign corporation; the Matador Ranch, a concern of over a million acres on the forks of the Pease River, was owned by a Scottish syndicate. There and elsewhere, foreign investment in Texas land and cattle marked a shift in ranching power away from local pioneers and toward corporate board rooms. Foreign owners had little feel for the romantic cultural aspects of ranching, and conflicts between the two factions helped to hasten the end of the era. The XIT Syndicate itself, true to Babcock's plan, began divesting itself of its land in 1901, and sold the last of its cattle in 1912.

DUST STORM. Increased ranching brought more and more people to northwest Texas, a vast, flat prairie of titanic weather forms. Blasting by tornadoes was one frequent hazard; another was dust storms like the one shown here approaching the town of Midland. Winters could be bitter; the most regular event was the "norther," and nowhere in Texas were they more abrupt than on the treeless plains: "First, a chilly whiff; then a puff, the grass bends flat, and, bang, it is upon us—a blast that would have taken a top-gallant sail smack out of the bolt-ropes, and cold as if blowing across a sea of ice. We gallopped to the nearest ravine, and hurried on all the clothing we could muster. . . .

"A thermometer . . . showed a fall of sixty degrees in seven hours."

This photo also depicts an important stage in the evolution of West Texas: windmills, pumping water from a vast underground aquifer, opened the plains to farmers as well as ranchers. With them came intensified competition for land and the "sodbusters'" determination to fence their fields against the herds of cattle.

Range Wars

BEGINNING in the 1860s and increasing through the 1870s, cattle spreads great and small found themselves facing a challenge they regarded as more threatening than either Indian attacks or thieves from Mexico. That was the advent of sheep ranches encroaching into the cattle range.

This was a conflict that erupted all across the American frontier, but Texas was a particularly volatile place for it. A good deal of the Texas range, particularly the Hill Country west of San Antonio and Austin, was better suited to raising sheep than it was cattle. And that region was largely settled by ethnic immigrants like Germans and Alsatians, who had not acquired the cultural revulsion against sheep that inflamed diehard cattlemen.

It is not clear exactly when the bias against sheep overtook consideration of using the range efficiently. Mifflin Kenedy, cofounder of the King Ranch, had imported ten thousand Merinos in 1854, but sold them off a couple of years later. But by the time the open range began to be limited by the growing population, it was instinctive for those who had adopted the "cowboy culture" to claim all the remaining grazing for themselves and expect the state to sustain them. They did indeed have some valid arguments against the sheep. First, although sheep could subsist on rocky hills that could not support cattle, good open range on which the sheep had grazed were often ruined for the cows' use. Sheep ate all the grass cover down to the roots, unlike the cattle, and their small, sharp hooves chopped into soil that would be left relatively undisturbed by the passage of a herd of longhorns. The cattlemen's principal complaint, though, was infection of the range with sheep scab, and laws pushed through the legislature worked to quarantine sheep within their county, and thus block the necessary changes in pasture, unless they were inspected by a state agent.

Other factors, cultural ones just as powerful, were also at work, however. Sheep raising was thought unmanly and ridiculous. Most sheepmen were foreigners, either Mexicans or Europeans, and were already objects of disgust and derision. They had no counterpart to the bunkhouse fraternity that warmed and encouraged cow hands. Since most shepherds worked alone in isolated camps, they were easy victims of cowboy gangs. Houses were burned, camps wrecked, and woollies slaughtered. Shepherds, who often went unarmed, were beaten and whipped; some who tried to resist, or who refused to clear out, were killed. Every culture has its ugliness; this was the seamy side of the cowboy.

Some ranchers, like Charles Goodnight, reached accords with local sheepmen and abided by them, but as Texas entered the 1880s, thousands of sheep every year had their throats cut, or were shot, poisoned, or rimrocked—stampeded over cliffs. Still, the profit potential in sheep herding, as much as $1,850 per year on a thousand-head herd, was too great for the cattlemen to wipe it out, and the number of sheep in Texas increased dramatically, from about 1.25 million head in 1870 to over 6 million in 1880.

While cattlemen were unanimous in their opinion of sheepmen—that they were "just too low down for any use," as one remarked—all was not harmony among the ranchers themselves. As competition for land increased, it became clear that the business' major flaw, that most of them depended on the public range without owning an acre, was a fatal one for that class.

Mifflin Kenedy was one of the first large-scale ranchers to improve his herds with crossbreeding. Not coincidentally, he also pioneered the use of fences, when he enclosed his Laureles Ranch with thirty-six miles of smooth wire. Barbed wire, invented in 1873 and introduced to the Texas range in 1879, soon came into general use—and abuse. While the great corporate ranches like the XIT and the Matador had the funds to fence vast pasturage, the worst offenders were the landless cattlemen. They, too, were increasing their herds as fast as they could, encouraged by northern beef prices that rose from seven dollars a head in 1880 to twenty-five dollars in 1883. Some who owned

SHEEP RANCHING, while concentrated in the Texas Hill Country, also complicated land questions on the Staked Plains, where the prevalence of Hispanic shepherds on the New Mexico side of the line sometimes created conflicts with ranchers on the Texas side.

On the JA Ranch Charles Goodnight reached a peaceable settlement with them. Indeed, on those ranches that were owned by foreign investors who did not share the cowman's hatred of the sheep culture, herds of woollies began to appear among the cattle, once it was apparent that the two were not antithetical range enemies. They even cropped up on the JA; those shown here grazed the largest of the Panhandle's kingpin ranches, the XIT.

BARBED WIRE FENCING. This road through the JA Ranch lands, flanked by fences on both sides, illustrates the end of the public range era. Charles Goodnight was among the first in the Panhandle to employ fences, at least in part to control his intricate breeding experiments. He also, however, was an example of moderation, a proponent of fencing effectively but not abusively.

small acreage fenced that, then drove their herds onto public range until the grazing was exhausted, then fenced them into protected pastures, shutting out other open-range herds. Several ranchers who owned no land at all took to fencing in thousands of acres to which they had neither title nor lease. Farmers, whom the ranchers ranked barely above sheepmen in respectability, small landowning ranchers, and sometimes whole towns found themselves completely enclosed in "pastures" that had not even a gate for exit. Mail and transportation were disrupted as roads were blocked, and fence cutting, done at the risk of one's life, became general.

A drought in the summer of 1883 made it imperative for open-range cattlemen to reach water and grazing for their dying herds. By autumn it was estimated that fences valued at $20 million had been ruined, often several miles every night snipped by organized groups like the "Javelinas" and the "Owls." The situation was so volatile that Governor John Ireland called a special session of the legislature for the following January to settle the matter for good. After passionate debate, the legislature made fence cutting a felony, but also outlawed the fencing of unowned land and required fences that crossed public roads to have gates every three miles. The law had the desired effect, but hard feelings lasted for years.

The legislature soon outlawed the open-range practice itself, requiring every rancher to own or lease his grazing land. It was the only way to permanently settle the range wars, although it wrote an end to a colorful frontier era. It also ended sheep drives across cattle ranges to change pastures, which also ended the land disputes with, if not the visceral disgust toward, the sheep ranchers.

The Apache Menace Fades

DURING the period when the great ranches of the Panhandle were flourishing, the area of Texas between the Pecos and Rio Grande rivers remained unredeemed desert. In part this was due to the hostility of the climate, but an equally significant factor was the hostility of Lipan and Mescalero Apaches who clustered about the higher mountain ranges. These were the Indians whom the Comanches had driven from the Plains in the mid-eighteenth century, but long after the latter succumbed to the Anglos' power, the Apaches retained a truculent independence and raided more or less at will. With their sharp wits and close attunement to the desert environment, they were a formidable obstacle to settlement.

After the close of the war with Mexico, an army column sent to survey a route from San Antonio to El Paso covered two thirds of the distance when they were forced to turn back. In the Davis Mountains they had run afoul of a powerful Mescalero chief named Gómez. After bartering for their lives with two subchiefs, the engineers made good a rain-soaked night escape. Another nearby chief turned back another army column by convincing the officer in charge that he commanded two thousand warriors in

THE CHISOS MOUNTAINS in West Texas were a favorite Mescalero camping place.

the field, a brag that must have raised guffaws in the *ranchería* after the troops hiked out at the double.

When the American Government sent out commissioners to draw a line between the United States and Mexico, they greeted these quick and practical people with introductions like, "The Great Chief of the American people lives far, very far, toward the rising sun." It was a toss-up who was more disgusted, the Apaches themselves or the white frontiersmen who knew them. As John Woodland, the British-born interpreter at Fort Inge, grumped in 1854: "Why do people . . . always make Indians talk in that hifalutin way they do? Indians don't talk so, and when folks talk that way to them they don't understand it. They don't like it neither. I went up with Lieutenant ———, when he tried to make a treaty with the . . . Apaches. He had been talking up in the clouds, all nonsense, for half an hour, and I was trying to translate it just as foolish as he said it. An old Indian jumped up and stopped me—'What does your chief talk to us in this way for? We an't babies, we are fighting men; if he has got anything to tell us we will hear it, but we didn't come here to be amused, we came here to be made drunk, and to get some blankets and tobacco.' "

To help control Apache depredations Fort Davis was put on the defense line in 1854, and the Apaches were quick to learn what was expected of them. One chief, a Gómez confederate named Nicolás, entered Fort Davis on invitation and concluded a treaty. He was then bundled onto a stagecoach for El Paso, where he was wined and dined, and Nicolás obligingly furnished enough blarney to choke on: "I am glad I have come. My heart is full of love for my white brothers. They have not spoken with forked tongues. We have made a treaty of peace and friendship. When I lie down at night the treaty will be in my heart, and when I arise in the morning it will still be there. And I will be glad I am at peace with my white brothers. It is well!"

On the return trip, twenty miles from Fort Davis, Nicolás suddenly yanked a colonel's revolver from its holster, leaped from the coach, and disappeared. The next day he and his warriors killed two of the herd guard as they made off with most of the post's stock. A detachment of fourteen raced out after them and recaptured about one hundred head of horses, but the lieutenant in command pulled up short in the face of a forbidding canyon that had ambush written all over it. His men, all volunteers from Texas acting true to their heritage, prevailed on his manhood to lead them into the canyon. None of their bodies were ever found.

That method of Apache fighting, dashing out after them in consequence of a raid, seldom netted more than frustrated officers and fagged horses. Not until 1880 was a successful innovation employed.

The catalyst was Beduiat, called Victorio, a powerful chief of the Eastern Chiricahua Apaches, who led a large following of warriors also from the Mescalero Reservation. Driven to hostility by years of government duplicity, his raids during 1879 in Arizona, New Mexico, and Chihuahua led the Army to order most of the troops out of Fort Davis to New Mexico to help in the pursuit.

The commander at Fort Davis, General Benjamin Grierson, had a better idea, however. Instead of forever galloping out into probable ambush, Grierson advised the army to anticipate Victorio's moves and seize the waterholes in his projected path, thus turning against the Apaches the desert climate that was usually to their advantage. Grierson knew that Victorio was being slowly squeezed between columns of 9th Cavalry in southern New Mexico and a Mexican army pressuring his Chihuahua hideouts.

SAN JUAN, a Mescalero Apache chief, in traditional dress.

Grierson expected him to attempt an end run northward through West Texas in an attempt to reach fresh supplies at the Mescalero Reservation in New Mexico. The Army approved the plan, and instructed Grierson to position his forces accordingly.

True to prediction, Victorio crossed the Rio Grande late in July 1880; Grierson was holding the Tinaja de las Palmas waterhole in Quitman Canyon with two dozen soldiers. Learning that he was directly in Victorio's path, he had fortifications flung up and sent for reinforcements. The Apaches tried mightily to drive Grierson away, but fled instead themselves when cavalry columns charged into the melee from both sides. Victorio recrossed into Mexico, leaving seven dead.

He came back on August 2, spent two days eluding Grierson's scouts and raced north. Grierson drove his men sixty-five miles in less than a day, not chasing him, but moving to seize the critical Rattlesnake Springs before Victorio reached them. He succeeded, and after another blistering firefight Victorio was forced back into Mexico, again without supplies. Out of ammunition, Victorio and his following were trapped by a Mexican army and slaughtered.

VICTORIO *(left)*, a chief of the Eastern Chiricahuas, was not just a walleyed raider. The Apache agent in New Mexico knew him to be sincere and peaceable when left alone in his homeland; among his own people he was known for his fastidious grooming. BENJAMIN GRIERSON *(center)* had a reputation in Indian fighting even before coming to FORT DAVIS *(below)*, having been in command at Fort Sill during the Satanta arrest in 1871; still, he had difficulty getting his Apache scheme approved. Many other officers disliked him for his not being a West Pointer, and snickered unfairly at his all-Negro regiment, the 10th Cavalry. Grierson's teenaged son, ROBERT *(right)* was present at the Tinaja de las Palmas Fight, recording in his diary that as Victorio's warriors chased a cavalry platoon up the valley, "We let fly from our fortifications at the Indians about 300 yds. off & golly!! you ought to've seen 'em turn tail & strike for the hills."

"By Gobs, That's My Rulin' "
—Judge Roy Bean

AFTER the Apaches retreated from the vast desert stretches of western Texas and Anglos arrived in greater numbers, courts of law were slower to follow. The most important legal entity, as the saying went, was Judge Lynch. There were vigilantes, and feuds, and companies of Texas Rangers galloping from one trouble spot to another. When authority did arrive, usually in the form of a justice of the peace responsible for a huge district, the equity dispensed often scandalized more urban folks. Some early-day JPs became legends for the pragmatism, not to say larceny, of their decisions, but none more so than Judge Roy Bean of Langtry. Accordingly, it is more difficult with him to separate truth from apocrypha. It is not true that he ever hanged anybody; those who think of him as a "hanging judge" have him confused with Isaac Parker of Fort Smith, Arkansas. (He did sentence a few to death, but allowed them to escape.) On the other hand, when a man fell from the high railroad bridge over the Pecos River and his body was brought to Judge Bean for disposition, he went through the corpse's pockets and found forty dollars and a revolver. It is true that he impounded the firearm and fined the body the forty dollars for carrying a concealed weapon.

Born in Kentucky around 1825, his adventures began at the end of the Mexican War, when he and his brother Sam outfitted a trade caravan to Chihuahua. Unexplained trouble there caused them to vacate in a hustle; all that Bean would ever say was that his horse disliked the water. Sam reappeared as a bartender in New Mexico mining towns, and Roy went to San Diego to stay with his other brother, Joshua, a noted citizen and militia officer. Jailed briefly in the spring of 1852 for dueling, Roy Bean escaped and rejoined Joshua, now operating a saloon in San Gabriel, California. After Josh's murder Roy continued the business for several years. Shortly before the Civil War he showed up at Sam's establishment in Mesilla, penniless and with a stiff neck from having nearly been hanged by a rival for the affections of a *señorita.* After the war he settled in San Antonio, earning a shady living from his residence on South Flores Street—a neighborhood still known as Beanville. At various times he operated a dairy, the profitability of which was explained when a customer discovered a minnow in his milk, a woodyard (not his trees), and a butcher shop (not his cattle). Also, of course, he operated a saloon. He married one Virginia Chavez in October of 1866 and had four children.

By early 1882 Bean had enough domesticity; he obtained a stock of whiskey and followed the construction crews of the Sunset Railroad as they built west toward El Paso. After a short stay at the transient village of Vinegaroon he relocated at Eagle Nest Springs and thence, a short distance away, established a permanent refreshment stop at Langtry, on the Rio Grande about seventy miles above Del Rio. Railroad officials main-

LILLIE LANGTRY. Born Emilie Charlotte Le Breton on the Isle of Jersey in 1852, her birthplace and fair complexion were the source of her nickname, the Jersey Lily. Finally able to visit Judge Bean's Langtry late in 1903, she noted that the "afternoon sun was blazing down on the parched sandy plain, with its monotonous clotting of sage-brush and low-growing cactus, when the Sunset Express came to a sudden stop. . . . I hurriedly alighted, just as a cloud of sand heralded the approach of a numerous throng of citizens ploughing their way along to give me the 'glad hand.' The cowboys were garbed in their finest leathers and most flamboyant shirts, one loosing off his gun as he passed me, in tangible proof of his appreciation of my visit."

tained that the town was named for a crew foreman; Bean asserted that he named the place in honor of Lillie Langtry, a lovely British actress (and mistress of the Prince of Wales), whom Bean revered. During one of her American tours, Bean went so far as to send an invitation to visit. The famous "Jersey Lily" sent her apologies that it was impossible to add Langtry to her itinerary, but she offered to send the town an ornamental drinking fountain. This Bean refused, however, explaining that "the only thing the citizens of Langtry did not drink was water."

Texas Rangers who patrolled the thinly settled districts began bringing suspects to Bean for disposition, rather than carting them two hundred miles to Fort Stockton. His frequent legal trouble in San Antonio made him conversant with enough terminology to sound judicial, and after the Rangers obtained his official appointment, Bean obtained a small collection of law volumes. He also began compiling his "Statoot Book," one entry of which pronounced cheating at cards "a hangin offense, if ketched."

Bean lived out his life as the "Law West of the Pecos" with only two interruptions
—he failed reelection in 1886 and 1896. He continued to function during these times,
however. "Once a justice," he explained, "always a justice." From his courthouse-
saloon, the Jersey Lilly, Bean's law became famous for its opprobrious eccentricity, but
often as not he had common sense on his side. He granted divorces without authority,
arguing that since a justice of the peace had power to marry people, he necessarily had
power to remedy his errors. He refused to remit to the state fines he collected, asserting
that as the state judiciary sent him no money, it must follow that he was expected to
maintain himself. Most of his business dealings were disreputable but relatively harm-
less: liquor route salesmen were bilked for rounds of drinks, jurors who failed to belly
up during court recesses were dropped from the rolls, and whistle-stop customers were
not given change—those who demanded it were fined for contempt, in the amount of
change due, just as the defendant's train was pulling out.

Judge Bean's most celebrated adventure happened in February of 1896, when he
outwitted Texas Rangers, federal marshals, and Mexican *rurales* to stage the champion-
ship fight between Peter Maher and Bob Fitzsimmons. Prizefighting was illegal in all
surrounding states, including Chihuahua, and a special session of the legislature outlawed it expressly to prevent the bout from taking place. Promoters announced the

Judge Roy Bean was a bullying swindler, but he took his judicial duties seriously.
Shown here is a defendant on trial for stealing the white horse at left. The closest
Judge Bean ever came to executing capital punishment was to place a noose around
the neck of one horse thief, to give him a good scare before letting him go. More
typical was a similar case wherein the defendant was found to have three hundred
dollars on his person. Upon conviction, Bean fined him only two hundred dollars,
with a grump that he could have at least stolen a decent horse.

fight for El Paso—or thereabouts—and as authorities converged to break it up, the fight party and spectators were entrained for Langtry. Judge Bean, first making sure he had enough liquid to sell, had constructed a temporary pontoon walk out to a sand bar in the middle of the international boundary. The fight itself, however, was a bust. Maher went down in less than two minutes.

Judge Bean never lived to meet the beacon of his existence, Lillie Langtry. The fifty-one-year-old stage legend scheduled a stop, but did not arrive until ten months after his death in March of 1903. She graciously received Bean's six-shooter as a memento, but was spared having to adopt his pet bear when the animal broke its tether and scattered the gathering.

Roy Bean, for all his larcenous foibles, tried when he could afford it to render proper justice. Elsewhere on the Texas scene in the rough-and-tumble eighties, it was not always easy to tell the good guys from the bad. A case in point was Ben Thompson, elected city marshal of Austin in December of 1880.

Born in Yorkshire in 1842, he was nine when his parents emigrated to Texas and settled in Austin. He was only thirteen when put to his first trial, for having shot a friend, but he served no time for the offense. He trained to become a printer before visiting New Orleans when he was eighteen. There he had a dispute with a Frenchman named De Tour; by consent the two were locked in a dark icehouse for a knife duel, and it was Thompson who emerged. Friends spirited him back to Austin, where what money he didn't make at his printing he won by gambling, a pastime at which he became a master. His kindness, wit, and affability won him friends of staunch loyalty, but even they learned to leave him alone when he had been imbibing. As a drunk he was mean and abusive; he picked fights and he killed people.

Thompson served in the Confederate army on the Rio Grande, where he operated monte banks for others in his regiment, and after the surrender he was off to Mexico to serve in Maximilian's army. Back in Austin he served again—two years in the penitentiary for attempting to murder his wife's brother—before going north to operate a gaming house in Abilene, Kansas, in partnership with a war buddy named Phil Coe. They became a well-known pair on the Kansas scene; one of the better stories of their stay involved Abilene's marshal, "Wild Bill" Hickok. Coe and Thompson's establishment, the Bull's Head on First Street, was identified over the door by a painting of a longhorn bull with some oversized anatomy. Hickok one day informed Thompson that the sign had given offense to some residents, and ordered it modified. Thompson protested that it was a Texas bull, and everything grew big in Texas. Hickok was not amused and the marquee was repainted. After Thompson returned to Austin to recuperate from a buggy accident, which also maimed his wife and son, he learned that Hickok had killed Coe in a dispute over either a gambling debt or a woman.

Thompson later drifted back to Kansas, serving a stint as house dealer at the Long Branch Saloon in Dodge City before heading to Colorado as a hired gun for the Atchison, Topeka and Santa Fe Railroad, then involved in a dispute with the Denver and Rio Grande over right-of-way to the goldfields. With the five-thousand-dollar fee he received he returned to Austin and bought a concession over the Iron Front Saloon on Congress Avenue, where the gambling marathons vied for local attention with Thompson's shooting sprees. Typically drunk one night, he observed a faro game for some

BEN THOMPSON.

minutes before whipping out his revolver. As patrons dove for cover he shot the chips off the table, shot out the lights, reloaded and sauntered down Congress, shooting out the streetlights. When he sobered up, he sheepishly paid his fine and damages, explaining that his faro equipment seemed defective, and he wanted to encourage his house dealer to buy some new.

Acquitted of another murder in 1876, Thompson was defeated in a race for city marshal, but was elected on his second try. The criminal elements in Austin were unwilling to tangle with someone vastly meaner than themselves; during his tenure they went into virtual seclusion and Austin enjoyed unprecedented peace. Thompson, however, was soon back in trouble.

He visited San Antonio, where he killed Jack Harris, a sometime gambling rival and locally prominent politico who owned the Vaudeville Variety Theater. He was held several months before being tried and acquitted; on his return to Austin he was greeted with a victory parade up Congress Avenue. During this difficulty he had resigned his office, and now lived by his gambling, a chronic troublemaker for the police department.

In March of 1884 he went back to San Antonio, in the company of another feared lawman-gunslinger, King Fisher of Uvalde. There was a rumor that Fisher had offered to mediate the dispute between Thompson and the Vaudeville Theater crowd. Once there, Fisher and Thompson chatted and shared a drink with the Vaudeville's two managers before retiring to an upstairs table with them and a house detective to discuss their differences. Suddenly, their voices rose and a fusillade of shots rang out. Although Fisher and Thompson managed to disable the bouncer and mortally wound one of the managers, they were blasted into the next world by a total of twenty-two slugs, mostly from a curtained theater box above them and opposite.

The murders of Thompson and Fisher caused a shock wave from one end of the state to the other, and touched off a lively, and sometimes profound, debate over whether society, to protect itself from crime, should resort to hiring characters more dangerous than the criminals.

Jay Birds vs. Woodpeckers

THE FORT BEND COUNTY COURTHOUSE in Richmond was one of scores of county seats that mimicked the statehouse in style and pink granite construction.

ALTHOUGH Coke's coup had ended the Reconstruction period of state government in 1874, there was one place where the carpetbag still ruled. Black people comprised the majority in Fort Bend County, on the Brazos River southwest of Houston. By the spring of 1888 the prolonged abuses of power by black Republicans and outsiders spurred white regular Democrats to organize. At the county seat of Richmond a newly formed Young Men's Democratic Club announced a grand parade and rally for July 7. From an initial strength of two hundred the organization grew quickly. In the cocky paramilitary romance of the times, they adopted showy uniforms, and became known as Jay Birds— they spelled it as two words. Woodpeckers, of course, nest in holes in trees, and popular ornithology had it that jays would scream and fuss until they drove woodpeckers from their nests. Thus, the carpetbaggers and black Republicans became known as Woodpeckers, and the last great Texas feud acquired its name.

Violence was sparked when the Jay Bird Democrats tried to woo the Negro vote away from the Republicans. On the night of August 29 a prominent white farmer, J. M. Shamblin, was shotgunned to death through his parlor window as he sat reading the Bible. (A black tenant was later tried and executed.) Less than a week later a Richmond storekeeper and prominent Jay Bird, Henry Frost, was shot and wounded on the street. The day after the Frost shooting, a rally brought out four hundred Jay Birds, and five black Woodpeckers were given ten hours to clear out of town. With an accurate sense of the popular drift, the Republicans declined to field candidates in the upcoming election.

But that was not the end of it. Not every ambitious Jay Bird who wanted to hold office could be nominated, and disgruntled would-be candidates formed an independent organization. The regular Jay Birds stood, in effect, for disenfranchising the black electorate as entirely as the white Democrats had been during Reconstruction; when the independents turned and courted the black vote, they inherited the Woodpecker name from the defunct Republican organization. During the campaign a black church was fired into, killing one and wounding a second, but the Woodpeckers won the election in spite of the intimidation. Still, the Jay Birds would not give up; the new county tax assessor wound up killing the man he had defeated, later to be killed himself by his victim's brother.

A climactic street battle occurred on August 16, 1889, before the Richmond courthouse, in which the Woodpecker sheriff and his uncle, formerly county treasurer, were killed, as was the Jay Bird wounded the year before, Henry Frost. After this the Woodpeckers vacated their offices precipitately, taking with them the last vestige of carpetbag rule. Texas Rangers were sent to prevent further violence, but with the Jay Birds in control the fighting ceased. Still, the Rangers made certain by appointing a Ranger sergeant, Ira Aten, sheriff.

The Jay Birds ruled Fort Bend County virtually unopposed until a decision by the federal Supreme Court forced them to integrate in 1953. The last meeting was held in 1959.

Texas in Transition

SERGEANT Aten was one of the last of a breed of frontier Texas Rangers that was slowly dying out, for as the range was fenced in and towns sprouted more thickly, the need for them diminished. One of the last great officers before the politicization of the department was Captain John Armstrong, who trailed John Wesley Hardin, the killer of at least forty men, to Alabama. Single handedly and under fire, in a railroad car, Armstrong killed one, captured Hardin and three others, and returned them to Texas for trial. It was left to Captain Bill McDonald, though, to speak the last word on Ranger composure. A Dallas sheriff, faced with unruly crowds over an illegal prizefight, "sent for the Rangers." When McDonald stepped off the train, the sheriff asked, aghast, whether he was the only one. McDonald's reply: "You only got one riot, don't you?"

Considerable significance can be found in the fact that McDonald was summoned, not to an outpost on the frontier, but to Dallas, and that he arrived not on a horse but a train. Texas was changing so fast—urbanizing and industrializing so fast that the old timers would hardly have recognized the place. In 1890 Dallas had some 38,000 people; Fort Worth, thirty miles west of Dallas, a railhead village at the end of the Civil War, had boomed to 23,000. San Antonio was virtually the same size as Dallas; Galveston had grown to 29,000, Houston to 27,000. Austin held 14,000 residents, the same as Waco, a town halfway to Dallas that had blossomed in the wake of the cattle boom.

Cotton, of course, had never been dethroned; indeed, it had transformed into an industry that would have amazed antebellum planters. The labor shortage brought on by freeing the slaves had proven a temporary setback. During the nineties the annual crop exceeded 3 million bales valued at well over $100 million, more than the value of all other agriculture combined. And perhaps a third of all industrial investment in Texas was connected in some way with cotton processing. The cattle empire had captured the spotlight, but cotton continued to pay the bills.

Texas' industrial capacity had turned older conditions on their ear. In the colonies and Republic, wheat flour was an almost unobtainable luxury; during the 1870s the flour industry, producing from more than five hundred mills, was the largest nonagricultural concern in the state. The tall pine forests of East Texas that stood over the early immigrants were now the seat of a lumber industry that, in the eighties, surpassed flour milling as the most important. One wage earner in six in Texas worked in a sawmill; Kirby Lumber Company near Beaumont, whose sawmills had an annual capacity of 400 million board feet, was chartered with capital stock of $10 million, making it the state's largest business concern.

Much of the industrial expansion was the result of the spread of railroads across Texas. In the case of lumber and cattle, benefits resulted from the availability of transportation directly to national and international streams of commerce. In 1893 more than a third of the cargo handled by trains in Texas was lumber—nearly 3 million tons of it.

And the establishment of railheads in Central Texas circumvented northern quarantine laws and gave Texas cattle a direct route to national markets, the last nail in the coffin of the cattle drive era. After 1876 the advent of refrigeration created a high-dollar meat-packing industry on the coast, and after the turn of the century, packing plants became the mainstay of Fort Worth's economy.

Other industries were the children of the railroads themselves. Extensive deposits of coal had long been known in Texas, but were not developed until the conversion of locomotive boilers from wood to coal. From that time, however, the industry boomed; richest of the early regions was the Cross Timbers, west of Fort Worth. At Coalville in Palo Pinto County a vein broached the surface; workers had only to load it into wagons and haul it to the nearest railhead to fuel the trains. Secondary industries like brickmaking and clay firing were also stimulated, as their development had been retarded by a lack of cheap, efficient fuel. By the early nineties, railroads in Texas were hauling nearly 2 million tons of coal a year, freight second in volume only to lumber.

There was a brief flurry of interest over Texas' possibilities to produce iron and copper, but the ventures failed to last. Explorations for other minerals sometimes yielded startling discoveries, however. In 1889 a drilling rig at Grand Saline punched

HIGH BRIDGE OVER THE PECOS. The pervasiveness of industrial change finally reached into Texas' arid, pastoral west with the completion of the Pecos River railroad bridge. The opportunity to ship beef direct from ranch to market spelled the end of open range and overland cattle drives.

over a hundred feet into pure rock salt without finding the bottom of the deposit. Up to that time salt production had been limited to small solar evaporating plants capable of making a few hundred pounds a day; they fell by the wayside and Grand Saline became a major national producer.

The spread of railroads across Texas was not cheap. After 1850 a variety of county bonds and state land grants were issued to railroads as inducements for construction, and the process was accelerated when the Constitution of 1876 did away with them in favor of a general provision to grant sixteen sections of land for each mile of line laid. Thus, the land grants that reached scandalous proportions across the country occurred in Texas in like measure; under the 1876 provisions alone railroads were compensated for their Texas construction with more than 32 million acres of public domain.

What Texas got for its investment was an extensive, efficient, and profitable rail system, but the blessing was not unmixed. Not only did towns bypassed by the lines wither and die, the railroads began to abuse their position with consistent daring. Operating virtually unregulated through the seventies and eighties, railroads in Texas granted free passes by the thousands as thinly disguised bribes to politicians and influential community leaders. Operating largely through the Texas Traffic Association, routes were pooled to avoid competition, and freight rates to farmers on noncompetitive routes were inflated almost to ruination.

Farmers began organizing in opposition, not just to railroads but to the other perceived abuses of the pro-business Gilded Age, as early as the summer of 1873, when the state Grange, or "Patrons of Husbandry," organized at Salado. In three years the Texas Grange ballooned to forty thousand members, sometimes in competition with and sometimes in league with other organizations such as the Farmers' Union and Farmers' Alliance. Most notable for their work in improving the educational system, the Grangers broadened their political agenda to include support of a pure food and drug law, popular election of senators, inflation of the money supply, and a host of business and land reforms.

An inevitable coalescence of virtually all disaffected groups came together as the People's or Populist Party in 1892. It consisted of farmers, sheepmen, and small ranchers who finally found themselves on a common ground against giant, foreign-owned cattle operations; laborers and Greenbackers suffering from big-business practices; and a porridge pot of Prohibitionists, Socialists, Republicans, and Jeffersonian Democrats. Their high tide rose in 1894 in Texas, when they carried a number of local slates and put two dozen men in the state legislature—two in the Senate and twenty-two in the House. They were not effective, however. Regular Democrats killed all their measures save four of little consequence, and at the local level Populist incompetence quickly disillusioned most of their following. The party declined rapidly after 1896 and carried no state offices after 1900. By then, however, they had managed to force the mainstream of the Democratic Party to come around to Populist positions on many issues, so their labor was far from wasted.

The man most responsible for giving the Democratic Party in Texas its populist tint was James Stephen Hogg, a huge, fleshy tankard of a man elected governor, at the age of thirty-nine, in 1890. The son of a Confederate general killed in the war, Hogg had studied law as his family sold their plantation piecemeal to make ends meet. A highly successful district attorney—once shot in the back by outlaws—and then Attorney General, Hogg as governor curbed speculation by alien and corporate landholders, improved the educational system, and organized the State Archives. His principal accomplishment, however, was the creation of the Texas Railroad Commission to regulate that industry. While farmers had long been clamoring for such a body, legislative steps began only in the session before Hogg's election, when a commission bill passed the House but died in the Senate. Constitutional obstacles delayed further action until the 1890 election saw the triumph of Hogg, a commission bill and an enabling amendment to the constitution.

Hogg persuaded U.S. Senator John Reagan, the old Indian fighter and more recently an architect of the Interstate Commerce Act, to resign his seat, return to Texas, and undertake the formidable task of bringing the railroads to heel. Reagan complied, but reluctantly. Industry opponents still challenged the legality of the Railroad Commission and enjoined its operation for a year and a half. The federal Supreme Court upheld the constitutionality of the commission itself, but because of a tactical blunder by the state, struck down the actual rates set, thus causing the commission to operate for some time with probably undue caution.

Governor Hogg retired after two terms in 1895 and turned his attention to rebuilding the family fortune. He remained politically active until he was disabled in—ironically—a railroad accident nine years later. He died in March of 1906.

COUGAR HUNT, NORTH TEXAS. Texas' monolithic Governor Hogg had a reputation for holding center stage, and also for blowing his own horn. When Hogg held court, even such other populist trumpeters as William Jennings Bryan (in vest and bow tie) could only gaze on in rapture. Texas was kind to Bryan, giving him huge majorities in each of his three presidential races.

In addition to his populist-leaning politics, Jim Hogg was also notable as the first native-born governor of Texas, for purchasing and restoring the old Varner Plantation in West Columbia in 1901 and for handicapping his daughter with the name Ima. He claimed not to have realized the blunder until after the fact.

The Madwoman of Austin

WHEN the German sculptress Elisabet Ney arrived in Texas in 1872, the niece of Napoleon's marshal was at thirty-nine already acclaimed as one of the great portraitists of her time. In Europe her subjects had included Garibaldi, Humboldt, Bismarck, Liebig, Schopenhauer, and the Kings of Bavaria, Hanover, and Prussia. She enjoyed a rent-free studio in the latter's palace. The scandal over her relationship with Dr. Edmund Montgomery, a Scottish scientist she had met while a student, abated only a

NEY HOUSE, AUSTIN.

little when she finally married him, in Madeira in 1863. Gossip forced them to America, and after two years at a German colony in Georgia they purchased Liendo Plantation, once the property of the Groce family, where Houston had fed and rested his army during the Runaway Scrape. There Ney turned her attention to literary subjects—Lady Macbeth and Prometheus—and heroic standing marbles of Austin and Houston, commissioned for the Chicago World's Fair of 1893.

The twenty years at Liendo were hard ones for Ney. She continued to scandalize local society, in part with her insistence that she be addressed by her maiden name. She raised a family, but grew bored from the lack of public attention she had once loved. She tried her hand at social work, attempting to "elevate" local Negroes, and was hurt and angered when they repaid her with thievery and mimicry.

Striking out on her own, she moved to Austin in 1892, designing her own stocky

NEY IN STUDIO.

house and studio in the woods north of the city. The photo above was taken in this house, as she finished a bust of William Jennings Bryan.

At last she was in her element. She returned in triumph to Europe in 1895 and 1902. At home, on the shaded lawns and terraces, she delighted in hosting visitors fascinated by legends of her eccentricity—some said madness—which she alternately confirmed or denied, with equal vehemence. One story that passed around Austin was that she had once cremated her own stillborn infant in a fireplace at Liendo. The truth was that it was her elder son who had died, probably of typhoid, and it was the physician who, fearing an epidemic, ordered it done. With her husband away, Ney did the job herself.

She never believed in funerals, anyway. She was hustled away for burial at Liendo immediately after her death in Austin in 1907.

The Secret Life of Will Porter

WILLIAM SYDNEY PORTER.

IF Elisabet Ney exemplified the celebrity of Austin's artistic life in the 1890s, William Sydney Porter represented the struggle. A native of North Carolina, Porter moved for his health—there was a family history of tuberculosis—to a sheep ranch in South Texas in 1882. The ranch was owned by family friends, who noticed Porter flipping through his new dictionary and writing stories when he got the chance.

He settled in Austin two years later, aged twenty-two. Sensitive and gregarious, Porter joined the Hill City Quartette to serenade society girls. He spent other time drinking and playing poker with his pals, and in spare moments continued to try to write funny anecdotes. To finance his habits he took a succession of odd jobs, mostly provided by friends—in a cigar store, a drugstore (he'd become a licensed pharmacist before arriving in Texas), a real estate company, and the state land office.

With his marriage to a winsome consumptive, Athol Estes, in July of 1887, and the birth of his daughter Margaret two years later, Porter's increasing responsibilities forced him to slow his social whirl. He took a job he detested, as a teller for the First

National Bank of Austin, and tried hard to get his stories published, without much success. His writing never earned more than ten dollars in a month.

The Porters rented a cottage in early 1893; in 1894 Will and a friend bought out a broke magazine and began publishing the weekly *Rolling Stone*, featuring much of his own work. Although it gained some critical notice, it failed within a year, and Porter lost his bank job because of consistent shortages at his window. Athol's health began to fail; she worried and nagged.

ATHOL ESTES PORTER.

Late in 1895 Porter landed a job with the Houston *Post*. He resettled his family there, but after only eight months he was indicted back in Austin on a charge of embezzlement. Athol and Margaret were sent back, but Porter, apparently besieged from every quarter, quietly boarded a banana boat for Honduras. An acquaintance there found him "very quiet; he was scared." He considered sending for his family, but a letter from his mother-in-law that Athol was dying brought him back to Austin. She passed away on July 25, 1897.

Crushed by this tragedy, and unwilling to implicate higher bank officials because of their previous kindness to him, Porter was useless to the attorneys who tried to defend him. The charges were technical, and even after having fled prosecution, he could possibly have beaten them had he fought. The Assistant United States Attorney who prosecuted him said fifty years later: "I do not believe that William Sydney Porter was dishonest. Banking laws at that time were such that any employe [sic] could 'borrow' from the bank, provided he returned it promptly. It was common practice and

I think he was just the unlucky example in order to stop the practice." This opinion was later seconded by the foremen of both the indicting and convicting juries. He was given the minimum sentence, five years' imprisonment.

Porter arrived in the federal section of the Ohio State Penitentiary in April 1898. There was no beer or caviar sandwiches, no parties or singing quartets or girls to serenade. Humiliated and depressed, Porter turned again to his writing, submitting short stories to national publications under a variety of pen names before settling on one he stayed with: O. Henry. Without the distractions of Austin society, Porter found himself as a writer and gained wide fame. (Many people later claimed to be the source of his famous pseudonym. Best evidence favors Étienne Ossian Henry, a French chemist whose subscription, "O. Henry," appeared in the *United States Dispensary* under his articles on different drugs. Porter had known the name since working in his uncle's drugstore in North Carolina, and signed it in an autograph book as early as 1886.)

Released from prison in July of 1901, Porter settled in New York to enjoy the universal acclaim he had earned. He died there nine years later, the author of nearly four hundred short stories, including such classics of Americana as "The Ransom of Red Chief" and "The Gift of the Magi." Some forty of the stories bear Texas settings.

PORTER AS BANK TELLER.

The Rough Riders

With the closing of the frontier, American military command had passed to a new generation. Sherman and Sheridan were dead. NELSON MILES *(left)*, who during the 1874 Red River War outran his supply lines to beat Ranald Mackenzie to the Comanches, became General of the Army in 1895. It was the pinnacle of a career dogged by controversy and scandal. The year previous it was he who commanded the troops at the Chicago Pullman strike. His last "victory" in the field had been in 1886, over Geronimo's Apaches in Arizona, where he had used friendly Apache scouts to capture the band, then imprisoned the scouts along with the renegades and claimed success for his theory that white troops were superior to native "savages" even in their own element.

Shortly after Miles assumed the Arizona command, surgeon LEONARD WOOD *(right)* was one of two officers selected, largely on the basis of their impressive physiques, to head into Mexico and bring Geronimo out. After the scouts arranged the surrender, Miles, his protégés, and the White Olympian ideal were extensively lionized in the popular press, to the disgust of officers who knew what had happened.

THEODORE ROOSEVELT enjoyed considerable personal popularity in Texas, but when he ran for President in 1904, he could not overcome Texans' hatred of the Republican Party. He got only 50,000 votes out of more than 230,000 cast. He narrowly carried the state, however, when he ran as a Populist on the fractionated ballot in 1912. This speech was delivered in Austin in April of 1905.

ROUGH RIDER HEADQUARTERS.

THE United States declared war on Spain in April of 1898. The reason was largely popular indignation over Spain's treatment of political prisoners in Cuba, but also there was pressure to protect American business interests and, although it was denied, a desire to establish an American empire to share the stage with European powers.

With the outbreak of hostilities, Miles' protégé on the race issue, Colonel Wood, was sent to Texas to recruit a regiment of frontier he-men to serve as the 1st United States Cavalry Volunteers. Aided by a former civil service commissioner and Assistant Secretary of the Navy, writer, rancher, and popular character named Theodore Roosevelt, Wood set up a headquarters at the San Antonio fairgrounds *(above)* and signed up cowboys, ex-Texas Rangers, virtually anybody who could ride and shoot.

Amid massive press coverage, the regiment was garbed up in boots, leggings, brown pants, blue flannel shirts, slouch hats, and bandannas. Apart from personal sidearms, some carried Winchester rifles; most had standard Krag-Jorgenson carbines. The Rough Riders were not required to wield the cavalry sabers usually issued, but the Texans accustomed to the western saddle grumped savagely at being forced to use the McClellan army saddle.

After brief training exercises in San Antonio, the Rough Riders—and their press entourage—embarked to a staging area at Tampa, Florida. There supply and transport snarls nearly unhinged the whole effort. Virtually all the horses and about half the regiment never left Florida. Those who did ship out to Cuba fought with unconventional tactics from Las Guásimas, for which action Colonel Wood was promoted to brigadier, to the famous charge up San Juan Hill.

By the end of the war Texas had contributed about ten thousand recruits.

Galveston Destroyed

BISHOP'S PALACE. Just beyond the cathedral ruins in the foreground, the opulent, turreted "Bishop's Palace" rode out the storm with only minor damage. The granite residence was built not by the church, but by a local magnate and congressman.

THE island city of Galveston was no stranger to the power of tropical hurricanes. One in September of 1766 destroyed a Spanish mission. Another in September of 1818 raised a storm tide that flooded the entire island four feet deep; the pirate Jean Lafitte moved aboard a damaged ship in the harbor so his "Maison Rouge" could be used as a hospital. The modern town, begun in 1836 and which briefly eclipsed San Antonio as Texas' largest during the 1850s, reached a population of about ten thousand when it was struck again in October of 1867. An eight-foot tide accompanied another storm in 1875.

By the end of the century Galveston boasted a population of thirty-seven thousand. Linked to the mainland by dual causeways, she was fulfilling early boosters' claims that she would be the Queen City of the Gulf. Wharfside warehouses were clogged with cotton. The port was one of the nation's busiest, and in September 1900 a special sight loomed over the harbor—the state's naval namesake, the great white battleship USS *Texas,* wallowed at anchor.

On the other side of the island, the Gulf side, fawn-colored beaches were dotted with bathhouses, fishing piers, and concessions of a burgeoning tourist industry. Bisecting the island was Broadway, a palm-lined boulevard studded with magnificent Romanesque mansions. In outlying neighborhoods, frame villas and summer cottages crowded so close on their narrow lots that dripping gingerbread bargeboards faced each other within inches over the property lines.

The people in Galveston had never held hurricanes in too much awe. The arrival of a storm was an occasion for school to let out, for children to slosh in the streets—most of the city was less than ten feet above sea level—and for crowds to gather at the beach and watch waves crash onto the shore. Thus, on September 4 when the telegraph in the Galveston weather station began ticking out a routine storm advisory, there was little concern. A hurricane was tracking northwest across Cuba and would probably strike Florida. Over the next couple of days the storm veered toward the west, and Galveston was included in the warning, but the pennant over the weather office was still white: the wind would come from the northwest. If one had to be in a hurricane, that was the best side, for at that point in the circular flow, the forward speed of the storm subtracted from the wind speed, and in Galveston's location would work to break up incoming swells.

By 4 A.M. Saturday, with the eye still two hundred miles away, a storm tide began to back up on the harbor side. Isaac Cline, senior weatherman at the Galveston station, was awakened by his brother, who had stirred from his bed with a premonition of disaster. An hour later Cline was on the beach, scribbling a telegram to Washington: "Unusually heavy swells from the southeast, intervals one to five minutes, overflowing low places south portion of the city three to four blocks from beach." With eighteen years in the weather service, he added, "Such high water with opposing winds never observed previously." This would be a wicked storm.

Cline rode through his surfside neighborhood warning people to seek the sturdiest shelter they could find. By seven, however, the Saturday morning work traffic detoured to the beach to watch monster waves splinter the piers and bathhouses. Not until ten did the weather station receive instructions to change the wind warning from north-

THE WATERWORKS PLANT.

A STREET DOWNTOWN.

THE RAILWAY POWERHOUSE.

west to northeast, and a new pennant was run up. At eleven there was a thirty-mile-per-hour wind with heavy rain. The last train rumbled in from Houston on tracks only two feet above the water. Only an hour later, at noon, the storm tide was rising at over a foot per hour, and the wind was gusting to seventy-five miles per hour. People now took the storm seriously and sought shelter. Some went home; others more sensible struggled their way into the city, seeking refuge in St. Mary's Cathedral, the granite mansions along Broadway—any building substantial enough to ride out the storm. Windows began to shatter; roofing slate tore free and whirled about like guillotine blades. Many people were hacked down before reaching safety.

Pounded by still-increasing surf on the Gulf side and encroached by the inexorable storm tide from the harbor, by 4 P.M. the entire island was inundated. Wooden houses began to wrench from their foundations, floating briefly before capsizing and, driven before the wind, battering buildings still standing. The wind reached ninety-six miles per hour at a quarter past five, shortly before the anemometer blew away. By eight, the paper curling from the self-registering barometer read 28.48 inches of pressure, the lowest ever recorded in North America. The water in Union Station was more than ten feet deep.

This was the time the critical edge of the hurricane, where the wind velocity was increased by the forward momentum of the storm, swept over the city. Estimated at 120 miles per hour, the wind shifted suddenly from east to southeast, sending a five-foot tidal wave rolling over the city. It was the instant of greatest destruction. In the large buildings where many had sought shelter, brick walls gave way to the wall of

FOURTEENTH STREET PIER.

water or were battered down by surging debris. Sections of streetcar trestle, one of them two hundred feet long, swept along like scythes. Hundreds were crushed or drowned at a time. Ironically, the wind shift that killed thousands also saved some. Many people, helpless passengers clinging to their houses, which had been blowing out to sea, stopped and ploughed back to the island until grounding on other wreckage.

After the eye passed ashore west of Galveston at 10 P.M., the change was dramatic. By morning the weather was little more than a bad rainstorm. The tide drained out of the harbor, leaving a scene of the most wretched devastation. The worst natural disaster in American history claimed between six thousand and eight thousand lives; half the city was reduced to lumber and rubble.

With so many dead, orderly disposal was impossible. Men who survived the storm were conscripted—some were forced at gunpoint—to load bodies onto barges for burial at sea. Many corpses were insufficiently weighted and washed back ashore, where they were cremated.

Seventy-eight-year-old Clara Barton, founder of the American Red Cross, arrived to oversee relief work, her last public appearance in that capacity. Then Galveston underwent massive preparation before rebuilding started. Sand pumped in from the floor of the Gulf raised the city's grade several feet, and all surviving structures, some weighing thousands of tons, were jacked up and put on new foundations some six feet higher than before. Over the years a massive seawall was raised along the Gulf beach. The innovations were a success, for when a hurricane of approximately equal intensity blasted Galveston fifteen years later, loss of life was held to only a dozen in the city.

The New Age

THAT there was oil in Texas had never been any secret; Spanish ships had put in at Sabine Bay to caulk leaks with oil oozing near the shore. Petroleum was discovered near Nacogdoches some two years before the famous Drake Well in Pennsylvania began producing, but very little commercial use was made of early strikes. There were no refineries nearby to make it useful, and no economical means to transport it. Crude was sold as a lubricant or bottled as patent medicine; one East Texas farmer used his natural oil seep as a hog wallow.

Frequently it happened that wells being sunk for water struck oil first, only to be capped in disgust and the search continued for water. This was the case in the east central Texas town of Corsicana in 1894, only here, a local land business decided to take a risk on commercial development of the petroleum. After leasing the mineral rights on some 30,000 acres around the town, their first two wells failed before the third finally dribbled out a steady 22 barrels per day. Dozens more drilling derricks were raised, and the first year's production of 1,450 barrels ballooned the next year to a market-busting 66,000. Construction of an on-site refinery, which produced mostly kerosene, pushed the crude price back up to almost a dollar a barrel, and experiments were successful in building an oil-burning locomotive.

In southeast Texas, meanwhile, a mining engineer named Patillo Higgins had been drilling for oil—deliberately—near Beaumont. Convinced from his studies that petroleum should gather about the geologic features called salt domes, he had been probing the giant dome known as Spindletop since 1892. Eventually, he was defeated by subterranean quicksands that foiled his drill. Higgins' work was taken up by an Austrian immigrant, Captain A. F. Lucas. Raising capital was difficult, because eastern oil magnates scoffed at Texas' oil possibilities, and virtually all the leading geologists in the country vilified Higgins' salt dome theory as a hoodoo. Lucas finally raised the money from the Pittsburgh wildcatting firm of Guffey and Galey, who first got the permission of the Standard Oil monopoly and reassurance that the Rockefellers couldn't care less about Texas.

Armed with the new rotary bit to penetrate the quicksands, Lucas drilled into the Spindletop in autumn of 1900. On January 10, 1901, the tenth day of the new century, the ground began to shake. "At exactly 10:30 a.m., the well . . . burst upon the astonished view of those engaged in boring it, with a volume of water, sand, rocks, gas and oil that sped upward with such tremendous force as to tear the crossbars of the derrick to pieces, and scattered the mixed properties from its bowels, together with timbers, pieces of well casing, etc., for hundreds of feet in all directions.

"For nine days the phenomenon was the wonder and puzzle of the world. It flowed unceasingly and with ever increasing force and volume until when it was finally controlled it was shooting upward a tower of pure crude oil, of the first quality, quite two hundred feet."

SPINDLETOP GUSHER.

In the nine days it took to cap the "Discovery Well," the thundering gusher had blown out as much oil as the entire Corsicana field had produced the previous year—at least eight hundred thousand barrels.

Standard Oil, one of the country's most ruthless monopolies, stopped laughing, confronted by one well—a single well, which they didn't own, that outproduced every field on earth except Baku in southern Russia. By the end of 1901 the State of Texas had chartered nearly five hundred oil companies with an authorized stock issue of 1.25 billion dollars. The next year oil production topped 20 million barrels and increased geometrically thereafter.

With such a massive supply available, the whole thrust of the petroleum industry shifted from lamp oil to fuel oil, and the explosion of secondary industries changed Texas' economy forever. Oil drums were insufficient for transport; by 1904 fifteen hundred rail tankers were built. Locomotives were converted to burn oil, and the coal industry, up to that time one of the state's largest, declined to await another day. There were wells to drill and maintain, factories to retool, refineries to construct and harbors to dredge, a vast new population to provision and settle. Beaumont's population tripled instantly, fueled by the making and breaking of fabulous sums overnight. Further discoveries, each more wondrous than the last, made millionaires out of hog callers. Things were never the same again.

In 1820 an aging Thomas Jefferson had written President Monroe that, if it could be acquired, "the province of Techas will be the richest state of our union, without any exception." Would that the old revolutionary had lived to see it—Stephen Austin and his leatherstockings, the Alamo and the Lone Star, buffalo hunters, Texas Rangers, and cowboys driving longhorn cattle across open ranges.

To all these things Spindletop was a great rubric of finality, at once asserting their grandeur while finishing their chapter of dominance. Texas entered the twentieth century with two gifts for the world: a universal fuel to rejuvenate its industry, and a magnetic heritage to enrich its imagination. Only more time—the "veil of futurity," as Sam Houston loved to say—has shown which gift to be the more lasting.

Only a year after the Discovery Well blew in, the Spindletop field sprouted
a virtual forest of derricks.

At Spindletop and other early fields the frantic development and lack of experience sometimes resulted in spectacular disasters like this one.

Notes

GENERAL works on Texas history are so numerous that it is not easy to steer the reader toward a next step. The most factually complete of them tend to date from an era when historical writing, to be respected, could not be terribly stylish. Of that genre one would certainly include Thrall, *Pictorial History of Texas,* and the bibliographical root ball of Wooten, Wortham, and Yoakum. Of latter-day works, T. R. Fehrenbach's *Lone Star* is probably the best known and most highly recommended, and *The Texans,* from David Nevin and the editors of Time-Life Books, is very engaging indeed.

Of general documentary histories, Wallace and Vigness, eds., *Documents of Texas History,* gives a broad cross-section of social as well as political papers over a lengthy time span.

INTRODUCTION

Alonso de Leon's account is most readily available in Wallace and Vigness, eds., *Documents of Texas History;* Peter Ellis Bean's memoir, edited by Henderson Yoakum, was published in 1930. The Comanche sacking of the San Saba mission is best summarized in Dunn, "The Apache Mission on the San Saba River." Of the destruction of the Green Flag Republic, one can see Mattie Austin Hatcher, ed., "Joaquin de Arredondo's Report on the Battle of the Medina."

MOSES AND THE PROMISED LAND

The advent of Moses and Stephen Austin on the Texas scene is recognized as the special territory of the great Texas historian Eugene C. Barker. Most of the Austin material quoted here is found in either his *Life of Stephen F. Austin,* which is still regarded as the standard, or his editing of *The Austin Papers.* Of firsthand accounts of life in the Texas colonies, the reader cannot do better than Noah Smithwick, *The Evolution of a State.*

AUSTIN'S DREAM TURNS SOUR

As Austin's organized introduction of colonists gave way to a stampede of emigrants, Texas travelogues appeared on the American scene with ever greater frequency. Frederick Law Olmsted's *A Journey Through Texas* remains the best of them, witty and insightful. Stephen Austin's cousin, Mary Austin Holley, wrote an 1836 equivalent of a best seller with her *Texas.* I have excerpted material from both. Of the political difficulties with Mexico during this period, Ohland Morton's *Terán and Texas* gives a good view of it; additional insight may be gained from Alleine Howren's "Causes and Origin of the Decree of April 6, 1830." Revisionists will love Margaret Swett Henson's *Juan Davis Bradburn: A Reappraisal.*

REVOLUTION

The bibliography following contains a representative selection of collated documents concerning the revolutionary period. The largest clump of them is in Jenkins' *Papers of the Texas Revolution* in 10 volumes. However, a significant amount is also to be gleaned from such sources as Gulick's *Papers of Mirabeau Buonaparte Lamar,* in 6 volumes, and Barker and Williams' *The Writings of Sam Houston,* in 8 volumes.

Of specific events during the revolution, Lon Tinkle's *Thirteen Days to Glory* is still the best account of the siege and fall of the Alamo. Additionally, I have quoted Captain Saldaña's account from the F. C. Chabot Papers at the University of Texas, Private William Zuber's recollection from the Zuber Papers at the University of Texas at Arlington, and Francisco Ruiz' account from the *Texas Almanac* of 1859. President-General Santa Anna's fanciful account is from Carlos Castañeda's unique *Mexican Side of the Texas Revolution.*

So, too, is the excerpt from the diary of General Urrea, recalling the Battle of Coleto. Dick Ehrenburg's memoir, *With Milam and Fannin,* is one of the most vivid accounts of the Goliad massacre. Of accounts of the Runaway Scrape, I have selected excerpts from the most moving, "The Reminiscences of Mrs. Dilue Harris." For a general account of the Battle of San Jacinto the reader can refer to Frank X. Tolbert's *The Day of San Jacinto,* or a number of personal memoirs, such as J. W. Winters' "An Account of the Battle of San Jacinto."

THE REPUBLIC OF TEXAS

Of Sam Houston biographies, Marquis James' *The Raven* and Llerena Friend's *Sam Houston: The Great Designer* are the two musts; as a first-book introduction I would recommend Sue Flanagan's *Sam Houston's Texas.* Of other discussions I have introduced here, Walter Prescott Webb's *The Texas Rangers* is still the best book, even though some of his research has been superseded. Information on the Sam Lewis Stopping Place is from R. Henderson Shuffler's "Winedale Inn."

Oddly, Mirabeau Lamar was probably his own best biographer, and the six volumes of his *Papers* are probably the most succinct picture he would care to give of himself. Accounts from which I have quoted excerpts concerning his Indian wars are John Holland Jenkins' *Recollections of Early Texas* and John Henry Brown's *Indian Wars and Pioneers of Texas.* Pro-Noble Savage revisionists who, I expect, will take exception to my dredging up the subject of Tonkawa cannibalism, may see a particularly appetizing account of a Tonkawa barbecue in Herman Lehmann, *Nine Years Among the Indians.* Mary Maverick's observations of what the Comanches did to Matilda Lockhart are quoted from Rena Maverick Green, *Samuel Maverick: Texan.*

Of Lamar's expansionist ventures, I have quoted excerpts from Falconer, *Letters and Notes on the Texan Santa Fe Expedition,* and Green, *Journal of the Texian Expedition Against Mier.*

More detailed accounts of the Regulator-Moderator War and of feuds in general can be found in Wayne Gard, *Frontier Justice,* and C. L. Sonnichsen, *I'll Die Before I'll Run.* I have excerpted brief selections from both, as well as the contemporary W. B. Dewees, *Letters from Texas.*

A general look at German colonization is Gilbert Benjamin, *The Germans in Texas;* an exceptionally interesting look at a German family in Texas is Minetta Goyne, *Lone Star and Double Eagle.* The best account of an American's visit to the German settlements has to be Olmsted's. The Comte de Saligny's papers concerning Texas and the Pig War are published in Mary Barker, *The French Legation in Texas,* and Katherine Hart, *Alphonse in Austin.*

THE LONE STAR STATE

Further information on the cotton industry is contained in W. H. Johnson, *Cotton and Its Production,* with historical insight to be gained in James Scherer, *Cotton as a World Power.* An excellent book on the early development of the Cattle Empire is Tom Lea's authorized *The King Ranch.* The material excerpted is from an early travelogue, Orceneth Fisher's *Sketches: Texas in 1840.* Most of the information excerpted about secession is from Sam Houston's *Writings;* there are also brief quotes from W. M. Baker, "A Pivotal Point," and Nevin, *The Texans.*

TEXAS IN THE CIVIL WAR

Civil War sources consulted included, of course, *The War of the Rebellion,* Army and Navy series, Robert M. Franklin, *The Battle of Galveston,* and May M. Pray, *Dick Dowling's Battle.* Additional material on the Battle of Sabine Pass was obtained from manuscripts at the United Daughters of the Confederacy Museum in Austin.

RECONSTRUCTION

Probably the best single work on this era is Charles Ramsdell's *Reconstruction in Texas.* Most of the documents concerning the Warren Wagontrain Massacre are reproduced and thoroughly analyzed in Ben Capps' *The Warren Wagontrain Raid.* The documents as altered are in the Letter File "Satanta and Big Tree" at the Oklahoma Historical Society. A more general account of the South Plains Indian problem, factually solid if less than compassionate, is W. S. Nye, *Carbine and Lance.*

BUFFALO DAYS

Walter Webb's recounting of the Oberwetter recollection was published as "A Buffalo Hunt" in *Holland's Magazine* of October 1927. Another highly interesting account of Staked Plains buffalo hunting is Wright Mooar's "Buffalo Days" in four issues of the same journal, January to April 1933.

THE RED RIVER WAR—1874

The book that focuses most closely on this conflict is my own *The Buffalo War.* However, an excellent broader and more regional overview is William Leckie, *Military Conquest of the South Plains.* In this chapter I have reproduced some material from *The Buffalo War,* also from Bard's *Life of Billy Dixon* and Carnal's "Reminiscences of a Texas Ranger." Quanah's account is from the Hugh L. Scott Papers in the Library of Congress. The manuscript accounts of Captain Hatfield and Lieutenant Baldwin are in the Panhandle-Plains Historical Museum in Canyon, Texas. Much documentation of this war is contained in Joe F. Taylor, ed., *The Indian Campaign on the Staked Plains.*

TEXAS COMES OF AGE

The most consulted biography of Charles Goodnight, with good reason, is J. Evetts Haley, *Charles Goodnight: Cowman and Plainsman.* For a biography of a ranch instead of a rancher, the same author's *The XIT Ranch of Texas* is hard to beat. The standard biography of Sam Bass is Wayne Gard's *Sam Bass;* the quoted excerpt here is from an unidentified newspaper clipping in the Austin History Center.

Two of the best brief overviews of the range wars are Wayne Gard, "The Fence Cutters," and T. R. Havins, "Sheepmen-Cattlemen Antagonisms on the Texas Frontier." Gard also considers the sheep problem in *Frontier Justice.*

Excerpts quoted on the expulsion of the Apaches from West Texas include Olmsted, *A Journey Through Texas,* and Raht, *Romance of the Davis Mountains.* The excerpt from Robert Grierson's diary is by permission of Frank M. Temple of Lubbock, Texas.

The standard Judge Roy Bean work to consult is C. L. Sonnichsen, *Roy Bean, Law West of the Pecos,* and one might also see Everett Lloyd's *Law West of the Pecos.* Sonnichsen's *I'll Die Before I'll Run* contains material on the Jay Bird–Woodpecker War; a more thorough examination is Pauline Yelderman's *The Jay Birds of Fort Bend County.*

TEXAS IN TRANSITION

John Stricklin Spratt's *The Road to Spindletop* is probably the best discussion of the change in economics and politics in Texas before 1900; John D. Hicks' *The Populist Revolt* is also good, as are Ralph Smith's articles in the *Southwestern Historical Quarterly.* Quoted material on Elisabet Ney and O. Henry are taken from vertical files at the Austin History Center. John E. Weems' *A Weekend in September* is a fascinating account of the Galveston hurricane. The discovery of oil in Texas is recounted in Boyce House's "Spindletop." Quoted excerpt here is from C. W. Raines' *Yearbook for Texas, 1901.*

Selected Bibliography

I. Primary Sources
  A. Manuscripts
    Stephen F. Austin papers. University of Texas. Austin, Texas.
    Frank D. Baldwin manuscripts. Panhandle-Plains Museum. Canyon, Texas.
    Vertical file "Sam Bass." Austin-Travis County Collection. Austin Public Library. Austin, Texas.
    Battle of Sabine Pass manuscripts. Museum of the United Daughters of the Confederacy. Austin, Texas.
    W. C. Brown papers. Western History Collections. University of Colorado. Boulder, Colorado.
    F. C. Chabot papers. Eugene C. Barker Texas History Center. University of Texas. Austin, Texas.
    Charles A. P. Hatfield manuscripts. Panhandle-Plains Historical Museum. Canyon, Texas.
    Letter File "Satanta and Big Tree." Oklahoma Historical Society. Oklahoma City.
    Hugh L. Scott papers. Library of Congress. Washington, D.C.
    Texas Army papers. Texas State Library. Austin, Texas.
    Zuber papers. University of Texas. Arlington, Texas.

  B. Published Documents
    (Books)
    Barker, Eugene C., ed. *The Austin Papers.* 3 vols. Washington, D.C.: United States Government Printing Office, 1924–28.
    ———, and Williams, Amelia W., eds. *The Writings of Sam Houston.* 8 vols. Austin, Tex.: University of Texas Press, 1938–43.
    Barker, Mary Nicholls, trans. and ed. *The French Legation in Texas.* Austin, Tex.: Texas State Historical Association, 1971.
    Gammel, H. P. N., comp. *Laws of Texas.* 10 vols. Austin, Tex.: Gammel Book Store, 1898.
    Garrison, George P., ed. *Diplomatic Correspondence of the Republic of Texas.* 3 vols. Washington, D.C.: United States Government Printing Office, 1908–11.
    Gulick, Charles Adams, Jr., et al, eds. *The Papers of Mirabeau Buonaparte Lamar.* 6 vols. Austin, Tex.: Von Boeckmann-Jones Co., 1921–27.
    Hart, Katherine, trans. and ed. *Alphonse in Austin.* Austin, Tex.: Encino Press, 1967.
    Jenkins, John H., ed. *Papers of the Texas Revolution.* 10 vols. Austin, Tex.: Presidial Press, 1973.
    Official Records of the Union and Confederate Navies in the War of the Rebellion. 30 vols. Washington, D.C.: United States Government Printing Office, 1897–1927.
    Taylor, Joe F., ed. *The Indian Campaign on the Staked Plains, 1874–75: Military Correspondence from the War Department Adjutant General's Office, File 2815-1874.* Canyon, Tex.: Panhandle-Plains Historical Society, 1962.
    Wallace, Ernest, and Vigness, David, eds. *Documents of Texas History.* Austin, Tex.: The Steck Co., 1960.
    War of the Rebellion: A Compilation of the Official Records of the Union and Confederate Armies. 128 vols. Washington, D.C.: United States Government Printing Office, 1880–1901.

(Articles)

Adams, E. D., ed. "British Correspondence Concerning Texas." *Southwestern Historical Quarterly,* vol. XV, no. 3 to vol. XXI, no. 2 (January 1912 to October 1917).

Barker, Eugene C., ed. "Journal of the Permanent Council." *Southwestern Historical Quarterly,* vol. VII, no. 4 (April 1904).

Hatcher, Mattie Austin, ed. "Joaquin de Arredondo's Report on the Battle of the Medina." *Southwestern Historical Quarterly,* vol. XI, no. 3 (January 1908).

C. Diaries and Memoirs
(Books)

Bean, Peter Ellis. *Memoir of Col. Ellis P. Bean, Written by Himself, About the Year 1816.* Edited by W. P. Yoakum. Dallas, Tex.: The Book Club of Texas, 1930.

Dewees, W. B. *Letters from Texas.* Louisville, Ky.: New Albany Tribune Plant, 1852.

Ehrenburg, Herman. *With Milam and Fannin: Adventures of a German Boy in Texas Revolution.* Edited by Henry Smith. Dallas, Tex.: Tardy Publishing Co., 1935.

Falconer, Thomas. *Letters and Notes on the Texan Santa Fe Expedition, 1841–42.* New York: Dauber & Pine Bookshops, 1930.

Fisher, Orceneth. *Sketches: Texas in 1840.* Springfield, Ill.: Walters & Weber, 1841.

Ford, John Salmon. *Rip Ford's Texas.* Edited by Stephen B. Oates. Austin, Tex.: University of Texas Press, 1967.

Gillett, James B. *Six Years with the Texas Rangers.* Austin, Tex.: Von Boeckmann-Jones Co., 1921.

Goyne, Minetta Altgelt, ed. *Lone Star and Double Eagle: Civil War Letters of a German-Texas Family.* Fort Worth, Tex.: Texas Christian University Press, 1982.

Green, Thomas Jefferson. *Journal of the Texian Expedition Against Mier.* New York: Harper & Brothers, 1845.

Hardin, John Wesley. *The Life of John Wesley Hardin.* Seguin, Tex.: Smith & Maine, 1896.

Holley, Mary Austin. *Texas.* Lexington, Ky.: J. Clarke & Co., 1836.

Jenkins, John Holland. *Recollections of Early Texas.* Austin, Tex.: University of Texas Press, 1958.

Jones, Anson. *The Republic of Texas, Its History and Annexation.* New York: D. Appleton & Co., 1859.

Langtry, Lillie. *The Days I Knew.* New York: George H. Doran, 1925.

Lanning, Jim, and Lanning, Judy, eds. *Texas Cowboys: Memories of the Early Days.* College Station, Tex.: Texas A & M University Press, 1984.

Lehmann, Herman. *Nine Years Among the Indians, 1870–79.* Austin, Tex.: J. M. Hunter, 1927.

Lubbock, Francis Richard. *Six Decades in Texas.* Austin, Tex.: Ben C. Jones & Co., 1900.

Miles, Nelson A. *Personal Recollections and Observations.* Chicago: Werner Co., 1896.

Olmsted, Frederick Law. *A Journey Through Texas; Or, A Saddle-Trip on the Southwestern Frontier.* New York: Dix, Edwards & Co., 1857.

Santa Anna, Antonio López de. *The Eagle: The Autobiography of Santa Anna.* Edited by Ann Fears Crawford. Austin, Tex.: Pemberton Press, 1967.

Seguin, John N. *Personal Memoirs of John N. Seguin.* Ledger Book and Job Office, 1858.

Smithwick, Noah. *The Evolution of a State.* Austin, Tex.: Gammel Book Co., 1900.

(Articles)

Austin, Stephen F. "Journal of Stephen F. Austin on His First Trip to Texas, 1821." *Southwestern Historical Quarterly,* vol. VII, no. 4 (April 1904).

Burnam, Jesse. "Reminiscences of Jesse Burnam." *Southwestern Historical Quarterly,* vol. V, no. 1 (July 1901).

Carnal, Ed. "Reminiscences of a Texas Ranger." *Frontier Times,* vol. I, no. 3 (December 1923).

Harris, Dilue Rose. "The Reminiscences of Mrs. Dilue Harris." *Southwestern Historical Quarterly,* vol. IV, nos. 1, 2 (October 1900 and January 1901).

Kuykendall, James H. "Reminiscences of Early Texans," *Southwestern Historical Quarterly,* vol. VII, no. 1 (July 1903).

Mooar, J. Wright. "Buffalo Days." Edited by James Winfred Hunt. *Holland's Magazine,* vol. LII, nos. 1–4 (January–April 1933).

Oberwetter, Emil. "A Buffalo Hunt." Edited by Walter Prescott Webb. *Holland's Magazine,* vol. XLVI, no. 10 (October 1927).

Waller, Edwin. "Reminiscences of Judge Edwin Waller." Edited by P. E. Pearson. *Quarterly of the Texas State Historical Association,* vol. IV, no. 1 (July 1900).

Winters, James Washington. "An Account of the Battle of San Jacinto." *Southwestern Historical Quarterly,* vol. VI, no. 2 (October 1902).

II. Secondary Sources

(Books)

Anderson, Charles G. *In Search of the Buffalo: The Story of J. Wright Mooar.* Seagraves, Tex.: Pioneer Book Publishers, 1974.

Atkinson, Mary Jordan. *The Texas Indians.* San Antonio: Naylor Company, 1935.

Bancroft, Hubert Howe. *History of the North Mexican States and Texas.* 2 vols. San Francisco: History Co., 1884, 1889.

Bard, Frederick S. *Life and Adventures of Billy Dixon of Adobe Walls, Panhandle, Texas.* Guthrie, Okla.: Cooperative Publishing Co., 1914.

Barker, Eugene C. *The Life of Stephen F. Austin.* Dallas: P. L. Turner Co., 1925.

———. *Mexico and Texas, 1821–1835.* Dallas: P. L. Turner Co., 1928.

———, ed. *Texas History for High Schools and Colleges.* Dallas: The Southwest Press, 1929.

Baylor, George Wythe. *John Robert Baylor, Confederate Governor of Arizona.* Tucson, Ariz.: Arizona Pioneers' Historical Society, 1966.

Benjamin, Gilbert Giddings. *The Germans in Texas.* Austin, Tex.: Jenkins Publishing Co., 1974.

Brown, John Henry. *Indian Wars and Pioneers of Texas.* Austin, Tex.: L. E. Daniell, n.d.

Buck, Solon J. *The Granger Movement, 1870–1880.* Cambridge, Mass.: Harvard University Press, 1933.

Capps, Benjamin. *The Warren Wagontrain Raid.* New York: Dial Press, 1974.

Castañeda, Carlos E. *Our Catholic Heritage in Texas, 1519–1936.* Austin, Tex.: Von Boeckmann-Jones Co., 1936.

———, trans. and ed. *The Mexican Side of the Texas Revolution.* Dallas: P. L. Turner Co., 1928.

Dale, Edward Everett. *Cow Country.* Norman, Okla.: University of Oklahoma Press, 1942.

De Shields, James T. *Cynthia Ann Parker, The Story of Her Capture.* St. Louis: Charles B. Woodward, 1886.

Fehrenbach, T. R. *Lone Star: A History of Texas and the Texans.* New York: Macmillan Co., 1968.

Flanagan, Sue. *Sam Houston's Texas.* Austin, Tex.: University of Texas Press, 1964.

Fornell, Earl Wesley. *The Galveston Era: The Texas Crescent on the Eve of Secession.* Austin, Tex.: University of Texas Press, 1961.

Franklin, Robert M. *The Battle of Galveston.* Galveston, Tex.: The Galveston *News,* 1911.

Friend, Llerena B. *Sam Houston: The Great Designer.* Austin, Tex.: University of Texas Press, 1954.

Gard, Wayne. *Frontier Justice.* Norman, Okla.: University of Oklahoma Press, 1949.

———. *Sam Bass.* Boston: Houghton Mifflin Co., 1936.

Garrett, Kathryn. *Green Flag Over Texas.* New York: Cordova Press, 1939.

Green, Rena Maverick, ed. *Samuel Maverick, Texan: 1803–1870.* San Antonio: Privately printed, 1952.

Haley, J. Evetts. *Charles Goodnight: Cowman and Plainsman.* Boston: Houghton Mifflin Co., 1936.

———. *The XIT Ranch of Texas and the Early Days of the Llano Estacado.* Chicago: Lakeside Press, 1929.

Haley, James L. *The Buffalo War: The History of the Red River Indian Uprising of 1874.* Garden City, N.Y.: Doubleday & Co., 1976.

Henson, Margaret Swett. *Juan Davis Bradburn: A Reappraisal of the Mexican Commander at Anahuac.* College Station, Tex.: Texas A & M University Press, 1982.

Hicks, John D. *The Populist Revolt.* Minneapolis: University of Minnesota Press, 1931.

Hobby, A. M. *Life and Times of David G. Burnet, First President of the Republic of Texas.* Galveston, Tex.: Galveston *News* Office, 1871.

James, Marquis. *The Raven: A Biography of Sam Houston.* New York: Bobbs-Merrill Co., 1929.

Johnson, Frank W. *History of Texas and Texans, 1799–1884.* Rev. ed. 5 vols. New York: American Historical Society, 1914.

Johnson, W. H. *Cotton and Its Production.* London: Macmillan & Co., 1926.

Kemp, Louis Wiltz. *The Signers of the Texas Declaration of Independence.* Houston: The Anson Jones Press, 1944.

King, Irene Marschall. *John O. Meusebach, Colonizer in Texas.* Austin, Tex.: University of Texas Press, 1967.

Lea, Tom. *The King Ranch.* Boston: Little, Brown & Co., 1957.

Lloyd, Everett. *Law West of the Pecos: The Story of Judge Roy Bean.* San Antonio: Naylor Co., 1935.

Lord, Walter. *A Time to Stand.* New York: Harper & Bros., 1961.

Morton, Ohland. *Terán and Texas.* Austin, Tex.: Texas State Historical Association, 1948.

Nevin, David, and the Editors of Time-Life Books. *The Texans.* New York: Time-Life Books, 1975.

Nye, Col. Wilbur Sturtevant. *Carbine and Lance: The Story of Old Fort Sill.* Norman, Okla.: University of Oklahoma Press, 1937.

Pierce, Frank C. *A Brief History of the Rio Grande Valley.* Menasha, Wis.: George Banta Publishing Co., 1917.

Raht, Carlyle Graham. *The Romance of the Davis Mountains and the Big Bend Country.* El Paso, Tex.: Rahtbooks Co., 1919.

Raines, C. W., ed. *Yearbook for Texas, 1901.* Austin, Tex.: Gammel Book Co., 1902.

Ramsdell, Charles W. *Reconstruction in Texas.* New York: Columbia University Press, 1916.

Reed, S. G. *A History of Texas Railroads.* Houston: St. Clair Publishing Co., 1941.

Richardson, Rupert Norval. *The Comanche Barrier to South Plains Settlement.* Glendale, Calif.: Arthur H. Clark Co., 1933.

———. *Texas, the Lone Star State.* 2nd ed. Englewood Cliffs, N.J.: Prentice-Hall, 1958.

Rister, Carl Coke. *Oil! Titan of the Southwest.* Norman, Okla.: University of Oklahoma Press, 1949.

———. *The Southwest Frontier, 1865–1881.* Glendale, Calif.: Arthur H. Clark Co., 1928.

Robinson, Duncan W. *Judge Robert McAlpin Williamson: Texas' Three-Legged Willie.* Austin, Tex.: Texas State Historical Association, 1948.

Scherer, James A. B. *Cotton as a World Power.* New York: Frederick A. Stokes Co., 1916.

Sibley, Marilyn McAdams. *Travelers in Texas 1761–1860.* Austin, Tex.: University of Texas Press, 1967.

Silverthorne, Elizabeth. *Ashbel Smith of Texas.* College Station, Tex.: Texas A & M University Press, 1982.

Sonnichsen, C. L. *I'll Die Before I'll Run.* New York: Harper, 1951.

———. *Pass of the North.* El Paso, Tex.: Texas Western Press, 1968.

———. *Roy Bean, Law West of the Pecos.* New York: Macmillan Co., 1943.

Spratt, John Stricklin. *The Road to Spindletop: Economic Change in Texas, 1875–1901.* Dallas: Southern Methodist University Press, 1955.

Streeter, Thomas W. *Bibliography of Texas, 1795–1845, Part 1, Texas Imprints.* Cambridge, Mass.: Harvard University Press, 1956.

Texas Almanac. Galveston, Tex.: Galveston *News,* Annual Editions 1857–1873.

Thrall, H. S. *Pictorial History of Texas.* St. Louis: N. D. Thompson & Co., 1879.

Tinkle, Lon. *Thirteen Days to Glory: The Siege of the Alamo.* New York: McGraw-Hill Book Co., 1958.

Tolbert, Frank X. *The Day of San Jacinto.* New York: McGraw-Hill Book Co., 1959.

Wallace, Ernest, and Hoebel, E. Adamson. *Comanches, Lords of the South Plains.* Norman, Okla.: University of Oklahoma Press, 1952.

Walton, William M. *Life and Adventures of Ben Thompson, the Famous Texan.* Austin, Tex.: Privately printed, 1884.

Webb, Walter Prescott. *The Great Plains.* Boston: Ginn and Company, 1931.

———. *The Texas Rangers: A Century of Frontier Defense.* Boston: Houghton Mifflin Co., 1935.

———, and Carroll, H. Bailey, eds. *The Handbook of Texas.* 2 vols. Austin, Tex.: Texas State Historical Association, 1952.

Weems, John E. *A Weekend in September.* New York: Holt, 1957.

Weyand, Leonie Rummel, and Wade, Houston. *History of Early Fayette County.* La Grange, Tex.: La Grange Journal, 1936.

Wilbarger, Josiah W. *Indian Depredations in Texas.* Austin, Tex.: Hutchings Printing House, 1889.

Williams, Clayton W. *Texas' Last Frontier: Fort Stockton and the Trans-Pecos, 1861–1895.* Edited by Ernest Wallace. College Station, Tex.: Texas A & M University Press, 1982.

Wooten, Dudley G. *A Comprehensive History of Texas, 1685–1897.* 2 vols. Dallas: Texas History Co., 1898.

Wortham, Louis J. *A History of Texas from Wilderness to Commonwealth.* 5 vols. Fort Worth, Tex.: Wortham-Molyneaux Co., 1924.

Yelderman, Pauline. *The Jay Birds of Fort Bend County.* Priv. pub., 1981.

Yoakum, Henderson. *History of Texas, from Its First Settlement in 1685 to Its Annexation to the United States in 1846.* 2 vols. New York: J. S. Redfield, 1855.

(Articles)

Adams, Paul. "The Unsolved Mystery of Ben Thompson." *Southwestern Historical Quarterly,* vol. XLVIII, no. 3 (January 1945).

Baker, William Mumford. "A Pivotal Point." *Lippincott's Magazine,* vol. XXVI (November 1880).

Barker, Eugene C. "The Annexation of Texas." *Southwestern Historical Quarterly,* vol. L, no. 1 (July 1946).

———. "The Government of Texas, 1821–1835." *Southwestern Historical Quarterly,* vol. XXI, no. 3 (January 1918).

———. "The San Jacinto Campaign." *Quarterly of the Texas State Historical Association,* vol. IV, no. 4 (April 1901).

———. "Stephen F. Austin." *Southwestern Historical Quarterly,* vol. XXII, no. 1 (July 1918).

———. "The Texas Declaration of Causes for Taking Up Arms Against Mexico." *Southwestern Historical Quarterly,* vol. XV, no. 3 (January 1912).

Brite, Luke. "The Bob Fitzsimmons-Peter Maher Fight." *Password,* vol. X, no. 2 (Summer 1965).

Bugbee, Lester G. "The Old Three Hundred." *Quarterly of the Texas State Historical Association,* vol. I, no. 2 (October 1897).

Burton, Harley True. "A History of the JA Ranch." *Southwestern Historical Quarterly,* vol. XXXI, no. 2 to vol. XXXII, no. 1 (October 1927 to July 1928).

Carroll, H. Bailey, and Gutsch, Milton R., eds. "A Check List of Theses and Dissertations in Texas History Produced in the Department of History of the University of Texas." *Southwestern Historical Quarterly,* vol. LVI, nos. 1–4 (July 1952 to April 1953).

Corner, William. "John Crittenden Duval: The Last Survivor of the Goliad Massacre." *Quarterly of the Texas State Historical Association,* vol. I, no. 1 (July 1897).

Cumberland, Charles C. "The Confederate Loss and Recapture of Galveston, 1862–1863." *Southwestern Historical Quarterly,* vol. LI, no. 2 (October 1947).

Davidson, Col. Wilson T. "Some Sidelights in the Life of O. Henry." *The Alcalde,* 1957.

Dunn, William E. "The Apache Mission on the San Saba River." *Southwestern Historical Quarterly,* vol. XVII, no. 4 (April 1914).

Gard, Wayne. "The Fence Cutters." *Southwestern Historical Quarterly,* vol. LI, no. 1 (July 1947).

Garver, Lois. "Benjamin Rush Milam." *Southwestern Historical Quarterly,* vol. XXXVIII, nos. 2–3 (October 1934 to January 1935).

Havins, T. R. "Sheepmen-Cattlemen Antagonisms on the Texas Frontier." *West Texas Historical Association Yearbook,* vol. XVIII (1942).

Holt, Roy D. "Introduction of Barbed Wire into Texas and the Fence-Cutting War." *West Texas Historical Association Yearbook,* vol. VI (1930).

————. "The Saga of Barbed Wire in the Tom Green Country." *West Texas Historical Association Yearbook,* vol. IV (1928).

House, Boyce. "Spindletop." *Southwestern Historical Quarterly,* vol. L, no. 1 (July 1946).

Howren, Alleine. "Causes and Origin of the Decree of April 6, 1830." *Southwestern Historical Quarterly,* vol. XVI, no. 4 (April 1913).

Koch, Lena Clara. "The Federal Indian Policy in Texas." *Southwestern Historical Quarterly,* vol. XXVIII, nos. 3–4; vol. XXIX, nos. 1–2 (January to October 1925).

Love, Clara M. "History of the Cattle Industry in the Southwest." *Southwestern Historical Quarterly,* vol. XIX, no. 4; vol. XX, no. 1 (April to July 1916).

Morton, Ohland. "Life of General Don Manuel de Mier y Terán." *Southwestern Historical Quarterly,* vol. XLVII, nos. 1–3; vol. XLVIII, nos. 1–2, 4 (July 1943 to January 1944; July to October 1944; April 1945).

Muckleroy, Anna. "The Indian Policy of the Republic of Texas." *Southwestern Historical Quarterly,* vol. XXV, no. 4; vol. XXVI, nos. 1–3 (April to October 1922; January 1923).

Muller, Edwin. "The Great Galveston Storm." *North American Review,* vol. CXXI, no. 3 (Winter 1938).

Reed, S. G. "Land Grants and Other Aids to Texas Railroads." *Southwestern Historical Quarterly,* vol. XLIX, no. 4 (April 1946).

Rister, Carl Coke. "Fort Griffin." *West Texas Historical Association Yearbook,* vol. I (1925).

Roper, William L. "Was O. Henry Guilty?" *Texas Parade* (August 1955).

Rowe, Edna. "The Disturbances at Anahuac in 1832." *Quarterly of the Texas State Historical Association,* vol. VI, no. 4 (April 1903).

Shuffler, R. Henderson. "Winedale Inn." *The Texas Quarterly* (Summer 1965).

Smith, Ralph. "The Co-operative Movement in Texas, 1870–1900." *Southwestern Historical Quarterly,* vol. XLIV, no. 1 (July 1940).

————. "The Farmer's Alliance in Texas, 1875–1900." *Southwestern Historical Quarterly,* vol. XLVIII, no. 3 (January 1945).

————. "The Grange Movement in Texas, 1873–1900." *Southwestern Historical Quarterly,* vol. XLII, no. 4 (April 1930).

Steen, Ralph W. "Analysis of the Work of the General Council, 1835–36." *Southwestern Historical Quarterly,* vol. XLI, no. 3 (January 1938).

Taylor, Maude Wallis. "Captain Sam Highsmith, Ranger." *Frontier Times,* vol. XVII, no. 5 (April 1940).

United States Department of Agriculture, Weather Bureau. *Monthly Weather Review,* vol. XXVIII, no. 9 (September 1900).

Warner, C. A. "Texas and the Oil Industry." *Southwestern Historical Quarterly,* vol. L, no. 1 (July 1946).

Williams, Amelia. "A Critical Study of the Siege of the Alamo and the Personnel of Its Defenders." *Southwestern Historical Quarterly,* vol. XXXVI, no. 4; vol. XXXVII, nos. 1–4 (April to October 1933; January to April 1934).

Photographic Credits

Institutions from whom several images were obtained are listed by the following abbreviations:

AHC—Courtesy the Austin History Center of the Austin Public Library, Austin, Texas.

DRT—Courtesy the Library of the Daughters of the Republic of Texas, at the Alamo, San Antonio, Texas.

LC—Courtesy the Library of Congress, Washington, D. C.

MHI—Courtesy the Department of the Army, U. S. Army Military History Institute, Carlisle Barracks, Pennsylvania.

NA—Courtesy the National Archives, Washington, D. C.

NHC—Courtesy the Department of the Navy, Naval Historical Center, Washington, D. C.

PPHM—Courtesy the Panhandle-Plains Historical Museum, Canyon, Texas.

RL—Courtesy the Rosenberg Library, Galveston, Texas.

SFA—Courtesy Special Collections, Ralph W. Steen Library, Stephen F. Austin State University, Nacogdoches, Texas.

SI—Courtesy the Smithsonian Institution, National Anthropological Archives, Washington, D. C.

TSL—Courtesy the Texas State Library, Archives Division, Austin, Texas.

UTB—Courtesy the Barker Texas History Center, University of Texas, Austin, Texas.

Index

Page numbers in *italics* indicate illustrations and captions.